LV Polcic

CW00517577

Judged for Mercy

Romantic Period Drama

Author: LV Polcic

Prologue

Marina Rivalli was always an odd duck in her neighborhood, Vomero. She has been insulted everywhere she goes, ever since her dear brother tragically died. Because the young lady was now an only child, she would not be able to inherit her family's wealth, so she opted to marry a man who simply needed to smile at her to make her happy. She got engaged a few months ago to a man named Matias Marotta. He was quite handsome, charming, and intelligent. Everything a woman needed in a man. His alluring grey eyes were enough to seduce her and make her head over heels for him. Although he seemed like a kind person, he was in fact the most vain person anyone could've met. If only the unlucky Neapolitan girl knew what trouble she got herself into.

"To the bride and groom!" The happy father of Marina, who was also celebrating his daughter's upcoming wedding that evening, exclaimed. Everyone raised their full glasses of red wine in a toast to the joyful future of the couple. The young lady was worried as she kept pacing around the room and looking at every area. "Have you seen Matias?" she questioned her mother, Mrs. Annabella Rivalli. "No, sweetheart, I haven't. Perhaps he went to freshen up?"

"Oh, well, I suppose so. He hasn't been around for at least an hour."

"You're aware of how men are. Instead of celebrating with their loved ones, they'd rather go out with their friends." In response, Marina pursed her lips as she continued to wonder where her fiancé might be. As she couldn't seem to locate him anywhere and knew that his company would have helped her feel less apprehensive about the entire wedding, she longed to find him. "Goodness Matias, you're nowhere to be found just when I need you!" When the young lady continued to look around the hallway in search of her beloved fiancé, she sighed. In the meantime, Matias was in bed with another woman in a bedroom. He muttered, "Oh God—" as he started to perspire. He took a few long breaths and collapsed to the bed by her side after the woman he was with put her hands on his chest. She pulled a lock of ginger hair out of her face. The lady took quick sharp breaths before she asked "What are you going to do about that young girl?" In that instant, the man glanced at her "Marina? anything I desire. Like the rest of her family, she is pretty naive and foolish."

"I don't know why you're with her among all the women in the world."

"Lucia, I have good reasons. You don't have to tell me that." To smoke it, he pulled out a cigar and began lighting it "I understand, but—to be honest, she isn't appealing. She has terrible olive skin. In contrast to her dirty skin, a woman should have fair skin. Not to mention that hideous face of hers with the freckles. Ugh!" Matias used his fingers to tame his mustache "Her appearances are not important to me. I'm interested in her money." She crossed her legs and arms in frustration because she couldn't believe he was so determined to become richer that he was prepared to wed the worst woman in the kingdom. Miss Lucia spoke to him softly while placing her chest on his back and wrapping her arms over his chest, saying, "I hope our fun won't end once you become a married man." "Don't worry darling, just because I'm getting married does not mean I should be true to that brat." he said with a devious smile.

While continuing to look for him, Marina was on the verge of sobbing. She was afraid about the wedding, especially when her father continued urging her to wed Mr. Marotta because of his enormous fortune and how his charitable nature would greatly benefit them. Her passion for Matias was sincere. She wasn't quite ready to get married, though. The young lady nevertheless yearned for adventure and a taste of personal freedom. She will never be able to be free after the day of her wedding. She will be required to cook, clean, and carry children, all of which make her the most anxious. Amelia Mor, the lover of her brother, entered her home as she was in the hallway on the verge of tears from feeling so overwhelmed. Amelia was looking for her close friend Marina. She stumbled across the girl's fiancé opening the door to a bedroom with another lady as they were both walking down the hallway. She could tell something was awry because they both seemed disorganized. Amelia detected Matias' anxious glare, which was made worse by the fact that he gave her a quite stern expression as if to intimidate her.

After seeing Matias having an affair, Amelia hurried to her friend, and when she saw Marina, she was overjoyed to see her. "Marina! Do you please have a moment?"

"What is it, Mia?" While wiping tears from her eyes and not quite in the mood to converse, Marina questioned her. "I understand that this may seem absurd, but please trust me." Amelia halted before the young lady sternly demanded that she tell it to her already. "I'm afraid this will only add to your already high-stress levels, but I just saw Matias having an affair with another woman. Since we were kids, you know me well, so I could never lie to you! I make a solemn vow!"

"You are correct. It does sound absurd. You are not trustworthy to me.

"Marina I am aware of what I have witnessed!—"

"Oh, please halt! You're only envious because my brother passed away, and since I'm getting married to someone I love and he loves me, you cannot." Amelia stared at her with wide-open eyes and was completely speechless "I love my husband. In contrast to your fiancé, he still cares about me despite not being your brother. I cannot believe that you thought I would be envious of you after you turned into such a horrible person utterly baffles me. I will never get to the same level of vile as you." Amelia continued to stare at Marina while twisting her white gloves. Marina was maintaining a chilly gaze. Even after ten years of friendship, the young lady told her something like that, she still couldn't believe it. While she believed she knew her well, Marina's comments hurt her. "What you think of me doesn't matter to me. You might as well not attend my wedding if you're going to treat me so horribly."

Amelia gasped at that, but she soon shut her mouth and said, "Fine. I won't. I hope you're happy with who you are right now. Farewell, Marina." She swiftly departed because she didn't want to spend any more time with the Rivalli family. She despised the day she met Marina. Marina's twin brother, Rocco was the only decent member of the family. The only one who never mistreated her or had solely his interests in mind. The moment she departed, Marina erupted in wrath. She became so upset that she seized a vase that was put close by and slammed it to the ground, breaking it into pieces. The young lady began sobbing hysterically. She took a seat on the ground and started kicking it with her feet. "I despise her!" She said "Who does she think she is to inform me that my fiancé is unfaithful? He wouldn't ever do such a thing to me, and I know him well." She rose and hurried to the living room, where everyone was, as she started to take fast, harsh breaths out of rage. Everyone standing near her could tell that she was enraged and psychologically unstable.

When she first spotted Matias in the living room with everyone else, the young lady's lips were pursed. She moved over to him right away and continued to think to herself how wicked Amelia is for passing such harsh judgment on her beloved fiancé. "Matias, my love!—"

"Not now Marina. Be silent." Matias told her as she wanted to show him how much she loved and appreciated him "Oh, alright." At the table, where everyone sat down to converse and eat, she took a seat next to him. Then Matias cleared his throat and stepped up to speak. "I just wanted to thank my fiancée's parents for welcoming me over to their house and for giving me their full approval to marry their wonderful daughter. I feel tremendously privileged to be able to refer to

Marina as my wife starting tomorrow. I knew I had to make her my wife the moment I lay eyes on her at a ball. She utterly silenced me with her grace and beauty. In her presence, I had trouble breathing. Of course, a toast to Marina as well! My wife!" He drank from the glass of wine while everybody applauded and clapped. That made the young lady smile and feel special because he made a toast just for her. The instant she rose with a glass of wine, wanting to make a toast for him as well, and began to say, "And I would want to—," Mr. Marotta interrupted her, "Marina I told you to remain silent. Sit back down."

Marina was perplexed by what he told her and looked down. She immediately sat down after expressing regret to him for breaking her quiet. The young lady kept glancing around the room to see everyone having a good time and laughing. Because Matias had already told her to be quiet twice, she knew that if she didn't concentrate on others and found herself alone with her thoughts, she would begin crying. She kept telling herself that since he would soon become her husband, he was free to tell her that. Furthermore, she might have been quite irritating or speaking wasn't her place. Now that everyone in the room had seen a man quiet her. She wasn't sure anymore and felt utterly humiliated. Even the fact that he hadn't glanced at her all night crushed Marina's heart. She prayed he would at least smile comfortingly at her. Her parents approached her and Mr. Marotta as she started to breathe heavily from nervousness. "Matias, please join us in conversation." Matias questioned as he turned to face them "What is it?" He asked In an annoyed voice.

"We discovered we may have too many people as we started counting the guests once more. So we wanted to know if it's perfectly alright if we switch the party to maybe at your house? It is far bigger than ours, as you stated." Mr. Rivalli questioned Matias, who suddenly started to appear anxious, "M-my house?" He said, twisting the napkin fold, "N-no, I don't think so. Although it is now under construction, I don't want the guests to get the impression that we are potentially being impolite by sending them there." The idea to have the party take place outside was Marina's dream. She'd always wanted to get married in a forest or by the sea. Yet, she chose to remain silent with her suggestion rather than run the risk of provoking her fiancé.

"Yes, I suppose you're right." Cracking her knuckles, Mrs. Rivalli questioned what she would do with the visitors. "But, I hope the wedding will go off without a hitch. You two should enjoy your supper. We'll take care of the rest." Matias smiled at her and then let out a breath as she left. He was unable to reveal to them that he is insanely impoverished and lacks a large home. His future ambitions will all be destroyed if they learn the truth.

Chapter I

"Today is the big day, Marina. It's going to be a big big big day."

While eagerly contemplating and attempting to get ready, she circled in her room, making a loud thump whenever her heel stepped on the ground. "Oh, my god. It's my special day. I can't do it; what if he discovers that I'm a gigantic freak? I'm going to pass out." Marina began fluttering her hands in the air to obtain some fresh air and maintain her composure. Her mother stood up from the chair next to the bed and gently seized her wrists. The woman encouraged her to take it easy in a voice that might soothe a winter storm. If you paid close attention, you might notice a faint German accent in her mother's voice when she spoke, because she's from Austro-Hungarian Empire. "Don't worry, you'll be alright. On my wedding day with your father, I was exactly as scared as you were. And look at me, I have the most beautiful daughter any mother could want for."

Marina smiled softly as she looked down at what her mother had said. It gave her a glimmer of optimism for the future and the possibility that her wedding wouldn't be so horrible... Her smile faded as her gaze shifted to her brother's ring. The ring was primarily constructed of gold, with golden small flowers as shoulder embellishments. On the top was a royal blue colored gem with a golden flower engraved in the center and small zircons on the outlines. It was too large for her finger and it knew to slip away. She twisted it with her delicate thin fingers and toyed with it for a few seconds.

"I wish he was here..." says Marina. She groaned despondently and fought back tears that began to well up in her eyes.

She felt them falling on her reddish cheeks full of freckles. Grabbing a fold of her white silky wedding dress and squeezing it, the girl sniffed trying not to cry in front of her mother on her special day.

"I shouldn't have dragged him out that day. Now he'd be the one getting married, and our lives would be better." She attempted to talk without her voice cracking, but the remorse and memories racing through her thoughts made it impossible.

Her mother placed her palm on her daughter's cheek and wiped away the tears that streamed down her cheeks like a waterfall. "You need to stop crying, you're ruining the rice powder I applied on your face." The young lady looked down "I'm sorry, mother." She said with a quiet voice and softly rested her head on her hand, her muscles softening as she felt her mother's touch.

"And please don't say that. The past is no longer relevant. Of course, I miss Rocco every day and night, but we can't erase what happened in the past. My butterfly, you'll make a fantastic bride, and your brother would be proud of you."

Marina wiped the tears from her eyes with her hand and responded with a shaky forced grin to her mother.

"Alright, enough with the misery. It's the day of your wedding! You should be pleased with yourself! Come ahead, I've got something to show you."

Mrs. Rivalli spun around in her room, looking for a tiny box she had hidden somewhere. She strolled around the room looking for it. Eventually, she sat down at the bed's edge, sighed, and said she couldn't remember where she put it. Marina's black long-haired cat Cesare, however, emerged from beneath the bed. Dusty, and began flinging around something small and making a ruckus. The girl named him Giulio Cesare because she found it silly to name a cat such way. Her parents were against it at first because it's a ridiculous name for a cat, but she managed to convince them to let her name him that way. Her mother reached down then and grabbed the box.

"Oh, my goodness! It's right here!"

Mrs. Rivalli glared at Cesare, telling him that he was a nasty cat for stealing her belongings.

When Marina's mother discovered it, she snorted and said, "What's in it?" The woman removed a set of lovely golden earrings with sapphires in the center and zircons all around. Marina exclaimed when she saw them and commented on how lovely they are. She placed them in her hands and told her how well they would complement her ocean-blue eyes. "They've been in our family for decades, and every woman in the Herz family, including myself, got married with them. If you wore them on your wedding day, it would mean a lot to me."

"Thank you, mother." Marina said softly.

"I love them. Although I do have a question." Mrs. Rivalli nodded at her as a confirmation for her to ask. "Did you enjoy your wedding night? I'm quite nervous and excited about it. I've been waiting for months to experience it! I'm kind of curious about Matias' looks."

Her mother turned even paler than she already is and couldn't believe she was having this conversation with her eighteen years old daughter, Marina still felt to her as if she were a five-year-old little girl. "Oh my goodness, you can't just ask your mother things like that!"

"Yeah but, was it or wasn't it good?"

"It was *fine,* I don't know what else to tell you." Annabella's entire face turned red and wished for this conversation to end already as it started to make her feel uncomfortable and awkward. She didn't want to talk about her daughter's father in such a sexual manner.

A sudden hasty knock on the bedroom doors was heard and her mother immediately got straight up so she could avoid that very unpleasant conversation.

"Anna, could you spare a moment?"

"Of course love, what is it?"

Her mother stood up and began heading towards the doors in a perplexing manner. Her husband stood next to them, waiting for her to exit so he could close the door.

"Mari, it'll only take a minute." Her father said as he shut the doors behind them. Marina walked around her room, looking at every single detail carved on her light blue walls. It was fascinating to her to see all of the different symbols and figures carved on them and to speculate on what they could be. She moved closer to the window and rested against it and placed her elbows on the edge. She looked at the sea and the city from afar and listened to the crowd and all kinds of sounds coming from it, while letting the breeze blow over her thick dark brown curly hair; she took a long breath and exhaled, attempting to feel the freedom outside of her home that she had never experienced before. And that she would most likely never experience again now that she is getting married. The blue Rigneck parrot appeared out of nowhere and rested on her window next to her.

"It's a pity you're in a cage like me, Blu. Perhaps you prefer it, after all. You've been confined your entire life and have become accustomed to it. If only I had done the same."

She sobbed on her window and kept caressing and twisting her brother's golden ring on her finger, which calmed her down and distracted her for a minute.

Meanwhile, the girl's parents. Mrs. Annabella and Mr. Adriano Rivalli were debating the wedding, as well as the relationship between the bride and the groom as they were walking in the halls. Mr. Rivalli kept talking about it from an economical standpoint, whereas Mrs. Rivalli kept talking about it from a romantic standpoint. And whether or not her fiancé was the right person to be with her.

"What are you talking about, dearest? He's flawless! He's well-behaved, has been educated by the best teachers in Italy, and is fluent in seven languages, seven! And I barely managed to learn English. And he's fantastic at politics; he's truly one-of-a-kind."

"I'm not sure, darling. It's just the way he thinks about some things in life is so, peculiar. And Marina appears to be rather uneasy around him." she added as she crossed her arms and continued staring at the pictures of her family that were hung on the wall, trying to imagine Marina's point of view. "It's a young romance; she'll fall in love with him as they get to know each other better. You were as well shy the first time you met me; you barely said anything." He chuckled and jokingly tapped her on the shoulder with his elbow, while she rolled her eyes and snickered.

"Ah, I suppose you're right, and I'm just being dramatic."

"You always are." he added. Even though he was the one who tended to be more dramatic. "Not to mention that my restaurant isn't doing the best since Rocco died. And we could use financial help from Matias and his family, through Marina." Mrs Rivalli looked uneasy "I feel odd using our daughter for money." Her husband looked at her weirdly "We aren't using her. And I refuse to work for some low-paid job. I'd rather die poor than look poor."

Marina was still standing close to the window, gazing out at the city, when her father walked back in.

"I was hoping to speak with you."

He was holding the door handle and keeping the doors open for her. She stood up and inquired as to what was wrong, and if it was as a result of something she had done or said. She couldn't help but panic at this point about everything as the wedding, guests, and marriage keep on making her paranoid. Her father stopped her, put his hand on her shoulder, and chuckled saying "God, you're just like your mother." Out of concern, she bit her lower lip and asked "What is it then?" He had his hand behind her back, close to him as they began strolling into the hallway.

"Well, I figured we'd have that discussion."

Marina gave him a confused look.

"When I was your age, my father always wanted me to be something he wanted to be, instead of what I wanted. It didn't matter what I did, he was never satisfied, which put a lot of pressure on me and I never knew when was I enough. Until I met your mother, she made me feel as if insecurity didn't exist at all and finally filled that void of emptiness. And that's what marriage is all about: being able to trust and be confident around each other yet never feeling unequal. " he added "And I know you won't feel any pressure from me or your mother since we never are unsatisfied with you." Which was a lie. They constantly judged her, but they were too blind to see that as they kept thinking of themselves as much better parents than their own.

Marina bit her bottom lip once again and told her father how she's afraid of messing things up, and how she feels as if she isn't ready anymore for such committed things and that her fiancé will start despising her. "Calm down Marina. No one will hate you. And do you want to know why?" He put his hands on her shoulders and stated "Because I know you, you're my daughter. You're sweet, kind, and generous. The greatest of everything. He will adore you, every day and every night, and I have faith in you." Mr. Rivalli then let out a chuckle "You're also a Rivalli. It's the greatest pride possible." He kept boosting her confidence so she doesn't suddenly break the engagement with Matias. If she does, he's doomed financially.

She gave him a delicate kiss on the cheek and gently whispered how she loves him. "All right" he answered with a bright smile. "Now is the time to get ready; the ceremony is soon." Marina looked at him with a heartbroken look when he didn't tell her he loved her as well, but rather kept focusing on her getting married already. He led her to her bedroom, where he left her, and then headed away to his own. Marina opened the doors and sat in a chair next to her cluttered table. Which was piled with cosmetics, brushes, jewelry, and other trinkets. She examined herself in the mirror, pulling her eyes up with her fingers to examine her eyes, and then examined the box that her mother had placed for her on her table. She took the earrings out of the box and went to try them on, as Blu was flying around the room, making strange noises.

"Hello ?" A strange voice and knock were heard.

When Marina turned back and saw who was standing outside the doors, she couldn't believe her eyes.

"What are you doing in here? Seeing me in a bridal gown is bad luck!" She smiled widely, happy and concerned to see him at the same time.

"Does it make a difference?" Matias stated it while leaning against the doors, arms crossed and a cocky smile on his face.

The girl sighed and rolled her eyes not caring anymore about him being in the room with her, just half an hour before their ceremony.

"If you want negative Karma in our marriage, that's fine with me. A shame you won't be surprised to see me like this on our wedding night." She smirked at him.

While Marina was fixing her face, hair, jewelry, and other vital accessories for her appearance. They both looked at each other, keeping eye contact "Well, Matias. Since you're already here, which pair of earrings do you think would look better on me: sapphire or diamonds?"

Matias' blue-eyed eyes, squinted. "Diamonds, they are a sign of wealth." Marina returned her gaze to them and was disappointed that he didn't choose Sapphire. Her mother had requested that she wears them to her daughter's wedding, and she felt upset about not keeping the old family tradition. She still wanted her future husband's opinion, since he was going to be her husband after all, and not hearing from him what he thinks felt kind of dull.

"So, your father is a very emotional man." says he.

"He cried?" Marina exclaimed.

Matias laughed "Yea, I'd never claim he cries in front of others. He's completely inebriated already. And singing with his mates down there. Although it is quite a shame that he's such a naive man."

The girl was confused about what he said and didn't quite understand the meaning behind it. She looked in the mirror in front of her and continued to look at the young man through it. He shrugged and explained that it wasn't significant in the first place and that he had come for something else. Marina snickered and remarked, exaggeratedly, "Oh, what could that possibly be?"

He put his fingers on his handlebar-shaped mustache, slowly stroking it while looking at Marina. He seemed lost in his thoughts as his eyes wandered to the girl's body.

"I think this is a hint." He said as he moved closer to her and gently kissed her shoulder from behind.

Marina gave him a frightened faint smile and asked him to stop since they didn't have time and she wasn't ready yet and had already prepared everything for later tonight. Matias insisted on doing it and that no one would notice. Marina turned back and told him no in a harsher tone, starting to get annoyed by his repetitive question. She thought for a moment about how this is normal for men to feel such strong urges before the wedding. Unfortunately, she didn't know enough since her mother was too shy to tell her more. The young man became irritated, ran his hands through his blonde hair, and became colder as winter, saying:

"You're my wife, you'll follow my instructions. I don't want to hear from you disobeying *me*. Now stand up."

Marina became pale as snow and was unsure how to respond to him; she assumed he was kidding with her. He should know how much she despises it when people talk to her like that, so he wouldn't... Would he do it? ... The frightened bride lowered her head and told him it wasn't amusing.

He approached her and aggressively grasped her cheeks with his palm, saying, "I'm telling you once, and never again you ungrateful brat. Stand up." Marina recognized he wasn't joking at this moment. "Are you happy?" she asked as she stood up feeling confused. "Can you leave me alone now? I really don't want to argue with you now." The girl asked in an irritated voice. He became enraged at her and hit her at that point because of what she said. "What in the name of God is with you!?" The girl exclaimed in a brittle voice, clutching her chair as her eyes were full of tears, a few seconds from falling down like a waterfall and her hand on her red left cheek.

"You don't talk back to me. Understood? I suppose I should lay down some ground rules before we tie the knot. Do what I say, and be a good wife. You should've been taught that already. Oh right, you were mostly taught by maids."

He kept circling in her chamber with his white-gloved hands behind his back.

She took some bravery "And what if I don't?"

Matias stared at her with a cold expression on his face.

"You don't want to know"

Marina cried and covered her mouth with her palm, unable to believe what she was about to marry.

"I thought— I thought you loved me—"

"Loved you? Why in the world would I love you? I would never marry you out of love, not even in a million years." he scoffed

The terrifying fiance of hers observed. "Do you realize how difficult it is to be in the same room with you? The nonsense, the chatting the idiocy. And you're so incredibly *loud*. Lord, do you realize how much of a horrible name you're going to give me? What will people say? That I married a murderer? A complete embarrassment?"

Marina became agitated and responded with an icy stare, "I'm not a murderer... It was a mishap..."

"Are you certain? Is it true or are you deceiving yourself? You were, after all the only eyewitness. Aren't you the one who said that? Regardless, my point is. I don't want you to ruin my reputation. The only reason I'm marrying you is because your idiotic father has some money that I'll inherit." Marina felt like having a nervous breakdown because she didn't know how to respond or say anything in general. Just thinking about her brother dying is triggering, but when she's blamed for it. It feels like thousands of knives have been stabbed into her entire body, all at once.

"Your parents are morons if they truly believe you are capable of getting married, but they don't have a choice since you're their only child. Fortunately, the only thing you have is your appearance." Marina averted her gaze and bit her bottom lip nervously; it became a horrible habit, and her lip began to bleed as a result of how hard she'd known to bite it when frightened, which is usual.

"Then what are you going to do with me? I'm not worth anything! Take a look around! Everyone despises me! Even going to a goddamn ball makes me feel like I'm being watched by everyone. I— I can't even say anything without being silenced—"

Because it made no sense for him to marry her, a lowlife young Neapolitan girl who is despised by everyone for her conduct and past.

"It's that easy. I marry you because you killed your brother, I get your parents' money, and all of the money will go to me, including the properties." He spoke about it as if he were a psychopath, a child with a passion for violent games and a man with a thirst for war. He strolled over to the window and gazed out at the sea, envisioning the moment when he signs the papers and becomes the legal owner of everything she owns. Hearing what he stated, the girl erupted in wrath, revealing his true nature. She began to scream and attack him, accusing him of lying to her and her entire family about how wealthy he is and how willing he is to help them and her. Matias pulled her away from him aggressively as possible with a hard glance. "It was honestly ridiculously simple to manipulate you. You're so naive that you fall in love with the first man who expresses even a smidgeon of care for you."

"How could you do such a thing to me!?" While looking at him, she screamed at the top of her lungs and fell into tears. "Please, you're so simple that everyone would do such a thing to you and keep you as some doll." he said, looking at her unamused. She took a deep breath and became even more agitated as he continued to speak.

A doll? She has no desire to be a doll! She wants to get out and experience life, go for a stroll alone for at least an hour, and travel to different countries and kingdoms. Rather than just being his wife. She was already being mocked, she didn't need a couple of more reasons for everyone to despise her. She became horrified at the prospect of it, and of how much more dreary her life would become. She didn't want that.

"I hate you!"

She'd soon regret ever saying those words after saying them. The man was so furious with her that he raised his leg and kicked her in the stomach as hard as he could with his knee to teach her a lesson and calm her down. Marina knelt on the ground, tears streaming down her face and a strong need to vomit as she grabbed her stomach. "Now now, be kind to me." he said as he knelt down and placed his hand on her chin, pulling her head up and forcing her to stand up again while in immense pain.

"Anyhow, where were we?" he asked, smirking as he clapped his hands.

Marina felt like sobbing as he forced his kiss onto her neck and shoulder, and she begged him to stop several times but he continued to ignore her. "Matias stop— stop please... Stop!" He kept grabbing her chest which made her insanely uncomfortable. The girl swerved around him and dashed for the doors, yelling for help, but Matias caught her and pushed her against the mirror. The slam was so strong that she broke it with her back, scattering glass pieces all over the place. Marina moaned in pain but all he did was grabbed her by her wrist and squeeze it. She gave up at one moment because she didn't know what to do and felt helpless. She tried to push him away with her hands on his chest, but he was too strong. The man pulled her into her bed, and she tried to kick him away and scream for help. But he overpowered her, grabbing her wrists and saying "You don't want to end up like your brother, do you?" She couldn't help but scream as he began loosening his belt and lowering his dark navy blue pants with golden details. She ordered him to stop it again at that point, but he refused. "Please stop..." she sobbed in a helpless voice "I-I don't want to do this." The young girl didn't know what to do because her heart was thumping so loudly. She shifted her head to the left and closed her eyes, unable to bear the sight of what he was about to do to her.

"I will kill you if you scream again." He threatened her. She desired to die at that time, dropped a tear, and surrendered.

The girl was startled by a sudden sharp pain and groaned. Marina looked down at her bed and noticed a pair of scissors close by from earlier when she was cutting a ribbon. She sighed as she tried with all of her power to get just a little bit closer so she could reach them. Matias grabbed her and instructed her to stay motionless when he discovered she was moving. She was overwhelmed with wrath at the time, as she cried she pressed her legs against herself and kicked him with her legs as hard as she could. Marina took the moment and grabbed the scissors immediately without thinking twice.

"You *whore!*" Matias grumbled.

He was outraged when she spat in his face and said "Go to hell." He was about to slam his fist into her. Marina stared at the scissors she was holding and then back at him as he proceeded to strike her as hard as he could.

"You'll be sorry." he warned her.

"No, you'll be."

When he drew close to her, she stabbed him in the neck with the scissors out of panic. Blood began to splatter in all directions... Her delicate freckled face was smeared with blood. Her white wedding gown turned bright red on her chest area as she looked down at Matias, who had collapsed and cried out for aid, gasping for air. Marina started grinning awkwardly as tears streamed down her cheeks. She was pleased with herself for stabbing him and watching him suffer in his final moments. The girl enjoyed him suffering the same way he made her, it felt like a wonderful feeling. "H-h-help m-m—" Matias tried speaking but he was running out of breath. The girl looked down at him at that moment and gave him nothing but a dead look. She sat down on top of him, tightly held her scissors, and stabbed him in the heart. She was humiliated enough by the man. He was dead in a matter of seconds, with no indications of life, and he couldn't have survived the scissors wound.

Her bedroom floor became a puddle of blood. The blood started coming all the way to where she was standing. Marina froze, she looked at her hands which were bloody, unable to believe she had once again killed someone. She knelt on her knees and kept looking at his dead body "I cared about you! Why did you do this to me!?" Marina screamed at him. This was the final straw. When the public finds out, she'll be arrested and her entire family will be humiliated. She didn't want others to look down on her parents because they didn't deserve it. It's all because of *Her*. Marina was on the verge of passing out as the blood began to flow faster and faster, the scent disgusting her, and she couldn't breathe.

She didn't know what to do anymore; everyone was expecting her and Matias to arrive and marry right away.

"I can't come down there and say how he tried to get me to bed without my permission, I killed him because of it. Therefore there won't be a wedding!" she nervously wide-smiled and sobbed, trying to come up with anything to say. She kept frantically circling in her room, leaving trays of blood on the floor, wondering and thinking of ways to solve all of her issues, and she chose the riskiest and most immature option possible:

Running away

She had no choice but to hide for a while until things calmed down. She looked around her room, wondering if she had any more time to change. Marina took a red-colored handkerchief from Matias's dark navy blue suit's pocket and wiped the crimson from her face while staring into the mirror, looking cold and lifeless in her eyes. She searched her room for some precious jewelry to have In case she needs to exchange money for a possible occasion. She finished it all and then took her animals, Cesare and Blu outside her room so they wouldn't be terrified. The girl walked quickly towards the exit, closing the doors behind her and wishing to never come back to her bedroom.

She locked the doors three times as she closed them behind her, just in case. She sighed and leaned against the doors, unsure of what to do next. Should she run away? Should she bite her tongue and go public with her murder of her fiancé, risking severe repercussions? She was unsure, and all she could think of at the time was whether anyone was nearby so she could sneak out of the house discreetly.

She inhaled deeply and clenched her fist, forming a deep crescent moon symbol on her palm due to her fingernails. She adjusted the cloak's hood and began walking quickly.

Every step she took left a crimson footprint on the floor, indicating the direction and destination of her walk. She didn't change her heels since she didn't know there was still fresh blood on them and proceeded on her way nervously.

Chapter II

S he continued to sweat and look around to see if anyone in the house was making too much eye contact with her. Fortunately, she was due to marry right now, and everyone was gathered in the nearby church, waiting for her and Matias to arrive and happily marry.

Meanwhile, her mother and father stayed put, waiting for Marina to finish getting ready so they could accompany her to the church. The middle-aged frustrated woman was apprehensive about the whole situation with Matias and his family, and she knew something wasn't quite right. What makes an insanely wealthy family marry an average young girl? That was a question she couldn't answer herself. She kept attempting to reason with her husband, wondering whether they should find someone else for Marina and how she didn't want their daughter to be sad ever again.

Mr. Rivalli fixed his suit while looking at her.

"Dear, it's no longer our decision; the wedding is today, Marina wanted this anyways. And Matias is quite wealthy so I could really use some money from his family. I already convinced Marina to marry him and she agreed with me!" Annabella irritatedly stared at him and exclaimed, "We're her parents, we're allowed to do something!" She continued in a harsh tone. "Anything!?—Do you disagree with me?"

"I wish I could believe you Bella, but it's ridiculous; perhaps they're only trying to help? Not everything needs to have a reason. You do know that people can love each other, right?" She groaned and sat on the edge of their bed, her palm on her head, "I just—I want her to be happy, I feel terrible knowing she's unhappy with her life. I don't want her to live the same life that I did or marry a man for his money." The man felt terrible and tried to show her empathy by moving her light blonde hair with few visible grays, away from her face and gently kissing her cheek. "I know, don't be concerned. She'll be just fine. Please don't overwork yourself and try to keep upbeat." Even tho he himself only wanted Marina to marry the man, purely for his money.

Mrs. Rivalli softly smiled and placed her hand on his cheek, gazing into his emerald green eyes, which were as mysterious as a forest. "I love you." she said softly. "I love you more." He gave her a sweet grin and rested his head on her hand that was gently placed on his cheek.

"We should be ready."

"You're right. We've already lost much too much time."

She assisted him in adjusting and repairing his outfit, snickering to herself as she did so. He wondered aloud, "What's so funny?"

"Ohh nothing, it just reminded me of when we were younger and I used to avoid you like the plague." she sniffed.

"Me? "How dare you," he said theatrically and sarcastically, "I always believed you loved me." The woman snickered at him "Oh no, you were insanely annoying." He gazed at her with such love in his eyes, as if he had just seen her for the first time in his father's workshop when neither of them had the courage to speak to each other properly. "And you're still the same scoundrel you were twenty years ago." She blushed as she proceeded to tease him, "Oh, stop it—"

"Hold on, dear, what time is it?" Mr. Rivalli paused in his suit-fixing and squinted his eyes, attempting to see the clock, but he was nearsighted and couldn't see the time without his glasses, since he refused to wear them, thinking he looks hideous with them.

"It's twenty to 1 pm"

"We have to go" he grumbled as he frantically tried to straighten his thick brown curly hair.

Mr. Rivalli sobbed again as they walked out of their room, unable to believe that his little girl is getting married today; it seemed like only yesterday that they were in the forest, and Marina would climb the trees, and he'd continuously fret trying to grab her without injuring her. His wife observed him crying and put her arm around his back, assuring him that everything will be fine. He wiped the tears from his eyes and cleared his throat, adding, "I'll go get her, just wait for me in the living room." She nodded and proceeded to the living room, where she awaited his and Marina's arrival. Mr. Rivalli knocked on Marina's bedroom door as she walked away.

"Mari, do you mind if I come in?" He inquired as he leaned against the doors.

There was no reaction. He attempted to open the doors, but they were shut. He was perplexed and couldn't understand why she would lock herself up. He kept trying to open the door violently and demanding her to open the darn doors immediately in a serious tone. There was no reaction this time. He dashed to a stool on which sat a ceramic plate containing keys to every bedroom, closet, etc... The man grabbed the keys to her bedroom in a hurry, thinking of the worst possibilities. "I'm going to count to three, if you don't open the doors right now, I'm coming in, and you better start praying." Her father said in a severe tone.

And, once again, there has been no reaction. He eventually became enraged and began unlocking the doors. He smelled something strange and nasty as he walked in. A body lay on the ground, surrounded by a large puddle of blood, as he glanced down. He began to breathe heavily and placed his palm on his chest, almost fainting out, as he tried to catch his breath. He kept his balance by leaning against the wall.

"*Marina!*" He yelled so loudly that the entire house could hear him, and his voice echoed throughout the halls.

Mrs. Rivalli sprung from her couch, startled by her husband's yell. She began sprinting towards him, and along the way, she noticed a swarm of crimson footsteps in the corridor. As soon as she entered Marina's room, her husband seized her and demanded to know where his daughter was in a menacing tone. As she witnessed the awful picture in the room, she exclaimed, "What in the name of God happened— Oh my good God! W—who was it that did this? And, more importantly, where is our daughter?—"

"I was hoping you'd know. I keep thinking only of the worst that she has been kidnapped. Because the window is open wide, her room looks as if she was fighting back and her animals aren't in the room." He commented as he looked down at the bloody scissors. His wife burst into tears and cried on her husband's shoulder, blaming him for not being cautious enough. Mr. Rivalli felt terrible, and because he didn't want the same event to happen again, he began to have deja vu, as if everything had happened before... He clutched his wife tightly and attempted to reassure her with a calm voice that they'd find her. He went to take a few steps outside of the room, checking if there was anything unusual, and just as he did, he look down to his left and spotted blood throughout the hallway.

As he looked down, he wasn't the most certain if they were Marina's. But judging by it, he just prayed to God that it wasn't what he was thinking. Mrs. Rivalli knelt next to Matias and placed her fingers on his neck, attempting to check his pulse. Her two oldest brothers were surgeons and she was quite familiar with the medical field because of it. But she could tell he was dead a long time ago by his pale lips.

In the meantime, Marina hid behind the curtains near the front doors. Hearing her father yell so loudly terrified her. And she was even more scared of being discovered. She began to cry silently and glanced down at the floor as tears streamed down her face. She noticed a red stain on the ground, she was confused because everything was fuzzy at the time, and brushed her tears away. When the girl realized the blood was coming from her heels, she gasped and peered out from behind the curtains, turning pale as she saw blood everywhere. Then harsh footsteps sound began to get louder and louder, and the sound of the wooden floors cracking could be heard too. She figured that it was either her parents or someone else from her family.

Marina kicked off her shoes, took a big breath, and ran as she'd never run before in her life. As soon as she opened the doors a loud familiar voice was heard

"Marina!—"

The girl turned around, in fright and shame looking at her parents. They were pale and confused as to what she was doing. She looked at them as if she was about to tear up any second. Her parents just stood by the staircases not knowing how to react, until her mother spoke up. "Sweetheart ...please...What is happening?—" While staring at her as if she were the murderer, her mother felt a piece of apple lodged in her throat.

"I'm sorry. You wouldn't understand."

She started running towards the city, but kept changing directions in case anyone follows her, got ahead of her, and couldn't tell which way she was heading. Her parents shouted as loud as possible for her to stop this mess, but they got no reply or reaction from her. Because of aging, they weren't able to go after by legs, and Mr. Rivalli grabbed his wife's hand and rushed towards their carriage.

"Darn, where do I go now!?" she said while petrified, not knowing where to go now. Her heart was racing and she was pumped up with adrenaline. She noticed an older gentleman with a carriage and a horse close. Marina dashed up to him and yelled as loudly as she could, "Stop the carriage!" As soon as he heard her yell, the man came to a complete halt. He was irritated since he was going to leave for home.

He exclaimed, "What do you want, young girl?" Marina hurriedly took out her bag that was tied up around her torso, containing valuable jewelry, and showed him diamond earrings in exchange for a quick ride into the city. The old man didn't hesitate to tell her to come in as soon as he saw her offering. She sat next to him, tapped him on the shoulder, and pleaded with him to get the horse moving as quickly as possible.

The tired-looking man wanted to get noisy and question her if she ran away from her wedding, by the looks of her gown "I don't have time to chat." she exclaimed, as adrenaline was still coursing through her veins. They soon arrived in the center of Naples. Fortunately, her parents were nowhere in sight. Marina alighted from the carriage and started mumbling to herself about how annoying the old man was. He waved goodbye to her as he removed his tattered black hat.

When the young lady began walking quickly towards the city's center, the inhabitants became perplexed and intrigued, asking themselves, "What is a young lady wearing an over-detailed and rich-looking bridal gown doing here, shouldn't she be getting married now?" Meanwhile, her parents arrived in the city and began asking residents whether they had seen a young bride anywhere, to which they responded with a point or a denial, as they had no idea where she was.

Marina became fatigued while running, gulped, and desired to sit for only fifty seconds. But she couldn't, and if she did, it would be the last of her. She continued rushing to her escape and then, *Dead End*. She came in the marine. The girl felt liberated for a little moment, seeing the sea so bright and sparkling that day, smelling the wind and salt in the air, and it all felt so...calming. However, on the other hand, she began to panic and looked around her; there was a large crowd in the marine, as a large number of goods had arrived that day from England, Spain, South America, China, and other countries.

She could hear many people whispering and talking about her since she looked quite unusual and everyone wondered what was that crimson on her white dress, so she kept walking quickly and glancing around. And then a loud thump.

" Ow! Oh, goodness that hurt! Watch it you—

"What's the matter with you?"

Marina looked up as she landed on her bottom on the ground. She kept angrily mumbling and had no idea what was going on. "Hello? Are you perhaps deaf?" The man spoke to her again, this time with a puzzled expression on his face and his arms crossed. "Did you not see me coming by!? That hurt a lot and I'm running out of time all because of you!" she explained. He halted her;

"Look, ma'am, I do not have time for small talk. Keep an eye out the next time when you walk" Marina rolled her eyes and expressed her displeasure with his demeanor, particularly when he sarcastically spoke *ma'am*. She looked around, unsure of what she should do next. The sound of ships, crowds yelling, pushing enormous boxes around, and arguing distracted her, and she was unable to concentrate if her parents approach her. She chewed her bottom lip again till it started to bleed.

She was annoyed because she had managed to run so far only to come to a halt. As the girl was overthinking herself, a middle-aged man approached a local citizen not far away and asked if they had seen a young-looking bride with brunette hair. "I assume that's her, I saw her wearing jewels and a white gown so, I'm assuming that is her." he said, returning his gaze to the man, who was narrowing his eyes in an attempt to detect Marina.

Marina was terrified and very anxious, and she didn't know how to react quickly. She looked around once more for a hiding spot, and she recognized the guy she had run into before. He was on his way to a ship, lugging heavy wooden boxes. He went to retrieve the last box and then yelled:

"All right crew, she's sailing astern towards Greece. Clear the decks"

"Captain? This is incredible!" She pondered her thoughts. And she dashed over to him, hoping without hope that he wouldn't tell her to go home. "Greetings." She waved and smiled at him all nicely as the young man turned around to her confused. "Oh, you're back? What do you want now? To yell at me again?" He scoffed and gave the heavy wooden box to one of his crew members. He told him "Get this to Hold right away, please."

"I'm aware that we've only just met, in an embarrassing manner. But! Would you be willing to let me board your ship perhaps?" She gave an uneasy smile and hoped for a positive response and she twirled a strand of her hair on her finger. "And why would I do something like that?" He furrowed his brow and wished she would just leave him alone.

"Well, you see, I'm in a bit of a...er—... in a hurry, and it would be fantastic if you let me in! You would help me a lot!" She pleaded with him to let her stay and tried to hurry up because her parents were about to arrive and take her back home, where she would never hear from her father and mother again.

He arrogantly looked her in the eyes

"The answer is no, ma'am. This isn't some kind of a holiday ship that you higher class people take."

"What—No! Please! I beg of you!" tears started falling from her face "I-I have nowhere else to go and I'm terrified." He was undecided about allowing her to board the ship. He sighed and consented, seeing how eager she was to get on it. He told her she needed to get on it right now because the ship is departing in a few minutes. She was ecstatic and delighted at the time. She reached out to shake his hand, but he flinched and made an uneasy look. She was confused as to why he acted in such a way and found him quite odd. She quickly got onto the ship and waited for him to appear on the deck.

Her parents approached her as she stood there looking at the marine; luckily, she was saved just in time. But they were heartbroken and confused because they couldn't find her anywhere. The ship began to cruise southward as the wind blasted through the sails. She leaned on the banister and removed the pins from her hair, allowing the wind to blow through her hair and the air. She exhaled and breathed with such joy and contentment at having finally escaped. She is no longer anyone's prisoner. There would be no more courtship responsibilities, no more shame on her chest, and no more anxiety about getting married. Or, at the very least, that's how she hoped it would be.

The captain suddenly approached her.

"I see you're already settling in." he said, half-smiling and crossing his arms. "Yes, even though this place smells so disgusting, like urine. How about washing this ship?" Gagging at the idea of having to stay here, Marina asked. The man was insulted and rendered mute. That comment seemed curiously pointless. He recognized the differences between a ship and a typical home, but for it to smell like urine? Especially because he takes great care of the ship and hygiene. Quite impolite of her to say.

He tried shrugging it off "Well, since you'll be working for me, I figured we'd get to know each other. Gabriel Santarelli, captain of this vessel." He extended his hand to shake hands.

"Marina Rivalli." she said as she extended her hand for a handshake.

Gabriel paused for a while to consider his comment. "Say, why does your dress have red on it?" He was stunned and speechless. The girl panicked and tried to come up with something as quickly as possible "Oh I accidentally spilled wine all over me when running away" The man was very suspicious of her and didn't trust her. He squinted his eyes at her and kept looking up and down at her. "So, you come from a wealthy family by the looks of you."

She gave him a troubled face as if it were a bad thing.

"Yeah? What about it?

"Nothing just," he snickered, "have you ever worked in your life, princess? How old are you even? "

"Eighteenth, but, what does work have to do with my age?" Marina was uncomfortable and averted her gaze while clumsily wiping her hand on her arm. He was underwhelmed. He grumbled to himself, "It is because you'll work for me." What will he do with her? She's a wealthy brat, after all. She almost certainly never cleaned up after herself. He moaned and clenched his hand, hating every decision he had made in his life. "Work!? I most certainly won't! My hands are too delicate for such stuff!" she inquired, upset and Mr.

Santarelli was beginning to get quite irritated by her "Do not think I'm letting you stay here for free. I'm even being incredibly generous." She looked up and peered at his strange and seductive dark nut brown eyes, black as a summer night and honey-like under the sun's rays whenever he stood under it. She peered into his eyes too long but quickly snapped out of it, looked in a new direction, and felt butterflies in her stomach just by gazing at them. The captain exhaled deeply, regretting what he was about to say, "You'll start cleaning the decks tomorrow. Did you understand? And for the love of God, go change, you're gonna scare my crew mates."

"Are you serious, Mr. Santarelli? I must work here?" The young lady inquired because she believed he would give her a free stay out of sympathy for her miserable life. "Yes you will, you're not on a vacation here. And please don't wreck my ship." he grinned at her, and Marina rolled her eyes in irritation. She approached him and sheepishly prodded his arm with her index finger as he was going to walk away to his cabin and prepare the ship's location.

"What is it now?" He turned to face her.

"Could you please inform me where I'm supposed to sleep? Is it even possible to find a room on a ship?"

"In the bottom deck, you'll sleep with other men. However, because you're new, you'll most likely sleep on the ground."

"On the ground!" she exclaimed aloud. "That's utterly disgusting?! Do you have a private room only for me? I require a private room." her ocean-blue eyes widened and she gave him a worried look.

The captain smirked and shrugged it off, asking if she wanted to visit her cabin or sleep on the deck outside. She immediately nodded, following him, and became enthralled by the fact that he was kidding. They walked down a wooden staircase to the Lower deck. Marina was awestruck; she had never been on a ship like this before, and the timber style of the ship felt attractive and intriguing, as well as oddly cozy. She grinned as she caressed the ship's walls, and the captain, who was perplexed by what she was doing, decided that it was best to remain silent and not even try to dispute with her.

"Well, we've arrived." he stated as he came to a halt in front of a cabin and opened its doors. Marina peered through the doors and was startled as she realized there were people inside.

"I thought I was going to be alone?" she exclaimed, her face flushed with embarrassment.

"Yeah, that's a good one; I'm the only one sleeping alone. Get used to it." Gabriel murmured as he placed his hand on the door to keep it open for her. "Francesca, Margherita, and Giordana are three women you should get to know. Ask them to lend you some of their clothes" Marina was uneasy. And questioned him why does she need their clothes.

"If you don't mind being noticed for wearing a wedding gown, then go ahead, I don't mind." He crossed his arms. Marina sighed and felt guilty about having to borrow someone else's clothes; strangely, she had never borrowed anyone's clothes before; instead, she had custom-made dresses and shoes fashioned for her by the best dressmakers in the kingdom. The girl took a timid step inside, and he shut the doors behind her. She gave them an uneasy smile and waved as she introduced herself;

"Good afternoon, my name is Marina. I suppose I'm new on board—"

"So you were getting married today." a girl with fiery hair exclaimed, laying on the top of the wooden bunk bed. "Congratulations," She sarcastically asked, "where's the groom?" Marina was perplexed by what she said.

"It's not any of your business." the young lady said with a harsh tone and buried her hand in her thick dark brown curly hair.

Marina sat in her shared bunk bed with Francesca, which was now empty. Her corset was killing her and creating red blotches, so she couldn't wait to get rid of it since a maid accidentally tightened it too much. Marina inquired whether the red-haired girl had anything she could lend her. Francesca sighed and rolled her eyes. "I'm only doing it because Gabriel told me to. Otherwise, I won't even touch you." Marina gasped and didn't know what to reply. Margherita, a middle-aged woman in her late fifties, began an argument with Francesca, saying, "Just because you despise rich people doesn't mean you have to be so disrespectful to her. Come here dear; I may have something for you. I know it's ancient, but I hope you don't mind." She gave Marina a warm smile, and the girl was relieved that at least one person on the ship was being courteous to her. "I think this is going to fit you, you're petite like me when I was younger," Margherita said as she opened her chest and showed her a few garments.

Marina guffawed and immediately snatched the clothes. Margherita looked at her with disappointment since the young lady couldn't even say a simple thank you to her. "Fran, was that so difficult to do?" The old lady inquired, and the girl agreed, groaned angrily, and turned around to face the wall, continuing to sleep as she had been before Marina interrupted her. Marina despised Francesca because she was frightening and haughty... Her chilly, dark brown eyes frightened her.

She removed her long black oversized cloak and hung it on the bed; she then felt disgusted as she glanced at her bloody feet; the girl was still shocked by what had happened a while ago. She couldn't wait to get some rest; her feet hurt from running so much that day, and she wasn't used to it. She felt as if she were walking on glass with every step she took. The old woman became concerned and inquired if she was alright.

Marina looked down and said how her feet hurt a bit. Margherita sat down next to her and took a bottle of grappa from her box of clothes. Marina didn't understand why she needed alcohol; she assumed it was because she wanted to drink it, and she was nervous. She had never tried strong alcoholic drinks before, only wine, which she drank only on rare occasions, such as balls or other special occasions. As soon as she was about to ask what she needed alcohol for, Margherita raised her leg and positioned it on her knees, rubbing the alcohol into her feet. Marina screamed in agony, struggling to breathe, and started swearing. The woman rolled her eyes and urged her to pull up her other leg and stop being such a hypocrite. The girl felt as if her spirit was about to depart from her body, and she couldn't wait for it to happen. Marina's face was full of tears as Margherita finished bandaging her up; the anguish was too great for her to bear. But at the very least, she can now walk more confidently.

Margherita and Marina ended up having a brief conversation. The old woman had inquired;

"What did the captain tell you to do?" Marina is a young wealthy-looking girl, so she doubted she had ever done a physical job, she inquired.

She said, "Cleaning the decks. Although he was quite rude to me. The old woman looked at her "I'm sure he was maybe having a bad day. You'll probably be friendlier eventually." Margherita said, putting her hand on Marina's shoulder. Marina became angry at the thought of even having to talk to him. "There is no way that will ever happen, he insulted me too much." she said anxiously.

"Whatever you say." Margherita rolled her eyes. "Also, about your dress. Care to explain?"

"Ah, you know...wine." Margherita considered that the most heinous falsehood she had ever heard. But she opted to remain mute and avoid putting any pressure on her because she appeared to have had an incredibly difficult and stressful day. Marina began to undress after an awkward chat and tossed her bridal gown into a chest full of other things. She was provided a nightgown to go rest in because she wouldn't be working today and it would be pointless for her to start dressed up in something heavy. She spent the remainder of the day in the cabin, chatting with the other ladies and getting to know them better, which helped her relax and feel more at ease. Until it was time for the night.

Marina was sleeping on the ship for the first time when night fell. She was already homesick, and the bed was too little; she was used to her king-sized bed, which she considered to be the most comfortable item on the planet. She kept groaning due to the fact that she had to sleep on such a bed that wasn't up to her standards. The bed that feels like she is lying on a pile of rocks, perhaps even rocks are more comfortable than the bed. She couldn't sleep since she kept turning around all night. When she closed her eyes, all she could see was herself murdering Matias. She'll never be able to forgive herself for what she's done. To calm herself down, she extended her right hand and touched her brother's ring. It made her feel better, but she ended up crying. She couldn't cry out loud because she didn't want to wake anyone else up, so she had to cry quietly, which made her cry even harder because she couldn't cry naturally. What has become of her life?

She fled from her homeland, murdered her fiancé, and then became a cleaning lady all at once. She was also forced to sleep in a filthy wooden bed with a flat mattress and no private room. The girl sincerely hoped that the next day would be better. She eventually became tired and fell asleep after an hour of crying and regretting her life choices and the person she had become. A murderer.

Chapter III

When Marina opened her eyes, the smell of sea salt was all around her. As the day began, the sound of footsteps and loud voices could be heard from all directions. A faint sound of seagulls shrieking above the water could be heard in her slumber. Her face was buried in her pillow, and she was fast asleep.

"Sleeping Beauty, wake up!"

"What? What is happening?" Francesca shook her hard and spoke in a strong tone and she barely opened her eyes. Marina was confused. She had just been forced awake, and everything in her head was still spinning as she struggled to absorb what was going on.

"The sun hasn't even risen yet?" As her eyelids became heavier, she looked at the girl and said "Let me sleep."

"Oh, no more sleeping " She laughed.

"Here's a broom, a mop, and a bucket for you. Begin by cleaning the main deck." She gave her the broom and mop, as well as the pail of soapy water. Francesca was requested to hand them over by Mr. Santarelli himself. Marina whined and pleaded with her to sleep for another hour. Francesca was annoyed. She picked up the bucket and splashed the water on her face. The young lady loudly gasped

"Why!? What's the matter with you!?" She expressed her dissatisfaction in a worried and annoyed tone.

The water began to drip from her body. Her hair was dripping wet and flat. They completely covered her tear-streaked eyes. She looked down and snatched the hem of her nightgown, attempting to squeeze the water out.

The girl gave her a sneering stare.

"Good morning. Now is the time to get to work just like everyone else. Stop whining."

Marina bit her lower lip and looked down awkwardly, avoiding Francesca's sight. She was degraded once more. "I couldn't care less about you. The captain is the one who makes you work." To avoid more confrontation, the frightening girl hurriedly opened the door to their cabin and departed. She was on her own now. The young girl began considering her life again as she sat in her uncomfortable bed. She sighed and gazed at the chest full of clothing. Marina had no desire to dress up, but she was compelled to. After all, she had brought it upon herself. She got up and opened the old wooden chest, which was filled with Margherita's old clothes and belongings. She went through it looking for something pleasing to wear. Among other things, it was a huge change going from soft and elegant fabrics to old overused servant clothes. "What is this even exactly? Most of it is ripped. Argh! I despise this; I can't even put on a nice dress!" Looking at the garments irritated her. She always had the most up-to-date materials and finest things from all across the lands back at home. Her parents insisted on having the best tailors in the kingdom sew their garments.

She sighed as she removed a damaged garment from the wooden chest. Marina looked through the chest to see if there were any shoes that would suit her, but she couldn't locate anything. She wanted to do her hair, but she realized she didn't have much time, so she hurried outdoors. Marina walked out of the cabin barefoot, expecting nothing awful to happen. She thought to herself "It's just wood."

She was holding an old mop in her right hand and an empty bucket in her left hand. She also wanted to bring the broom, but it didn't fit in her hands. Marina had a peek around on the ship, everything seemed to be so calm and tranquil. She stood on the deck for a long time, just looking and marveling at everything. Being outside was a new experience for her. She was free of her gilded cage, with no one to defend her or tell her what to do. In some sense, she'd rather prefer being told around at work, than by her mother and father. Maybe running away was the correct decision after all, even if she knew she missed her home more than ever. It took her a while to come out of her funk. Looking around again, she noticed that practically everyone is staring at her with a filthy expression on their face. Probably because she was a new member, or because of her status which practically everyone knew about up until this point. She stared down at the empty bucket, uneasy, and wondered where she would get fresh water and soap to begin her new responsibilities.

A quick touch on her shoulder startled her.

"Is everything okay?" a soothing voice asked from behind her.

When she turned around, she noticed Margherita. Marina smiled uncomfortably. "All I can say is that I have no idea where to get fresh water. Since, well. We're in the middle of the sea." The elderly lady chuckled. "You're so hilarious." she said, her gaze falling on the bucket. Marina gave her a perplexed look that lasted only a few seconds before the woman in front of her resumed her conversation.

"How come you're barefoot! Do you realize that as the sun rises higher in the sky, walking on the deck will feel like walking on hot rocks? Not to mention the fact that glass shards and other debris will severely injure your foot." Marina's eyes expanded and her oval lips pouted. She felt even more humiliated and like a complete moron now. To be honest, she was terrified to ask anyone for anything in this place and because the elderly woman wasn't in the cabin when she awoke she didn't have the guts to ask someone else. Everyone was still throwing her ugly stares and side glances, clearly indicating that she wasn't welcome on board. She mustered the bravery to split her lips and ask softly, "Can you show me how to sweep the decks too? I've never done it before. I'd also love it if you could show me where I can obtain some fresh water and soap."

"Come on! You aren't a moron! I know you're a bright young lady who can think with her head if she so desires!" The kind old woman encouraged her to be more self-motivated and work on her own rather than relying on others for assistance. Cleaning isn't difficult if you have patience and take control of the situation. Even for a girl who had been born with the golden spoon in her mouth. The young girl eventually complained and apologized, but she still pleaded with her to show her something. Anything that could assist her in learning the fundamentals.

"First and foremost, you'll be putting on shoes. Second, you are not permitted to wear your hair down." Margherita took her hand in hers and guided her to their cabin. She sat down on her bed and walked out to acquire some hair and shoe accessories. Marina felt awful about dragging the poor old lady around and constantly asking for assistance. It was at this time that she began to reconsider her decisions over the previous twenty-four hours. The girl became lost in her thoughts and spaced off, failing to notice her senior clutching items and attempting to catch her attention. Margherita approached her and snapped her finger, causing the young girl to jump a little, her long lashes charming in a manner to bring her back to reality. "I couldn't think of anything else for you to wear. For the time being, you may wear Giordana's old boots. She's an old hag, she won't notice that it's hers anyways."

"Ah I suppose they're fine for old boots." says the young girl. Marina sighed as she gazed up at her. She put them on, but they were most likely two sizes too big. Margherita pushed her thumb on the boot's end to see how much bigger they were. She went to grab two socks and urged Marina to shove them into her boots so they wouldn't feel as huge and would be more comfortable to walk in throughout the day.

"Do you feel more at ease now?"

"Yeah, it does actually." Marina answered, with a faint smile on her lips. She ruffled her still-wet hair with her fingers. Margherita drew her attention "Why can't I let my hair down?" The girl was taken by the idea. It didn't make sense to her.

"Because your hair gets in the way when you're working. I don't want any hair in my food, either."

Marina's lips formed an O before she closed them. It made more sense to her now. Margherita snatched a towel and began rubbing it against the girl's hair to dry it. She sat down next to her and picked a nearby brush that the girl assumed was hers after she finished. "So, runaway bride hm? Why did you leave?"

"I suppose I just didn't like it."

Marina was in a panic. After all, confessing her fleeing because she killed her fiancé was a stretch. She was still unsure who she could trust. Especially because she's only been aboard the ship for one day. "Oh? I thought people like you have the time of their life. You know, servants in every corner, not having the need to pick up your glass."

"I mean, I suppose it's nice not to have to do much. However, after a while, it becomes tedious. It's a little upsetting to see your brother walk to school while you stay at home all day and talk to the maids." She grumbled and crossed her arms, exasperated at the thought of her very boring life. She screamed in her chamber after being chastised over and over that she isn't allowed to do certain things, such as venturing outdoors on her own, getting schooled again... "Oh, you have a brother?" Margherita inquired. Marina's eyes started to water up. Margherita's smile eventually faded as she realized what was going on.

"Twin brother. He passed away."

Marina lowered her head and pursed her lips. Due to the number of times, she had sobbed over her brother's death, she no longer cried. She remained silent throughout and clutched an apron fold.

"Please accept my apologies..." The lady sighed.

"No, it' is all right. I shouldn't have mentioned him in the first place." Marina felt a surge of remorse as she glanced at her brother's ring. Every time she thought of him, she was filled with guilt. She'd never be able to forgive herself. She was given a reassuring grin by the old woman, who was attempting to reassure her that she didn't have to feel so horrible about herself. The woman's warmth appealed to Marina. She may have just recently met her, but she was struck by how calm she is, how patient she is with her, and how willing she is to talk to her about anything. Marina expressed her gratitude to the thoughtful lady. She got up and attempted to straighten her outfit in preparation for her first day of work. Margherita placed her hand on her shoulder as she was about to grab the mop "What are you up to? I'm taking you to the kitchen." She couldn't understand what was going on. Didn't Francesca tell her to clean all of the decks? Despite this, she couldn't see herself in the kitchen just yet. The fear of poisoning everyone because she can't cook and has never done so before.

"But I am unable to prepare meals. Why did you choose me to be in the kitchen over everyone else?"

"It's not like you'll never cook. You'd eventually find your way around here. And it's now! I don't know what Gabriel told you, but you're coming with me." the woman joked.

In horror, Marina swallowed her saliva. She found the woman's complete lack of respect for the captain a little intimidating. Marina would understand if she didn't appreciate her because she was still new. Mr. Santarelli, on the other hand, is a captain and the ship's owner. Ensures that everyone and everything is safe, and accepts complete responsibility for everything. She couldn't imagine what it would be like if someone did that to her mother or even her father. Margherita took a step forward and opened the cabin's old wooden doors, which made a grating noise every time they were opened or closed.

"Please stick with me. The kitchen is located on the second deck."

Marina couldn't help but wonder as they went outdoors on the main deck, downwards with old wooden stairs, and began going lower towards the kitchen. "For how long have you worked here? Have you learned anything about the sea?" Margherita laughed at her curiosity "I did learn loads of stuff about it, it's very interesting. And I've been here for more than two decades."

Marina stopped her off in the middle of her gasp, "Oh? Has it been twenty years? How did you not grow tired of it?" Marina's pointy nose was mashed against the old woman's finger as she giggled. "You're very curious. If you're interested in learning more about nautical activities, I recommend speaking with the captain." The girl had no intention of conversing with him. When he spoke to her, he seemed arrogant and cocky. She'd rather die of curiosity than ask him a question. They quickly made their way to the kitchen. The main deck was only a couple of short steps away. The kitchen was nothing to be amazed at. The whole room was constructed of wood and appeared to be old and overused. Everything, even the ship, would go up in flames if just one tiny catastrophe occurred. Marina was frightened about that. She had also expected no one to be in the kitchen at this time, but there was one man at the table. Margherita was waved by a dark-skinned man with dark brown hair tied in a messy low ponytail.

"Good morning , Margherita. Is everything well?" Even in the morning, he appeared to be a happy man.

He quickly realized that they were accompanied by another individual. "Oh, Is this the woman Gabriel has mentioned?" Marina was becoming agitated by everyone's continual mention of Mr. Santarelli at this time. She let out a small irritated sigh. The man rose from his seat and approached her "Pleasure to meet you, D'Angelo Antoni" He smiled, revealing dimples on both cheeks. The smile was pleasant and affectionate.

"Marina, but I'm guessing Mr. Santarelli already informed you." she said as she held out her hand to him. Antoni laughed "He did. He actually mentioned you this morning." She rolled her eyes while pinching her lips. He softly took her hand in his and kissed it. "It was a pleasure to meet you." he added, smirking. Marina's face reddened. She was taken aback by the unexpected hand kiss. His enticing and lovely structures had rendered her speechless. This was a usual act by Antoni. He enjoyed tormenting people with his charms and making them laugh. He was particularly fond of their memorable reactions.

Judged For Mercy

"Antoni, leave the poor girl alone."

Antoni rolled his eyes and tightened his low ponytail. As the kind woman asked her to assist her in preparing breakfast, she slowly drew her hand away. Antoni sat down again, still laughing at himself. Marina approached Margherita and inquired, "What are your plans for breakfast? I just wanted to remind you that it's probably best if you don't let me cook just yet."

Marina was given a medium-sized knife with a wooden handle, as well as a lot of vegetables like carrots, tomatoes, mushrooms, and so on... Everything has to be cut. The young lady groaned at the fact that she needed to work a lot. The old woman reasoned that it would be better if she taught her how to do simple tasks. It was as if she were demonstrating how to prepare bread with marmalade to a five-year-old child. Marina regarded the knife, then the veggies, with trepidation. She had no idea where to start. She paused for a bit before picking up one onion, deciding that it would be the easiest to cut because all she had to do was peel it with her hands and chop it into small pieces. A tall charming guy with thick black hair slicked in the back and one strand of hair dropping on his face, walked in with the terrifying girl whose glare made your bones shiver, just as she started putting an onion on a wooden chopping board Marina gulped down her spit.

Unfortunately, her counter faced the dining table where the rest of the staff ate. She was even more neurotic than before, fearful of being judged by the captain and his companion for her folly. When the captain walked in, he appeared to be in a good mood. He waved to Margherita as he looked in her direction. She and Giordana were to him like mothers or aunts, they both acted that way toward him, which he adored. Marina was too shy to return the greeting and continued to cut the onion while looking down. He sat at the table with Antoni and Francesca, two of his best pals who are rarely seen apart. They all act like a family and try to help one another as much as they can. Antoni started cracking jokes as soon as he sat down, and Francesca was already annoyed by his presence. Even this early in the morning, she wasn't psychologically prepared for his god-awful jokes.

The elderly lady approached them and offered every one of them a freshly brewed cup of coffee. Margherita was everyone's favorite when it came to cooking and making coffee. Giordana could cook as well as Margherita, but her cooking lacked Margherita's warmth. She kissed them all on the forehead with a huge kiss. As usual, Mr. Santarelli received additional attention. Antoni gasped in disbelief and out of the blue, demanded another kiss, accusing her of having favorites. She rolled her eyes and stroked her hand through Antoni's hair, admonishing him to be more mature. The image in front, befuddled the young girl looking up at them, melting her heart. She gave them a soft smile because they reminded her of her family. The captain smirked at his good old friend's folly and gave Marina a quick glance. They shared a brief moment of eye contact. He gave her a disinterested expression.

Marina became agitated as a result of her embarrassment at staring him in the eyes. She looked down as quickly as she could after breaking eye contact. The man returned his buddies' stares as if nothing had happened.

Marina began peeling the onion, but she couldn't help but overhear what they were discussing. Francesca had been muttering her name here and there.

"It's only her first day, and she's already willing to give up!" The captain responded to the girl's exclamation "What exactly is she up to in the kitchen? I thought I told you to inform her that she needed to clean the decks." He was irritated and frustrated by her. He didn't want to put his life in danger because of some spoiled Neapolitan girl who couldn't cook. She didn't even bother to look at him; instead, she sat back in her chair and imitated him with hand-talking, telling him that he was bothering her. Antoni, on the other hand, pinched his lips and gave them both a cold stare. When they argued about little matters, they acted like children.

"Why are you two passing such harsh judgments on her? Give her some space. Maybe she will enjoy her time here as much as everybody else." As he exclaimed what he said, he established eye contact with Francesca. She, too, couldn't wait to get off the ship and didn't bother to heed anyone's commands when she first boarded. The tall man chuckled "Yes, indeed. I'll give her a week at most. She'll lose her mind at some point " The girl, as obnoxious and unconcerned as ever... She leaned against the table, pointing out her index and middle finger, and murmured

"I'm going to give her two days. I'm betting forty thousand lire."

They exchanged handshakes while Antoni expressed his disappointment in them. He bet as well, saying how if the girl stays for longer than they expected, all the money goes to him. Marina was completely taken aback by what they were saying. She was so irritated that she lost her focus and began cutting the onion too quickly, which was one of the primary blunders that caused her eyes to wet and she was unable to see anything... She slit her finger shortly after that. As blood began to drip down her finger, she screamed in pain. The sixty-year-old woman raced up to her, panicked, and asked her what the hell had happened. Marina sniffed, her left hand pressing on her right index finger. Margherita groaned, unable to believe she had messed up on such a basic task.

Francesca smirked quietly as she realized she was already a failure. D'Angelo became irritated at this point and gave her a chilly look, signaling that she had had enough. Mr. Santarelli got up and headed up to the counter, clearly concerned about what had transpired. Inquiring whether they require assistance. Marina's freckled face was dripping with tears, and she was too humiliated to admit she needed help. Margherita rummaged through the kitchen in search of bandages to help her cover the cut. She exclaimed as she rummaged through the shelf "Please, Gabriel, go get some sea for me. A cup of it will be enough." He grabbed a cup and walked down to the lower deck to fetch some seawater.

Marina was in a bad mood. She was humiliated by her inability to perform even the most basic tasks. She began profusely apologizing to the elderly lady, as well as for damaging the cutting board, which was now covered with blood smudges. As looking at the blood, she widened her thick-eyelashed eyes while being remembered the other day. She felt sick remembering Matias, the man who has ruined her life for good. Marina kept breathing heavily, trying to calm down and surpass her emotions. She was told to relax and that it wasn't the end of the world. Margherita was meant to make her infamous homemade veggie soup with grated parmesan cheese on top for breakfast, and she still felt awful for making everyone lose their appetite. She felt humiliated and glanced down.

"I'm terribly sorry. I became distracted. I couldn't help but be intrigued when I overheard Francesca mention me." She spoke softly in hushed silence. Margherita simply rolled her eyes and couldn't believe how easily distracted she is. Mr. Santarelli arrived after a few moments. "I've brought you some sea. It'll help with the wound." Marina looked at him perplexed "Thank you, I suppose." She kept gripping onto the towel which was wrapped around her wounded finger. The captain sighed at her rudeness "I'll need to double-check the coordinates. Antoni meet me in the cabin."

"Yes, Mr. Santarelli." Antoni retorted sarcastically.

He sighed and said, "Please. don't call me that."

Chapter IV

Marina was left alone in the kitchen with the old lady after all three companions had gone their ways. Antoni turned around and walked backward, blowing a kiss to Marina and winking as the trio walked away. She laughed at his folly. Marina got up and walked up to Margherita, asking if she needed any additional

assistance. The lady responded "For the time being, I suppose you might start sweeping the main deck. After that, wipe the windows, and then you can relax until three o'clock when I'll be starting lunch."

Marina, after hearing everything the woman has assigned to her, It made her sigh, and it was already difficult for her to picture the work. She inhaled deeply and began heading back to her cabin, where she had left the broom, mop, and bucket. She moved towards the main deck, holding the broom in her left hand. The majority of the crew had already gathered on the deck. Whether it's smoking or inspecting the sails here and there, etc... She feels more confident now, despite the fact that she has already embarrassed herself enough in the kitchen. She didn't want her mood to be ruined by unpleasant thoughts that rushed through her mind.

Marina was also perplexed as to why she had been so quiet the entire time; she is normally a very talkative and gregarious person. It could simply be stress from the previous day. She took a close look at the broom and began to analyze it. To decide where to put it and to begin cleaning. Marina, being the dumb girl she is, held it entirely incorrectly and began sweeping the deck like a moron. The crew members that were outside and observed her were very perplexed as to what she was doing.

"That is why he should not allow women to board the ship."

" You're absolutely correct."

The two sailors talked about the perplexed young lady.

When she was sweeping the deck, she looked like a complete imbecile. Mr. Santarelli happened to pass by at that same moment. "Wonderful." she exclaimed to herself. She didn't need him to respond with a retort about her inability to tidy. He palmed himself as soon as he saw her:

"Dear God!" He moaned, unable to believe that ladies like her exist at all. She was wary of him at this point and raised her voice, pointing her index finger at him. "Stop being so judgmental! I'm fed up with you! And Francesca, your friend! What exactly is your issue!? Just leave me alone!" He was surprised and gave her a chilly stare.

"I simply wanted to show you how to sweep the deck." Marina felt bad. She stood nervously next to him, handing him the broom and carefully watching him demonstrate. He took a position, rolling up the sleeves of his dark blue sweater. The man began gracefully demonstrating how to sweep, and Marina was taken aback by how simple it appeared when he did it. When he was finished, he handed the broom to her and said,

"This is it. I'm already kicking myself for letting you in."

Marina sighed as she snatched up the broom. She had a relaxed expression on her face "Yes, that's fantastic. Don't you have anything to do as a captain?"

His dark brown eyes expanded. "Oh no, I forgot to—" he was stopped off by the sound of smashing in the lower deck. He dashed downstairs to take care of the matter he had neglected before.

She continued to sweep the ancient wooden deck as he walked away. She observed while cleaning that nothing had been altered in heaven knows how long. Everything appeared to be old, at least two or three decades old. Perhaps even more. While cleaning, she smiled softly, grateful for the captain's assistance. Although she still doesn't fully trust him, because he's so unbelievably rude to her. She was just hoping he got off on the wrong foot the other day and is genuinely as sweet as everyone claims. Even when she was harmed in the kitchen, he offered to help immediately, instead of laughing at her.

She was entirely absorbed in her thoughts at this point. Marina was pondering all of the new folks she's met. That was a new score for her in terms of meeting a large number of individuals in a single day. The girl hardly ever spoke to anyone during balls or other social events. She wasn't interested in the first place and she wasn't fond of privileged brats, daughters of dukes, and such who always seemed to judge her harshly for everything. She jolted awake as she felt a peculiar sensation in her stomach. Because she wasn't used aboard the ship, it was going to happen at some point. The tearful girl dashed to the banisters, stood on her toes, and puked over the edge. Seasickness has taken hold of her; it's something that many individuals who aren't acclimated to ship life, experience. It goes away after a while, which Marina had hoped for.

She leaned on the banister while turned around, facing the deck. She groaned and wished to die. She didn't need seasickness to ruin her mood even more.

Everything was making her feel messed up. It's not easy adjusting to your new life. Working eight hours a day is exhausting, especially when you've never worked before and are now being forced to do duties you've never imagined doing in your life. Marina tried to bury her regrets. She kept telling herself that this was something she'd always desired and that something would always get in the way. She'll eventually depart the ship and go her own way, once she's become used to everything. Without the captain, her parents micromanaged her, or the entire city judged her for everything. She was fantasizing about the day when she would receive the keys to her own home and be able to dance freely in the living room or anywhere she pleased. She was ecstatic at the prospect of stepping outside in a little seaside town with few people, children running around, the scent of fresh air, and meeting new things and cultures.

The vivacious young lady continued to fantasize about her ideal future. All she had to do was say her goodbyes to her parents, get her cat and parrot, and flee the place that felt cursed at this point.

She gasped out as she realized she was sweeping the floor correctly. With a rush of adrenaline coursing through her veins, she hurriedly cleaned the deck. She was pleased with herself, unable to believe that she had once again done something decent. A little towel and a bucket filled with water and soap were left by the old woman some time ago. Marina grabbed the bucket and towel from the floor and walked over to the windows. She began cleaning the windows up and down, and up and down, attempting to clean every unclean area. While doing so, the girl became so comfortable that she began humming a few symphonies. It was soothing, and it made the job more appealing. While cleaning and humming like a hummingbird, she developed a contented expression on her face.

She walked over to the cabin room's window. As she cleaned, the curious girl couldn't help but peek inside the captain's room. Marina couldn't tell what was inside because she couldn't see it clearly. All she could do was make assumptions based on what she could see. Marina was nevertheless happy that he tried to help her twice, and she hoped he would soften up further on her. She didn't particularly enjoy being on bad terms with other people.

By the time she finished her responsibilities, which included washing all of the ship's windows and sweeping the main deck, she was exhausted. It was noon. Tiredness got to her, and headed back to her cabin, throwing herself into her uncomfortable bed for a little nap. She was so exhausted that she couldn't bring herself to remove her filthy clothing and ended up sleeping in them. Marina slept for three hours straight. She'd sleep till at least seven o'clock if she could, but she couldn't since she had obligations. A quick touch of a delicate female hand grasped her shoulder while she was deep in slumber, dreaming of whatnot.

"Marina, wake up." To wake her up, she was gently shackled.

"Is it three already?

- I feel like I've been run over by a train."

It was none other than Giordana who had jolted her awake. For her age, she was an extremely promiscuous woman. "Yes, it is. Now rise and proceed to the kitchen!" She yelled at her, pleading for her to wake up. "It's not the first time I've heard something like that."

The girl rolled her eyes and puffed at her 1800s-styled bangs, wishing they would move away from her face. The stern middle-aged lady marched away, shutting the doors behind her. Marina stood up as soon as she walked out the door and washed her face with water from the washbasin on the oak wood cabinet. She grabbed a dry little towel from the cabinet, cleaned her face, and left.

Marina began to walk away, her mind still on the kitchen. She hoped Margherita and Giordana had already done the cooking and that all she had to do was serve the food. She could smell all kinds of delectable dishes as she walked into the kitchen: pesto pasta, tomato soup, apple cake, and so on...

As she walked in, she waved and said, "Good afternoon." with a bright smile. Several others, including the captain, greeted her at the table. Marina approached Margherita and asked her if there was anything she needed to do right now. "Place them at the table, dear." the old woman said as she handed her two plates. Marina formed an O with her mouth, not expecting the plates to be so heavy or Margherita to provide her with something to do so quickly. Her hands were shaking as she confidently walked over to the dining table and served the platters. The captain's right-hand man rose to his feet "I'll assist you! Don't put yourself through this!" He felt horrible seeing her struggle for the first time with heavy plates and offered to assist her in placing them on the table.

"Leave it." the captain said coldly as he gazed up at
Antoni. He motioned him to take a seat with his hands.
The man was taken aback by his actions; he hadn't
expected it from him. To reach him, he got up a little and
bent over the table "What's the matter with you!? Isn't it
possible for a man to be courteous nowadays?" Mr.
Santarelli's hands were crossed "She isn't stupid enough
to not bring a few plates with her. That's something even
a child is capable of." He was quite harsh with Marina.
She overheard him saying that, but she decided to be an
adult and ignore him.

Marina took a stroll over to the two elderly ladies who
were busy cooking lunch for others. She gathered the
final few items for the table. The girl straightened up,
took a deep breath, and walked over to the table with
both hands full. She set down a large golden-colored
chicken with a generous amount of spice. All of the
items smelled fantastic when combined. The hungry
stomach of the fatigued girl began to growl; she hadn't
eaten anything and all the lovely food was making her
hungry. She was uneasy seeing everyone eating and
sitting at the table. She stared down, biting her bottom
lip hard, and dejectedly walked away to her cabin,
thinking the food wasn't for her. She moaned, wishing
she could just do something herself. Antoni then called
her over to sit down next to him. She smiled softly at
him and revealed both of her dimples. She sat down and
was patiently waiting for her dish to arrive so she could
finally begin eating for the first time today. Margherita

began cutting the roasted golden-colored chicken and dishing out pieces to everyone once everyone had seated down and was ready to eat. Marina was frightened as she took her plate and was going to give her a portion of it; she nervously looked over at the old lady and explained "I'm sorry but. I don't eat meat." She was always sensitive when it came to animals, one of her weakest spots. Just the thought of chewing on meat made her guts twist.

"What? Is something wrong?" Marina asked

Margherita made a confused and annoyed facial expression " Nothing, you could've just stated something sooner and I would've made you something different." Margherita exclaimed as she set her dish down, unable to think of anything more to give her. The captain chuckled, "We always have a salad." and Margherita smacked him behind his head, yelling at him that he isn't funny. The girl nervously giggled saying "It's fine— I'll just have some soup! It's not a big deal." She stood up and grabbed across the table tomato soup, pouring it on her plate and sitting back down, trying to enjoy eating in peace. Just as she thought that Antoni started asking her numerous questions. She let out a sharp sigh and rolled her eyes, at this point she can't even eat.

"What brought you here? Where did you formerly reside? Why do you choose to not eat meat?" He was becoming increasingly obnoxious with his questions, but for some reason, others were also interested in her responses. "I'm not sure, but I think I enjoy traveling. I'm from Naples." Marina took a spoon in her hand once more, only to realize that the spoon isn't made for soup. It bothered her for a moment since she got used to her parents correcting her on which fork or knife is the right one for any type of food. The girl sighed and tried to relax, since she isn't with her parents anymore, and attempted to take a drink of the soup. "Naples! That's very intriguing! I went there once and had a great time. I'll come back and you can show me around!" Antoni was ecstatic.

The girl on the run laughed at his response. "Of course." She said that, knowing full well that she would never return. She finally managed to eat something after answering all of his grueling questions. Lunch had a pleasant effect on her. Everyone was friendly and there were a few laughs. Plus, the meal was incredible. Despite the fact that the only thing she ate was regular tomato soup, she became ill once more. She reasoned that this meant she had consumed too much of it, but she was wrong. "Where's the washroom—" she hastily rose and excused herself. Francesca gestured with her finger and swiftly conveyed the directions to her. Marina ran to find it before she could finish. She was in the Head, which was also where the washroom was. She noticed a towel as she opened the washroom doors and hurriedly grabbed it, placed it on the toilet seat, and got down on her knees. Marina immediately puked and began sobbing. She couldn't take being unwell all the time any longer. Bad thoughts began to flood her mind, and she concluded that her persistent nausea was maybe caused by pregnancy.

Marina cried even harder as she placed her hand on her stomach, expressing her dissatisfaction with being pregnant. Not right now, and certainly not with him. The thought of Matias and her maybe getting pregnant made her feel even sicker. Margherita dashed towards her, frightened by Marina's reaction in the kitchen. When she saw her crying and down on her knees, she became even more worried. The elderly lady sat down and shifted her now messy bun away from her face. She tried to calm her down by telling her that seasickness is entirely normal and that everyone gets it at some point. Marina screamed as she sobbed "I'm not seasick at all! I'm pregnant—I believe I am." The woman's eyes widened, and she couldn't say anything. Marina was pregnant, and she couldn't believe it.

"H-How long have you been aware of this?"

"I'm not sure, for a day?

... I'm not sure if I'm expecting!" She brushed the tears away from her eyes.

"Well did you have, you know... that kind of a relationship with a man?" Margherita said it quietly because she was afraid Marina would be offended.

"N-no!—I'm not sure I want to talk about it..." Marina sighed and looked down, not wanting to think about what had happened the day before. But she needed to recall some facts in order to determine whether she was seasick or simply pregnant. Margherita shrugged it off, reasoning that she couldn't possibly be pregnant if she had never had intercourse. The lovely woman assisted her in cleaning up and walking to their cabin so she could rest for a while. Marina couldn't stare any longer, despite the fact that it was just four o'clock. Marina sat down on her bed as soon as they arrived at their cabin and began removing all of her clothes, including the boots she had borrowed from Giordana. The girl wore a long, comfortable nightgown that she received as a gift from Giordana because the unfortunate girl was without clothing. Marina began undoing her hair; she felt much more at ease with her long puffy, curly dark brown hair loose. It also kept her warm, which she appreciated, and it would come in handy now as she was about to lie down. Margherita quietly smiled as she laid down, pulling the blankets up over her and kissing her on the forehead, wishing her a restful night's sleep. "Get plenty of rest and don't dwell on the negative." As the old lady was going to walk away, Marina was mumbled

"I'm terrified!"

The woman glanced around, perplexed as to what she was afraid of. "What are you talking about?"

"I don't want to let anyone down…"

She yawned and was unable to communicate due to exhaustion, and by the time Margherita wanted to speak with her, she had fallen asleep.

Because the day had been long and exhausting, it was no wonder that she was already asleep. The woman began strolling towards her kitchen, intending to clean up the mess caused by the others. As she walked in, she noticed the captain and Antoni alone in the room, cleaning up after themselves. Antoni rushed over to Margherita and inquired about Marina's whereabouts.

"She's in good shape. She was simply seasick."

Mr. Santarelli said, "Of course she did."

Margherita clenched her fists in rage "I'm going to have a long conversation with you. I anticipated more from you." Her tone abruptly shifted, and it was threatening. "Good luck, wouldn't want to be you right now." Antoni chuckled as he clapped his friend on the back. He left them two fully alone in the room as he walked away. "What are you talking about? Why are you so irritated with me these days?" The man was more perplexed than defending himself; he believed Margherita's age had finally worn her down and made her insane. "What about me? Do you want to know the matter with me? What's the matter with you!? You've been treating the poor girl like she's an animal for the entire day! I was hoping for a lot more from you!" She continued to yell at him, unable to believe what he was saying.

"Nothing is wrong with me. I am just not letting anyone on my ship for free while still being absolutely rude to me and ungrateful." He continued to take deep breaths, angered by Marina's presence and the idea that Margherita, who had been like a mother to him, was not on my side. "Gabriel, my love. I understand your point, but it's not like she's to blame for her inability to cook or

clean!" She persisted in defending herself. "At the very
least, acknowledge that Marina is attempting to do
physical labor. When was the last time you saw girls like
her do something like that? And be thankful that she isn't
as spoiled as the others." Even though Marina was in
reality just as awful as the rest.

Margherita kept attempting to persuade him to change
his views, as well as seeing things from Marina's
perspective. If the captain continues to give her dirty
looks and harsh words, it's no surprise that she'll be a
wreck on the ship. "Goodnight Margherita." the man said
as he put the dishes in the sink and began heading out of
the kitchen. He appeared exhausted and irritated. "I
haven't finished speaking with you yet! I swear to God,
if you don't start treating her equally, I'm going to kill
you." She crossed her arms, as she watched him leave to
his lonely cabin. She was the only one left in the kitchen
at this point, so she went to continue cleaning up the
mess.

Margherita couldn't help but think of Marina as she
walked out the door to her cabin. What made the young
girl flee her wedding? What was the rationale behind it?
Why does she believe she's pregnant when she's never
had intercourse? None of it made sense to her; all she
wanted to know was that the girl hadn't done anything
strange and that everything would make sense shortly.

Chapter V

July 17th, 1908.

It was a beautiful, sunny summer morning, just like any other at this time of the season. The meadow was strewn with dandelions, and a variety of fresh aromas filled the air as all kinds of flowers started to bloom. It had rained the night before, so the ground was still wet and water drops were dropping from plants, trees, and other sources... The citizens of Naples have begun waking up and getting ready for their daily tasks. The children ran around, accompanied by stray dogs and cats who were just as excited as they were. Everyone was busy with their tasks: bakers were displaying freshly baked goods in the windows so that the entire city may admire their hard, wonderful labor. The newspaper delivery lad was distributing newspapers to every house in the city while riding his bike along the shore...

The young girl was still resting in her room, as the night before had been extremely stressful. Her black-haired cat Cesare slept quietly under her legs, coiled up like a ball, making him appear as if he were nothingness. Because he felt safer with her, he always slept by her side. The brunette girl clung to her large, soft pillow, which helped her feel more at ease while sleeping. Until her brother,

Rocco flung open the doors. He yelled at her to wake up, unconcerned that she was still sleeping. Marina ignored him since she didn't want to wake up and wanted to sleep some more. He grumbled angrily and rolled his green-eyed eyes, irritated by her laziness.

Her brother began shaking her violently, causing her cat to become enraged and leap from the bed. He stopped her off, adding, "Mother and father called you for breakfast." The tired girl's face was in her pillow as she whispered, "Leave me alone, you're annoying—" She snatched up the silky white sheets and wrapped herself in them completely. Marina's brother walked away with his hands behind his back, adding "So long as you say so. I'm guessing I'll go to the city by myself then." The girl's eyes widened as she grabbed her sheets and threw them away, leaping out of bed as quickly as she could. " You should have said it earlier!" She continued. Marina loved going outside of her home, she always took every single opportunity to go out. As he sat down on her double-sized wooden canopy bed with long curtains and gorgeous etching, the young man chuckled, flinging back his blonde-colored hair.

Marina strolled over to her enormous closet and rummaged through all of her garments, unsure of what she should wear. She picked two outfits from a hanger, unsure which one would be better for her. " Ah, the blue one is too dismal, and the white one makes me look like

Judged For Mercy

I'm getting married. God, I hate it when I can't find a dress for such basic situations." she lamented. " I don't know, just hurry up." He added. She ultimately chose the white gown and grabbed her hat that had poppies attached to it. Marina tossed the clothing on her bed and was going to remove her long white cotton long-sleeved nightgown when she realized her darling brother was there.

"Do you mind?"

"Mind what exactly?"

Marina grinned "I understand that we shared the same womb and that incest is a thing. However, I'm not interested in you in that sense."

"You're disgusting— " the boy muttered as he walked out of her chamber uneasily.

The girl waited for him to completely seal the doors so that no one could see her undress. She was finally alone. She began to gently pull up her long nightgown and remove it from her body. She tossed it on her bed for the maids to fold neatly because she wasn't very good at it nor did she wish to learn. Marina examined her reflection in the mirror, moving her gaze up and down her diminutive frame. She made an uneasy grimace with her hands on her chest, wishing she was more developed. The girl jolted awake and proceeded to put on her undergarments and long socks. Marina began altering her dress for a few moments until she was happy with it. She preferred to dress in simple, comfortable clothes rather than something more voluminous and inconvenient.

The girl noticed that her hair was still braided. She braids her hair before going to bed so that she wakes up with gorgeous curls. Marina sat on her bed, unbraiding her braids and inspecting herself in the mirror. She began humming as she worked, and soon she was finished and pleased with the appearance of her hair. The girl didn't feel like arranging her hair that day, so she braided on herself one long braid and was pleased with it. She as well added a lovely green ribbon on it for the finishing touch.

She got up, brushed her teeth, and prepared to meet up with her family. As she stepped out of her chamber, Rocco was standing by the doors, bored out of his mind

"Lovely blue ribbon but why did it take you so long?"
He continued to tap the glass on his wristwatch,
demonstrating how long she had been getting ready.
Marina seemed unconcerned and walked away into the
kitchen, prompting the impatient young man to pursue
her and telling him it was green instead of blue, and the
young man sighed in frustration. Marina's brother
approached her and mocked her, saying, "No red stain on
your lips or darkening your lashes today, I see."

"I wouldn't look like death right now if you hadn't rushed
me."

"It's not as if it would make any difference." he muttered
under his breath.

Marina locked her gaze on his, already irritated by his
demeanor. When he mocked her, she detested it, but then
again. She's the one who makes the most fun of him. As
her brother was ready to inquire, "So, where's Mia?" she
rolled her eyes and moaned as she gazed at the paintings
and decorations in the hallway

"You mean your beloved?" Marina smiled.

"Who else could it be? When will she be able to join us?" He was intrigued. He had been thinking about her all morning and was nervous to see her. "I'm sorry. She told me she was going to spend the weekend with her parents."

He sighed and sighed again, feeling horrible. "I couldn't wait to spend the entire day with her... to see her lovely dark brown eyes, kind smile, and just her in general. We hardly see each other anymore because I've gotten so busy. And I planned something special for her today." The girl made a snide remark. "She, too, is occupied. Her family needs a great deal of assistance." He agreed, knowing how difficult it would be for both of them to see each other.

"I wanted to express my regret for yesterday."

"What do you mean? For what purpose?" She was perplexed.

"For disregarding you when you needed me last night." Rocco was ashamed; he had always promised her that he would always be there for her, no matter what. However, he had broken his vow the night before... Marina put her hand on his shoulder, smiled, and reassured him that everything was great and that the other gals had mostly ignored her this time. They continued on their way to the dining area, conversing as they went. The girl couldn't stop herself from bombarding him with questions. She enjoyed asking others questions about everything that came to mind, but she disliked being in a dismal group of people."What's the status of your painting classes? When are you going to draw me again?" The girl grinned. She adored it when he drew her. It made her feel incredibly loved and valued, especially because he sketched her. It was his method of expressing love, just as it was for their mother. He learned how to sketch from her. Marina, on the other hand, lacked skill. She was brilliant at playing the flute and dancing, but neither of these activities made her happy. Dancing was pleasurable, but it didn't satisfy her sufficiently. When Rocco, on the other hand, picks up a brush or a pencil, it feels so natural to him. His strokes appeared to be quite pleasant and graceful. He liked to go outside in nature to acquire ideas and see what he could sketch next. He called his sister or Mia to come to be his muse whenever he ran out of ideas. Marina was unconcerned; in fact, she enjoyed messing around and posing in odd positions for reference...

"It's going well. He sighed, "I just completed painting Amelia yesterday and wanted to deliver it to her today. But, oh well, I'll most likely give it to her tomorrow." He made a pout and blew away a strand of hair that had fallen on his face. Marina gave a warm grin. She enjoyed watching her brother so enamored with a girl.

They made it to the kitchen in no time. Their parents were already seated at the table, talking about their ambitions for their job as well as their children. As they entered, their mother rose and moved closer to her beautiful children, hugging them both and kissing them on the cheeks. Marina snickered and wished their mother a good morning, while the boy whimpered at her devotion.

"Mother! Please, it isn't even ten o'clock yet."

"So what? Am I not permitted to show affection to my children anymore?" She had a gloomy expression and crossed her arms. You could notice a resemblance in each of them when they were standing next to their parents. The curly-haired girl resembled her father, who was similarly olive-skinned, short for a male, and shared her hair texture and color. Her brother, on the other hand, resembled their mother in appearance and behavior. He was as pale as she was, albeit she was even paler. Despite the fact that Rocco was more focused on his mother and Marina on her father, they both possessed the eyes of their respective parents. The daughter had her ocean blue eyes on their mother, while Rocco had the same emerald green eyes on their father. The fact that they both had something that showed a little bit of their parents was quite lovely to see. Marina's only weakness was that she possessed their father's anger, which was quite unpleasant. Hers was more steady, but Mr. Rivalli's rage issues were so severe that it took him years to settle them down.

His wife, on the other hand, is wonderfully peaceful and compassionate just like their son. She gradually tried to tone down his anger issues after they married and got to know each other.

Rocco approached Marina and pulled the chair away from the table, inviting her to sit and assuring her that he would assist her in sitting more comfortably. She smiled at his brotherly devotion and relished the opportunity to be spoiled. When they were both seated, their father put down the newspaper he had been reading for the past twenty minutes, placed it on the table, and proceeded to fix his pipe, puffing a few breaths of smoke. Even when he wasn't supposed to, he gave the impression of being intimidating. Mrs. Rivalli begged him to quit smoking at the table, saying that she couldn't stand the smell of tobacco so early in the morning, especially when she was going to eat breakfast.

A maid entered the room, softly pushing a trolley loaded with a variety of dishes. It smelled wonderful, and it made everyone's stomachs turn. Marina sat close to her mother, admiring her beautiful blonde hair, which was fashioned in a high, massive bun. She appeared to be quite young, and she would chuckle when people misjudged her age. Regardless, she liked it since it allowed her to feel young and beautiful. She stared at her pipe-smoking husband and warned him that if he didn't put down the pipe, she would shatter it and him. He shivered at her intimidation and gave it over to a maid who was standing next to him, setting the table. He didn't want to irritate her so early in the morning.

When Marina's parents fought, she couldn't help but snort. They made her burst out in laughter, especially when her mother became enraged which made everyone tremble.

When the plates were brought to the table, everyone began to eat. Marina swallowed her spit as she stabbed a cooked egg with her fork, just as her father opened his mouth and stated, "You're slicing food wrong, do it as a lady for goodness' sake." Marina to that mumbled, "Sorry papà." In a quiet voice. "I heard what happened at the event." She was afraid he would bring up the subject, and now that he had, she was at a loss for words.

"It's all right. It's not a major issue."

"It's not a major issue? I won't tolerate others laughing at you!" he said, puzzled.

"You're only saying that because you worry about our image." Marina was hesitant to hear her father say all of this because he had always encouraged her to calm down for certain things so that others wouldn't think she was crazy or God knows what else. He admired her feistiness but feared that others would not. Rocco was debating whether he should join in the conversation or go about his business and eat his breakfast.

"I am not. I just don't want other people to make fun of you."

"It makes no difference to me. At the very least, I'll be more relevant than anybody else in the room." Hearing that, Mrs. Rivalli choked on the wine she was sipping and began snickering at what Marina said.

Her father sighed, unsure what to do with his defiant
daughter any longer. He recognized her easygoing
attitude, but he knew there were some things he needed
to do. "Plus, no one seems to notice. Even though I was
calm, you saw what they did to me last night." As she
lost her appetite for food, the girl exclaimed while
looking down at the plate with food that was getting cold.
She was upset by what she remembered from the night
before and couldn't believe it had happened. All she
wanted was for everyone to stop talking about it and go
on with their lives. With worry in his eyes, the man
gazed at her. "Yes, what they did last night was heinous,
but you also have to mature and learn not to act on your
emotions. I'm sick of you always moaning about others."
he added. The girl exclaimed loudly, took a big breath,
and prepared to defend herself when her mother entered
the conversation.

"You are seventeen years old, he is right. You should
begin solving difficulties independently. At your age, I
was already courted by your father."

"We're telling you this because we care about you." As
he bit into the steak, the man exclaimed.

Marina was overly upset by everything and mistook their
assistance in the wrong way. "How could you say that?
The other girls poured a gallon of wine all over me. They
ruined my dress... as well as my hair and shoes... That

day, I even felt more confident and attempted to initiate interactions with others again." As she grabbed a fold of her dress and squeezed it, a tear began to fall from her rosy cheek. "I just don't understand what's wrong with me." she said. Her brother fixed his gaze on her "Oh please you're such a hypocrite. I heard you spread an ugly rumor about Letitia sleeping with her first cousin. You could've damaged her image for good." The girl remained deafeningly quiet. "Marina." While keeping her eyes down, fully focused on one location, she heard the faint sound of someone calling her name in her mind.

"Marina!" The sound has returned.

Her father clapped his fingers in front of her face, jolting her out of her reverie and bringing her back to the present. The girl apologized for ignoring him and glanced at him. "As I was saying. Are you sure that they poured wine on you just like that? It seems I don't know. Out of nowhere. Rocco is right, you do tend to act a bit... rude sometimes. And I hope you never said such a rumor."

Marina became enraged. "What came out of nowhere!? Rocco is making it up! I never said such a thing, it's nonsense! Papa! I was standing in the corridor talking to a boy when those—those gals appeared out of nowhere and made me look like a fool! Everyone began to laugh at me! I've done nothing to them, and they even threatened me the last time I approached them, saying that if I approached them again, I'd make everyone else hate them and that I'm a curse. Is that sufficient justification? Is it necessary for me to tell you what else they did to me? What about when—" Rocco cut her out "Will you stop playing a victim? I saw what you did which isn't the first time. Your crying won't work on our parents anymore." The girl lied, constantly to her parents and brother. She pretended to be innocent in front of her parents, but her brother has seen what happened and knows what she's like. Marina kept exaggerating the scenario and portraying herself as a victim, despite her initial insults to the other girls, and even meaning them. The young lady groaned. She thought to herself, "Of course." No one has tolerance for her, and she sometimes wishes she had been born as dull as she was, content to spend her entire existence at home, reading books and smiling at anything anyone said. Or simply not speaking at all, which would make everyone pleased since whatever she said, was seen as an insult.

She decided to be mature and simply finish the vexing topic by switching to a new one and asking "Is it okay if I accompany Rocco to the city this afternoon? I heard there was going to be a festival today, and— "her father snubbed her "Certainly not. You had a disaster last night and you act like a brat, and now you expect to be able to do whatever you want?" Marina's eyes widened as she felt trapped and broken. She had been looking forward to going on a stroll with her brother all morning, only to be reprimanded for something that was not her fault. The girl didn't even try forcing her father to say yes, because they were both going to say no because of what had transpired the night before. It was unjust, but she couldn't help but listen to her parents because they knew what was best for her.

But she can't help but think they've been in the wrong a couple of times. She never asks for anything when it comes to wishes. Unlike any gleaming jewels or the most delicate outfits that most girls her age would desire a simple flower is all she needs to brighten her day. Although she never asked for such things, she did abuse their kindness by constantly ungrounding her which at times was worse than asking to buy her things. As a result, she never understood why she couldn't, for example, go outside alone. She never realized that her parents were too scared of a young woman to go walk alone in Naples, especially when night came. It was far too dangerous. Marina was aware that it is customary for a lady to be escorted when stepping outside, which she accepted. Whether she was alone or with others, all she wanted to do was see new things. Her brother placed his hand on her shoulder and told her that they would go for a walk later.

"Besides, Rocco, you have a ton of work to do with me." Mr. Rivalli went on to say.

The young man moaned, unable to bear doing more tedious work with his father, who is quickly irritated by minor errors. And he was getting exhausted with his parents overworking him constantly. "See, even if you could go, I wouldn't be able to since I have things to do." he said to Marina. At that point, a maid arrived and began clearing the table, removing everyone's plates and washing them all in the kitchen. Marina paused for a moment, her gaze falling to the ground. "How about horseback riding?" she asked her parents, before shifting her gaze to Rocco.

"Riding a horse? Didn't you hear? I'm sorry, but I'm out of time."

"Yes, but... It'll be close to Vomero, among the streets and such. We'll also be brief. Of course, provided both father and mother are in agreement." Their parents exchanged glances, unsure whether to allow them or not. Rocco was hesitant at first because he was afraid of being overworked later and because he wanted his sister to be grounded fairly for once. When their parents answered no since Marina's behavior the night before was horrible, the girl burst into tears and exclaimed,

Judged For Mercy

"Why don't you love me!?" And threw tantrums like a little child.

The young lady would blame her parents' affection for her every time she was grounded. She made them believe that grounding her meant they didn't love her. Her father felt awful after hearing what she said, doubted himself as a good parent, and kept telling her how much he loved her, but she kept denying it because he wasn't even on her side. Marina's scheme eventually worked, and she was able to persuade her parents to agree thanks to guilt tripping. Marina bit her lower lip with glee and became a whirlwind of action. She snatched her brother's arm and yanked him up while beaming as wide as she could. They were about to leave when their mother raised her voice and remarked in worry "Please be careful! Because of the rain from last night, the ground is extremely wet today! Go on the left side of the neighborhood." She then added "Oh! Be back before dinner! We're having guests today and I want you two to prepare your violin and flute!" Rocco was horrified to watch his sister exploiting her parents' love for her to the point where it had become routine.

The twins began strolling outside their home to the stable barn, where they hoped to find their horse and go on a ride. They were greeted by a foul odor of animal feces as they arrived, which made both of them gag. Marina disliked the scent of animal farms and stables even though she adored animals and if she could, she wouldn't mind living with them. They split off to prepare their riding shoes, which were kept inside the stable. They kept it there in case they felt like going for a ride at any time. "Good day, my dear horse. Mr. Rossi appears to have cleaned you up. You look so handsome now!" The girl continued to flatter her horse while petting his black coat, which glistened in the light due to how immaculate it was. She sat in a tiny wooden chair, removing her shoes and replacing them with her black riding shoes. When the girl was finished, she adjusted the black stallion's grazing muzzle and took the rope attached to it, leading the horse out of his stable and meeting Rocco outside of it. "Are you all set?" He inquired, wanting to ensure that they had completed all of their preparations and were ready to depart. The girl smiled and nodded, then hesitated for a bit before asking, feeling embarrassed, but eventually summoning the strength to do so. "Could you assist me in mounting the horse?"

"Of course?" Rocco asked, perplexed. "There isn't a lot of things to stand on."

"I meant," Marina said, making an embarrassed expression and crossing her fingers. The young man groaned and face-palmed himself as hard as he could. "I climb on your hands and then you push me up." she said. He didn't want dirt on his clean hands because his sister is an idiot who is too short to hop on the horse by herself without assistance. He kept sighing and complaining that he didn't want to do it, but Marina's pushy side of herself insisted. When she stood up, she gazed down at him and said, "Was that so difficult, my brother?" Rocco raised his eyes to her, a cold expression on his face. "You're annoying." he said in the coldest voice he could muster. It took Rocco only a few moments to climb up on the horse, and after they were settled, they went for a calm ride. "God, mother, and father know to get so bothersome sometimes." the girl complained. "You mean, you are?" he asked, raising his brow. Marina was taken aback and couldn't believe what he said. Is she annoying? When their parents don't comprehend her challenges and simply yell at her for whatever she does or says, it's their parents who are to blame. Rocco attempted to reason with her, telling her, "Look, I'm just saying. You, too, are not an angel. They rarely yell at you because you give them your gorgeous eyes, and when they do, you cry as if you were abused." Marina raised her hands in the air and began flattering them, saying, "Can we not talk about this? I don't want to sabotage our get-together." Because if he says anything, she'll attack him, the young man rolled his eyes and did what she said and thought that was the most peaceful option.

Chapter VI

They had a moment of silence, and the girl was irritated with him for not standing up for her when it came to their parents. He should be aware that they are not always possible. Rocco took a deep breath and smiled slightly as he smelled the fresh air. He missed going on horseback rides with his sister and had forgotten how relaxing it is to gaze down at the city and the beautiful, sparkling clean sea. He grinned and asked, "Did you meet any boy last night?" He tried to transition to some pleasant themes so they didn't quarrel the entire time. Marina became flushed and scared, exclaiming, "Oh! I'm not sure— does it mean he likes me if he gives me a few glances?" She was inquisitive and wanted to know if the boy liked her, and since her brother was one, he should know. Rocco paused for a second before deciding to tell her the truth and make her happy by lying and answering, "Yes. You were, after all, the only girl in the nicest dress." Marina squealed with delight and was overjoyed at the time. A boy? Liking her? It seemed as if a fantasy had come true. She yearned for a companion, but she yearned much more for a lover. Her brother was overjoyed when he saw her so enthusiastic about anything. He has always longed for her happiness and makes every effort to spend time with her, but he is unable to do so consistently.

Marina couldn't help but inquire about Mia when they were discussing relationships. "How is it with Mia, though?" She had a devilish smirk on her face. She had a lot of fun tormenting him about her. When Rocco remembered his sweetheart, he grinned. His one and only love. He looked down and smiled for a bit before continuing, "I was meant to propose to her today." he reached into his suit pocket and took a little velvet box. His sister stared at him, her eyes wide with disbelief at what she had just heard.

"Propose?"

"Yes! I've been planning it for months! And I wanted to ask for your approval as well. She's after all, your best friend." When he opened the box, a stunning engagement ring that was exactly appropriate for her was inside it. Marina grinned, overjoyed to learn that Mia would be her sister-in-law and that her brother would be married. But then she had an awful realization. "Wait... you're getting married? So you're going to live with her?" Her question perplexed Rocco. "Isn't that what marriage is all about?" The girl couldn't say anything. This can't possibly be happening. He and Amelia were her only companionship, and now she'll have to say goodbye to them as well. "But, we won't spend much time together?"

"Don't be silly; I'm not going to the moon. I'll still see you, but not as frequently as you'd want." Marina was relieved that Amelia wasn't at their place today, since if she had been, they would have been engaged by now.

The girl felt terrible. Why now, of all times? Why is he getting married now? If only he could do it after she gets married to someone. Just not just now... Marina sank to her knees, unsure of how to feel. She became outraged at one point, blaming everyone but herself. She decided to do something against her parents' wishes and changed the direction of their journey. Marina tapped their horse to make it move quicker, and they began descending to the city. Her brother noticed her changing directions and screamed at her to tell him what she was up to. "I wanted to change roots, and I did, easy as that." Marina said, an irritated frown on her face. "You informed our parents that we're staying in the neighborhood!" he yelled at her. "And that we're going to be quick!" Marina pretended she didn't hear him by pressing her lips together and looking elsewhere. Going downhill, Rocco was a little nervous because everything was slick and the roads weren't as wide. He sighed, his frustration with her palpable.

"Can you tell me what's wrong with you today?" He inquired, angered by her actions at this moment.

"Do you want to know what's wrong with me? I'm furious! You're going to leave me alone!" Marina became enraged and yelled at him. Her brother couldn't stop giggling at her attitude. He couldn't believe her way of thinking at times. "Marina I'm about to tie the knot! I'm not going to war!"

"You know, I sent Mia home just so you and I may spend some time together," the girl smiled as she wiped tears from her eyes. "But in the end, all we've done is fight—" When Rocco heard that, he became pale.

"What did you do?" Marina panicked, forgetting that she hadn't told him the whole truth. She tried to make it seem better, but she ended up sounding just as selfish as before. "Ah, I was simply looking forward to spending some time with you! You constantly hang out with her, and I've always wanted to go out with you..."

"I knew it!" her brother exclaimed as he buried his palm in his hair and took a big breath. "I had a feeling she wouldn't just walk away without telling me anything!" Marina became envious when he only thought about her again, and she continued, "You constantly leave me for her..."

"You are the most immature person I've ever met in my entire life!" Rocco exclaimed as he glanced at her. "You only care about yourself and don't give a damn about how others feel! You have no right to send her home without informing me! I was the one who was supposed to see her today, not you. You have no right to send her home in general! You've officially crossed the line, I can't believe it." The girl began to cry, sniffed, and uncomfortably smiled as she said, "I see..."

"Yeah, and I can see why you don't have any friends."Rocco continued. Marina was shocked and enraged as he said it. "How dare you say that!" she exclaimed. "And how dare you send her away!" he yelled at her. "What's the matter with you?" The young girl tried to persuade him that she was just doing it because she adored him and wanted to spend time with him. Rocco began to lose focus on the horse and the road while fighting with her, and he began to get too close to the road's edge. She stretched out to rest her arm on his shoulder to express her gratitude, but all he did was twitch and say in a harsh tone, "Please just stop touching me. I'm no longer able to look at you. I just want to get this riding over already." To her, everything went black. Her own brother was disgusted by her. Perhaps the issue isn't with others but with herself.

She was too ashamed to blame herself for her actions, and she had no intention of ever admitting it. Marina kept averting her gaze from him as she was embarrassed. "I can't believe you're acting this way toward me, after everything I've done for you." she merely said. "You?" he asked, laughing. "You doing something for me? What about you being unappreciative of everything I've done for you? You wanted me to teach you the things I learned in school every day after school, which I did for a long time. I've always tried to make your life easier by introducing you to my pals. I even made sure you were safe from other people! And how are you going to repay me? By chasing Amelia away? Even though she did nothing to you and always tried spending time with you as well. In every way, I loathe you, truly."

"Fine," Marina said, her nose twisted as she stared at him with a shattered heart. "I loathe you as well." Rocco was still enraged, and he began insulting her, calling her names for being so irresponsible and dislikeable due to her nature and conduct. Marina continued to ignore the situation and couldn't wait to get home and retire to her bedroom, where no one would bother her. Then, in an instant, The horse moved too close to the edge, stepping on the ground and causing the earth to crumble. "Marina!—" he screamed in horror as they both and the horse plummeted downhill. This wasn't supposed to happen. This wasn't how he planned out his day and for him to fall into his doom. As soon as they slid off, the man collided with a large boulder, breaking his neck and falling to the ground. The horse got up and was terrified, so it started jumping around and then broke Rocco's ribs with its legs. Their horse bolted away, far away from him, but Rocco was gasping for air.

Marina was in immense pain from the fall and gasped for air in panic. When she turned around and saw her brother, she kept saying no to herself, unable to comprehend what was happening and wishing the fall had been less severe, despite the fact that it had been a massive fall. Marina instantly ran up to him although her legs hurt and got down on her knees, softly laying her hands on his face and breaking down in tears, assuring him that everything would be fine and that she would go get aid and return home, leaving him free to propose to Mia. Rocco scarcely looked at her; his eyes had stopped glistening and had lost all life. "Marina I'm terrified! I don't— I don't want to die." Rocco spoke as his lungs began to fill with blood, making it difficult for him to breathe and even speak... He drew his final pained breath and died in her arms. Marina was terrified as soon as he closed his eyes and stopped moving.

"No, Rocco! Do not close your eyes! Please! You can't treat me like this— No!" Everyone nearby heard her screams for help as she continued to scream in anguish and cry as loudly as she could. "Please... Don't leave me alone, I love you..." Some people recognized the twins and went to their house to alert their parents, banging on their doors. Mrs. Rivalli was the one who opened them and in confusion asked what happened so terribly, and when she heard what had happened, she immediately dropped everything she was holding at the time, and tears began to fall like a river. The wife grabbed her husband's arm and began sprinting to their children's location. She spent the entire time blaming herself for everything that had transpired, saying things like, "I shouldn't have let them leave! Everything is wet and slippery," she cried, "Oh God, I hope our boy is okay." Mr. Rivalli kept wiping tears from his eyes, not wanting to disturb his wife by crying in front of her. "I just hope he didn't break anything." the man expressed his hope that his son was still alive. They both sobbed as they descended the hill and saw their daughter kneeling next to Rocco. Mrs. Rivalli dashed over to her son, pushing Marina away, and knelt. Her hands were trembling as she reached out to touch his bloody face, and she burst into sobs even more. "Rocco, my love, please open your eyes—" she pleaded, her voice trembling and afraid. Mr. Rivalli covered his lips with his hand as soon as he realized he was dead and began crying as he had never done before.

His wife screamed in pain, resting her head on his crushed chest, pulling at his garments, and pleading with him to wake up. Mr. Rivalli collapsed to his knees, screaming and clutching his wife and children. Marina's mother gazed at Marina for a brief minute before becoming irritated and exclaiming, "I told you to watch out! And you said you'd stick with Vomero! Why were you both here in the first place!?" Marina cried out in an attempt to defend herself, covering her face with her hands and saying, "I'm sorry! I'm sorry! I just wanted to visit the city for a while!" Her mother wanted to slap her as hard as she could. She was overwhelmed by a variety of emotions and had no idea how to manage them. The man screamed at his wife to cut it right now, that now isn't the time to blame anyone for anything, and that it was the two who are to blame for allowing them to go out.

"We have to get out of here. I don't want people to congregate around me. You're aware of how old individuals are." As he grieved and stared at his dead son, the husband exclaimed. He gently kissed his wife's forehead and sobbed, telling her, "It's alright, it's going to be alright." He wiped her tears off her cheeks and softly kissed her forehead, then led his forehead on hers like cats and wept. Marina just stood there, terrified, holding herself in place because she didn't know what else to do. She felt terrible that her own mother blamed her for her brother's death and she didn't even bother asking her if she was fine or if she broke anything. As Mr. Rivalli stood up, the man placed his hands under Rocco, gently scooping him up and holding him. "I'm sorry, my son; I know you would have despised this." His wife couldn't stop crying; the entire walk to their house was difficult since she couldn't stop crying. Everyone kept staring at them, perplexed as to what had happened. Mr. Rivalli kept looking down at his child, when holding him in his arms he felt as if he were a newborn again. He cried as he remembered the days when he'd sleep in his arms, and now he'll sleep forever. Rocco looked so serene in his father's arms, his head resting on his father's chest, that he appeared to be sleeping. If only it weren't for the blood on his face. The young lady walked behind her parents, humiliated and horrified by the sight of Rocco. She was even afraid to approach her parents, fearing that they would keep blaming her for everything, as they always did. She rubbed her arm and sobbed, feeling bad about everything and how things had taken a turn for the worse in a matter of seconds.

Three days had gone since the horrifying event, and the Rivalli family was mentally and physically preparing for Rocco's funeral. No one could believe it was all genuine and happening right now. Mrs. Rivalli didn't speak much in those three days; she either cried or lay in bed, completely silent, not wanting to say anything. She would break down every time she passed by her children's room, and she couldn't bear to look at it because it reminded her of her only son. When her family asked her for assistance in preparing the burial, meals, and other details, she simply remained silent and felt dead on the inside. Not wanting to distress her any further, her husband tried as hard as he could to remain optimistic and not cry in front of her. He shut himself in the bathroom whenever he felt like sobbing, sat on the floor, and wailed till his eyes started to hurt. He'd rather cry in private than make his wife's depression worse.

He came up to her whenever she was upset and showered her with love, hugged her, or forced her to lay on him to calm down. Instead of her, he did all of the conversing with the guests. She'd pass out if she spoke with her relatives while offering condolences. His wife was insanely mentally bad, but Marina? No, he couldn't handle her seeing him crying or shaking, it would cause the poor girl even more trauma which he didn't want her to experience. Marina continued to blame herself for everything, claiming that if she had only listened to her parents once, none of this would have occurred. Her thoughts were consumed by the image of her brother, in his final moments of life, loathing her. She was devastated that he died disliking her. And, once again, she was the one who started the fight and was the one to blame.

Except for Marina, everyone wore black on the day of the funeral. She realized how much he would despise it if everyone dressed down for his funeral, so she wore a green gown instead. Green was blue to him instead, which the girl thought was amusing because he couldn't see that color. She smiled at the prospect of him constantly mixing colors or arguing with her because she kept forgetting that he doesn't see colors the same way the rest of us do. Her parents didn't mind if she wore something more cheerful; she was a child, after all, and they didn't want her to be melancholy. They couldn't wear something more cheerful, though, because everyone else would have criticized them for not wearing black. Her parents continued kissing her and telling her how much they loved her at the burial. The young lady was taken aback. Every second, there was so much going on.

That day, Mrs. Rivalli and her mother fought, and her mother chastised her, telling her that if she had been a better mother, this would not have happened. Out of wrath and agony, the lady sobbed and yelled at her mother to leave her alone and not to offer her any advice on how to be a good mother, because she should take notes herself. A quarrel was about to break out when her husband burst in, seizing his wife by the arms and leading her away to steam out. The woman sobbed in her husband's arms, telling him how much she wished her mother was gone, but they couldn't do anything. Almost everyone was frustrated that day because it was anything but a lucky day.

When the ceremony began, Rocco's casket was uncovered so that family members could see him and say their final goodbyes. Everyone began to arrange lovely bouquets around the casket, but Marina's parents chose to place a rose on his chest, to stay with him forever. Marina didn't bring any flowers; instead, she took a few of his painting supplies, assuming he'd appreciate having them with him in the afterlife. By his side, she laid his brushes, paints, and the best of his works. The girl sobbed as she did so, feeling terrible for doing so. "I love

you, brother." Marina kissed her index and middle fingers and placed them on his cheek. Her parents kissed his face without hesitation, not even horrified that they were touching a corpse. They continued to hold his cheeks, crying and telling him how much they cherish him. Mrs. Rivalli nearly fainted when they had to move so that others might show respect as well, but her husband caught her and walked her to a spot where she could sit and cool down. Then a young girl appeared, carrying a bouquet of just pink and blue flowers. She approached the casket with care, placing her bouquet alongside others. The girl slipped her palm from his cheek to his lips, drawing closer to his face and whispering to him a secret she didn't want anyone else to know about.

"Rocco, my one true love, you were the one and only person who cared about me."

When Marina's parents saw Amelia, they broke down in tears. She instantly reminded them of Rocco, since Amelia was his beloved. They've been together for such a long time, and their relationship was so wholesome. Amelia stepped over to Marina, hoping to console and keep her company.

As she approached Marina, Amelia asked, "How are you?" in a quiet, melancholy tone. Marina tried to avoid eye contact at first because she was too preoccupied with seeing Rocco's casket being lowered into his tomb. "No!" her mother screamed anguishedly. "Don't let him down! I beg of you!" The woman slumped on the ground, sobbing and pleading with her son not to abandon her; it was infuriating to witness her child being buried instead of her. Marina stared at Amelia, tears in her eyes, and said, "Well, we're here so.. not very well..." amid a brief moment of quiet. "I'm sorry you had to go through it. I never intended anything like this to happen to you, or for you to lose the love of your life." Marina looked down and bit her lower lip "Thank you, Marina. And please accept my deepest condolences on the loss of your brother, twin, and only sibling. I hope we can both find a way to overcome this catastrophe."

Amelia gave her a soft smile, but she didn't hold out much hope that things would get better any time soon, but she remained hopeful for the young lady. At the time, Amelia and Marina were both trying to say something but were cut off by each other's words. Marina's eyes widened as she thought to herself. She looked up at the girl and asked about her company and if she was going to come by. Amelia groaned and responded, "I'm not going to come to visit you anytime soon. I need time to recover from this, and I'm not sure when I'll be able to contact you again; nevertheless, I do want to hear from you ...I hope so." Marina sighed. Amelia couldn't believe the girl had asked her such a question at the moment she was grieving over her brother. It felt, heartless although she knew Marina didn't intend it to be that way.

Then, in the heat of the moment, Amelia looked at her wrist and seemed concerned, so she turned to Marina and asked her a question "However... How did Rocco and you end up at the wrong place? I don't believe he'd ever do something like that. With horses, he was always cautious."

The young lady's eyes widened and she became agitated; she clutched her arms and averted her gaze from Amelia. The tight atmosphere she was in made her uneasy, and she couldn't bring herself to tell the girl anything. Thankfully, Mr. Rivalli approached them before she could respond, explaining that they were ready to depart but still needed to attend church.

As they walked away, he gently placed his arm on Amelia's back, wanting to talk to her about her future with the Rivallis. The girl ended up following in, relieved that her father had interrupted the scene, but the entire day still hurt her greatly, with her mother's cries still echoing in her head. The freckled girl sobbed as she walked away, feeling as though she had lost a piece of herself when her brother was buried. What does it mean to be a twin if the other one isn't by your side any longer?

Everyone vanished as she approached the carriage, and she couldn't see anyone.

"Mother? Father? Where have you gone!?" While gazing around, the girl yelled. She started to get a shiver down her spine since the graveyard was terrifying without anybody else around. While searching for her parents, the ground began to disintegrate, as if it were devouring her. She began to sweat and scream in terror as she ran away to avoid falling into the infinite void. Unfortunately, she wasn't as quick, and the girl fell in, reaching for the sky with her hand as her tears began to float and she shouted for help.

July 27th , 1910.

Marina awoke terrified, clutching her chest and heavily breathing while sweating profusely. Her face was all moist from crying while sleeping. She covered her face with her hands and moaned, "God, why did I have to witness all of that again?" she moaned as tears welled up in her eyes. She took a peek around her cabin and discovered that it was deserted and that she was the only one there. The girl sighed, lonely and desiring a drink to take her mind off the agony. She got up and wrapped herself in Giordana's shawl to keep warm as she walked outside on the deck. She walked out barefoot once again after opening the doors. Everything was quiet when she stepped outside; the only sound she could hear was the waves and the sea crashing on the ship, which was quite soothing to the ears. She took a look around and noticed how gorgeous the night was. There were many stars in the sky, as well as a dazzling full moon. She felt more at ease as a result of it. She exhaled deeply as she rested her arms on the banister, gazing out at the sea and allowing the breeze to pass through her hair. Margherita noticed Marina outside, looking lonely, as she was finishing up cleaning the kitchen and getting ready to go to her cabin and sleep. She decided to approach her. Margherita laughed a little as the woman put her hands on her shoulder, startling her.

"So, what's the special occasion for you to be outside?"

"Just had a really bad nightmare..."

"You want to share it with me?" Margherita inquired since she wanted to assist her in feeling better. The girl quietly smiled at her and decided that if she wanted to be good with anyone here, she needed to stop being so secretive, and she decided to reveal her nightmare. Marina began to explain to her how she had a nightmare about a previous incident in which her brother died and how she couldn't stop blaming herself for it. It was her fault that he died. The girl ran her hand through her hair, barely smiling as she looked down, tears streaming down her cheeks. "I'm sorry for sobbing; I'm sure you're tired of me doing it all the time by now." "Ah, dear," the old woman groaned and hugged her. "It's fine to cry; there's no need to hide it." Marina felt warm in her arms and yearned for an embrace from her parents, but she'd gotten herself into a big mess and was now stranded here.

"I'm so tired of feeling bad about myself, I'd want a glass of wine right now." the girl said as Margherita released her. "Well, it just so happened that Gabriel and Antoni had a drink a while ago, and left an open bottle on the table." the old woman said, hinting that they should go get a drink to take their minds off things. Marina was ecstatic to learn this and to be having a drink with her. Margherita turned around and asked, "Are you coming?" as she went away to the kitchen. "I will in a moment." the girl said after pausing for a bit. While Margherita was busy preparing their drinks in the kitchen, the girl raised her eyes to the sky and sweetly smiled, saying

"Goodnight, brother."

Chapter VII

A couple of mornings later, the girl was already on her feet. She found it a little easier to wake up so early this time. She was sitting in the kitchen with Margherita and Giordana, drinking coffee, and grumbling about her terrible headache, which she assumed was the result of drinking too much lately. She already drank a lot a couple of nights ago with Margherita, but last night she has overdone it.

"I've never drank this much wine in my life, this is a record." she murmured, her hand deep in her hair and her head resting on her arm. The old ladies kept snickering at her, sometimes even finding her Neapolitan accent funny, and would repeat the words she had said. "Well, think twice before you have a drink next time." Giordana grinned as she dipped Margherita's baked biscuit in her bitter coffee. The girl leaned against the table, muttering about how bad she felt about herself and how she can't wait to get to land so she can stretch out and go for a walk, maybe even purchase a few trinkets to give to her parents if she decides she wants to talk to them. "Oh!" exclaimed Margherita. "Isn't it likely that we'll be in Marseille soon? Actually, in a few hours." Marina straightened up and slammed her hands on the table. "Marseille?" she exclaimed. "Is it the same city in France? We're heading to France!" The girl exclaimed. She grinned as big as she could, overjoyed at the prospect of finally visiting the land of love. She sighed as she realized she was traveling, seeing new places, and experiencing new things. Giordana took a sip while staring at the doors. "Yes, but it's a bit cloudy today." "I'm hoping there won't be any storms; I loathe them!" remarked the other woman.

Early this morning, they learned from the captain and his right-hand man that the clouds are unusually dark and that the birds are rushing towards the land. Marina was unconcerned about it because all she could think about was France. The adrenaline flowed through her body, and she couldn't wait to arrive at their destination. The girl then paused for a moment before placing her hand on her soft cheek and hesitantly asking, "Miss Margherita, do you perchance have a fresh pair of undergarments?" The woman looked at her with surprise but nodded and followed her to their cabin. Marina began to notice how low the walls are as they moved. They're acceptable for her height, but someone as tall as the captain would have a lot of trouble with them. Everything on the ship made her feel claustrophobic at times due to how strange everything is in comparison to a typical dwelling.

As they entered the cabin, the elderly lady got down on her knees and opened an old wooden chest, hoping to find for the girl undergarments. Marina sat on her bed, waiting for the lady to hand it over to her. She chuckled to herself as she realized that she asks the lady to do something for her practically every time they spend time together. The realization made her feel awful for appearing to be so reliant on others for everything, and also quite embarrassed. When it came to her behavior, it was exactly something her mother despised. While searching, the woman inquired of the young girl as to why she required a new pair of undergarments.

Marina seemed a little uneasy. She snatched a fold of her garment and squeezed it tightly as she uncomfortably expressed how she doesn't feel at ease in her own clothing. She didn't want to disclose the whole truth about how she feels disgusted when she looks in the mirror every morning and night while wearing the same undergarments in which Matias harmed her. The poor girl felt sick to her stomach just thinking about it. She was horrified by everything about herself at this moment, and all she could see was him. Margherita didn't want to get into too much detail because she could sense Marina wasn't feeling well, and nagging at her to reveal the truth would just make the girl feel even more distant from her. The young lady waited impatiently for Margherita to hand it over to her, and when she finally did, she was overjoyed.

Marina stood up to lead the woman away so she could change in peace, and as she reached for the doorknob, she noticed a stunning gown hanging on the hook. "Is this yours?" the girl inquired, puzzled. "No, and I don't think it's Francesca and Giordana's either." Margherita said. "Perhaps it was given to you."

"For me?" Marina was taken aback. "However, who bought it?"

"Who knows." the elderly lady began to snicker. "You'll find out in the end." She had a good idea who it was, but she didn't want to give anything away. Marina sat back down on the bed and softly smiled as Margherita walked out the door. "Perhaps it's the captain?" says the girl "He's quite charming, but he doesn't like me, so he's off of the list. And definitely not any other sailor. They could be my grandparents." Marina told herself, and as she was pondering who that man may be, she noticed a note hanging from the dress that read, "Take this as a welcoming gesture. Also, don't allow Gabriel and Francesca's statements to stick in your head too much." Marina exclaimed as she read the final sentence, "Signed, D'Angelo Antoni." she murmured to herself. She was overjoyed that Antoni had bought her a gown, and even happier that someone other than Margherita and Giordana was concerned about her and her sentiments. As soon as she changed, she dashed outside and began searching the ship for Antoni. She looked and looked for him, but he was nowhere to be found. She eventually went outside to the deck and simply exhaled in frustration, failing to look in the most obvious spot.

"Rina!" From the quarterdeck came a shout.

Marina looked up and covered her eyes with her hand since the sun was blinding her from that direction. She peered for a moment before realizing it was Antoni. She rushed up to him, carrying the gown in her hands, in a state of ecstasy. "D'Angelo!" She exclaimed joyfully. Antoni touched her on the shoulder and wished her a pleasant morning. When the gal turned around, she observed his hands on the steering wheel. She had not expected him to be in charge of the ship. "Shouldn't Mr. Santarelli be in control of the ship?" "Gabriel? No, he's not very good at it in the first place. But it's just me and another sailor who control it though." The girl made an O with her lips, she has yet to learn much about sailing, as much as she despises it. D'Angelo gave her a sidelong glance and asked if she needed him for anything. Marina blinked three times before recalling that she had meant to ask him about the dress.

"Yes! I found the gown you gave me!"

"Oh? Do you like it?"

"Of course, you didn't have to buy anything for me. It's a very thoughtful gesture."

When Antoni heard it, he snickered and burst out laughing, saying, "I did not buy it, I made it." Marina was taken aback and couldn't believe he had sewn it. All on his own? How did he do it in such a short period of time? She began to feel awful that he stitched such a beautiful garment just for her as if she deserved it. "Oh, I feel terrible!" She grumbled, "I don't have anything in return." "A kiss on the cheek would suffice." the man said as both of his dimples showed on his face. "Thank you D'Angelo Antoni." she concluded as she rose to her toes and gave the man a sweet kiss on the cheek. He helped her feel less insecure and more human, the realization that he's always been there for her since the beginning warmed her heart. Marina ran downstairs to put the garment back in her cabin and rush back to the kitchen to assist while D'Angelo continued with his work. Her smile illuminated the entire room when she returned to the kitchen. She was beaming so brightly that Giordana approached her and inquired as to what was making her so happy.

Marina averted her gaze and quickly summarized how she had a nice morning surprise. The elderly women bombarded her with a slew of washing demands. Those were the jobs she disliked the most. She could handle chopping vegetables and preparing the meal, but she

couldn't stand doing the dishes. How did her maids at
home manage to do it every day for so many years? The
girl sighed as she went to wash the dishes, and the
captain walked in again while she was performing her
task. "Great." She pondered her thoughts. She felt like
exploding with rage every time they were in the same
room. She was enraged just thinking about seeing him.
He didn't even say hello this time when he walked in;
instead, he sat down by the table and chatted with others,
like he did every morning.

Although the man looked different this morning, he
looked... tired, as if he isn't even present in his own body.
His always-perfect hair was now messy, and his dark
brown eyes which once looked full of love, now look as
if all hope was lost in life. Marina didn't want to pay too
much attention, but she couldn't help but be so curious
and keep on analyzing him. She went over to the captain
to bring him coffee after she finished washing the dishes.
She respectfully wished him a good morning while
pouring, and the captain added, "Good morning Mrs.
Rivalli." Marina was perplexed and irritated as she stared
at him "Mrs? I don't have a spouse." The captain
swallowed hard and looked down, "Ah, the wedding
gown puzzled me, and the ring you wear on your hand"
The girl gave him an uninterested look and sat down,
moaning. The man ignored her because he already had
too much on his plate and didn't need to hear her
whining anymore. Marina expected him to inquire about
her issue, but to her dismay, he did not. She began to

believe that he truly despises her for no reason, which saddened her because he isn't different from anyone else. The entire ship surely despises her, and now that she thinks about it, she suspects Antoni of being overly polite to her.

"Well, Naples," Mr. Santarelli said as he sipped his coffee. "I heard it's nice there?"

"Oh no," the girl replied, "It's a literal headache. The city is beautiful, but the people... not so much." The captain sighed and thought to himself about how, of course, no one suits her. Marina then started talking and recreating how incredibly beautiful the city is, while softly smiling and clutching a biscuit in her hands. Its architecture and culture, particularly the vistas, make her happy. Despite the fact that it was all fascinating, she couldn't help but get dissatisfied since she had seen the entire city thousands of times and wanted to see more. The man eventually realized that despite his several visits to Naples, he had never truly wandered around the city or gone sightseeing. He thought to himself that it was a missed opportunity, and would like to maybe one day visit it. Marina looked at Mr. Santarelli and smiled as she snapped out of it, asking him where he was from. The girl gasped as the man replied, "Rome." Marina began speaking quickly and asked him a slew of questions about Rome as if she wanted to know everything there was to know about the city. The man's cheeks flushed slightly; no one had ever shown such an interest in him before, and it had taken him by surprise. "There isn't much to know about it. It's just an insanely old city."

"Oh, I know. I just really enjoy visiting it. It's one of my favorite cities in the kingdom that I've seen."

D'Angelo disrupted the moment just as he was ready to answer all of her bothersome inquiries. He sang, "Marina Rivalli and Gabriel Santarelli!" Antoni rushed over to the captain and began rubbing his hands through his hair, causing the man's hair to become tangled. "Stop!" He was yelled at by him. "You're dull." Antoni grumbled as he averted his gaze. "Francesca is funnier than you."

"I'm not in the mood." said the captain, who was visibly upset. D'Angelo sighed; he didn't like it when his friend was upset, so he stopped fooling with him right away and sat down with the two of them to talk. Antoni shrugged as he put his hand behind his neck and looked at the captain, who was not in the mood for anything. With a sigh, Antoni asked "What is it that is bothering you? "

"I just wasn't feeling good, again, this early morning.." Mr. Santarelli stared at him with a tiny lack of interest, as he wasn't in the mood for a discussion, and turned

Judged For Mercy

away from Antoni, "I was barely able to drag myself out of bed." He went on... D'Angelo lowered his gaze, paused for a moment to consider his options, and then returned his gaze to the captain, his hand caressing his back. With a sweet smile, he said "But, alright. When I'm feeling down, you know what makes me feel better?—"

"You get sad?" the captain asked, puzzled. Antoni laughed and replied, "I mean, doesn't everyone? But, as I already stated... When I recall that I have *You* aboard this ship, it makes me feel a little better. Whenever I'm feeling confused and upset, I remind myself that I'm not alone. My dearest friend and I are both aboard the same ship! We're both on the same crew! Then those thoughts lead to me recalling our first meeting... Oh, the good times we had looking for work, stealing from the piazza, and surviving on the streets! What would I do if you weren't there?"

"Well, those were fairly pretty stressful times. I do not understand how you managed to find it fun." Mr. Santarelli said softly as he looked at Antoni. D'Angelo chuckled and shook him a little with his hand on his shoulder. He smiled proudly as he said, "I'm glad I helped you appear less sad." He was always quite upbeat and loved it when he was right. After a brief moment of looking away from him, the captain stopped smiling and simply studied the kitchen, thinking about the ship's next

location and the work he'll have to accomplish later.
Marina exchanged puzzled looks with both of them.
"Streets? Is it possible?" She had a sneaking suspicion
that Antoni and the captain were orphans who had grown
up on the streets. The girl sought to communicate with
them since she felt uncomfortable gazing at them and
staying silent. "Well, I always feel better after a walk— I
mean, not everyone enjoys them, but it's still relaxing,
isn't it?"The captain gave her a wry grin. He'd gone for a
lot of walks, but none of them had ever made him feel
better. D'Angelo violently punched him in the back and
exclaimed in a positive tone, "What are you talking
about? You feel a lot better every time you go out on a
walk with me or Margherita." The captain gave him a
squint and answered that they don't have much time to
chat about their unhappiness because they are arriving in
France in an hour and they need to prepare everything.
As the men rose from their seats, Antoni glanced
backward and waved to Marina as he walked. The girl
returned his wave with a sweet grin. She was alone in the
room once more, which made her feel lonely. She
groaned as she sat in the chair, thinking about how she
would never be able to help anyone get better since no
one thinks she was of any use, other than her body.

The crew had arrived in Marseille an hour earlier.
Everything about it was charming, just like the country
of France itself. The sailors were getting ready to carry
out the cargo, the captain was getting ready to drop the

anchor in the sea, and the women on the ship were finishing up their daily cleaning.

"Aha! You were five minutes late for your estimated time of arrival, calculation!" Antoni yelled, his gaze fixed on his wristwatch. "Please, I didn't say we'd be here in exactly an hour," Mr. Santarelli responded. "You actually informed me that you're always right when it comes to ETA," his best pal sneered. "How did you get to be so smart and great?"

"My lord, you make me sound dreadful!" the captain pressed him. Marina was ecstatic when she heard that they had finally arrived. The girl dashed outdoors to the main deck and proceeded to gaze at the city. She was moved by the fact that she was traveling and seeing new sights, but she desired her brother could be there with her right now. The captain decided to approach the girl who was leaning too close to the banisters.

"You know, you shouldn't be leaning on them too much?" he said when approached. "What if you slip and fall? No one is going to jump down after you." Marina smirked and turned her head to him, "Oh please, I can save myself. I'm also not a child. I'm aware that I shouldn't lean in too far." The captain shrugged and allowed her to do as she pleased. He leaned against the banisters as well, taking in the view of the city. He inquired as to if this was the young lady's first visit to Marseille. "Yes." the girl said, and she described it as "wonderful." She then inquired as to whether this was his first time as well. "Mine? No, no, no. I've probably been here tens of thousands of times... I believe I've memorized the city at this point." Marina grinned as she returned her gaze to the harbor. She inhaled in the fresh air and smiled because it was a beautiful day.

The captain took off right away to unload the cargo and receive cash for delivering it. Marina, meanwhile, sighed, wishing she could go out into the city, but she knew they'd be off to another city soon enough. She proceeded to the kitchen to see if there was anything more that needed cleaning, and Gabriel and Antoni came in shortly after. They were all talking about something. Margherita was perplexed and inquired as to what they were discussing. Antoni responded by saying they were going to stroll into the city and possibly stop at a restaurant later that evening. Marina slammed a towel on the table, which she was holding. "City? Restaurant?"

"Yeah?" Antoni asked, perplexed. "However, it is nothing special. Would you like to join us?" This month, the girl was ecstatically delighted. Everything got worse and worse over the month of June. However, Antoni's invitation to dinner made her quite delighted. She dashed back to her cabin to change into something more appropriate for a walk. She didn't want to be seen out in public in her cleaning and cooking garments, and she also smelled a lot.

She went straight to the men after changing and styling her hair well. Antoni was taken aback when he saw her wearing the gown he had sewn for her.

"You're dressed in the gown I made for you! It was obvious to me that it would suit you. And the fact that I made it without taking your measures. Doesn't it look great? I have God's hands." he remarked, kicking Mr. Santarelli in the arm. "Yes, great," the captain said, "I don't want to eat at the restaurant at midnight, so may we leave now?" Marina smiled softly and nodded, thanking Antoni for the comments. But she couldn't keep them all because he was the one who sewed the gown and made her appear so lovely. As they all started heading out, Antoni asked if she had ever been to the city before. The girl shook her head and stated that she had never been to France. The Austro-Hungarian Empire was the only country she had visited previously. Since he had been here thousands of times and said he wanted to show Marina the best things to see in the city. He quickly took her hand in his.

Marina and Antoni had a lovely time together while the captain kept mumbling to himself. The man took her to numerous interesting places, such as parks, monuments, and lovely streets, which she adored. Everything she saw that day was breathtakingly gorgeous. She also loved the fact that Antoni kept her company. The young lady came upon a post office while walking. She paused for a moment before deciding to enter. Antoni and the captain were waiting for her outside, and when she came, she was holding a postcard in her hand. "Oh, you're going to send it to a friend?" He inquired. "I thought of keeping it to myself." Marina said. "Every new place I see serves as a type of reminder." As they walked, the curious man continued to ask her countless questions about her life, which she both liked and disliked. She enjoyed that she could open up to him, but she loathed the fact that she was embarrassed by herself.

She inquired to the captain about their plans for the evening. The captain's mate began to tell how they had planned to have a pleasant evening in a nearby restaurant. "Oh, that reminds me, aren't we supposed to leave tonight? Will we even be able to go to a restaurant?" She inquired. "We're leaving tomorrow," Mr. Santarelli said. "I have plenty of time to get to my next destination, so I decided to take a rest." Marina grinned at the thought. She could use a little more stretching now that she's on the ship, which isn't quite as relaxing as she had hoped. Marina noticed a boutique and her eyes expanded. She put her palms on the shop's window and continued to examine the shoes.

Her present ones are too large for her, so a new pair would be ideal. She entered right away and promptly exited with a new pair of shoes. "Where in the world did you obtain that much money for such shoes?" The captain said strangely. The girl was perplexed and inquired, "What do you mean?"

"You didn't even bother offering me any money to let you on a ship?" says Gabriel. "I let you stay for free."

"I thought you sailors were always in need of any kind of money because you know..." Marina remarked, puzzled. "It's a well-known fact that you sailors are poor and money-hungry. So I thought it would be best to not even offer you any money or you might've robbed me, haha." The captain was offended at that point and looked to Antoni for a response. The man was perplexed by the girl's words, yet he couldn't help but laugh. Mr. Santarelli, on the other hand, felt hurt, particularly because he had been so generous to her, and yet she had insulted him in such a horrific way. Especially because she thinks that he'd rob her. The young girl was perplexed; she didn't understand why he became so enraged at her out of nowhere. Was it because of what she said that he felt this way? Most likely not, because he's pretty sensitive to anything she says. The captain took Antoni aside and informed him that he could no longer handle the girl and also that he really can not appear so polite to her when she was disrespecting them.

"How do you keep your cool around her?" He stated

"Maybe because I'm accustomed to it? When we first met, you were the same. I recall you getting sick to your stomach at the prospect of being a sailor. You constantly whined about being one."

For a brief while, the captain became silent; he had forgotten that he had been the same when he was younger. Antoni placed his arm around his friend's shoulder stating, "Plus, if you get to know her, she's nice and sweet. If you start being polite to her, I'm sure you'll like her more." Marina will eventually realize her mistakes.

Marina awkwardly strolled behind the captain and his mate as they conversed. She was uneasy by the captain's remarks about her, and she hoped Antoni wouldn't start thinking negatively about her as well. She began to lose

track of time while overthinking, and she had no idea
where she was walking as she was lost in her thoughts.
Then, all of a sudden, she looked up and saw a massive
crowd in the street. When she came to, she noticed a
man standing in the crowd, staring at her. The girl
squinted for a moment before widening her eyes.

The man resembled Matias a lot, and she was afraid he
was still alive, therefore he decided to follow her and get
revenge on her. Or even worse... hurt her again. Her
heart began to race as if she had run millions of miles,
and she began to breathe rapidly and she started to turn
pale as white bread. Antoni, who had been walking with
her the entire time, seemed worried and asked if she was
okay. He softly gripped her wrist with his hand. That
enraged Marina, who whirled back with weeping eyes
and smacked his hand, shouting, "Don't touch me!" in an
angry tone. The man was perplexed; all he wanted to do
was assist her. The girl continued to take deep breaths
and examine the area to see if Matias would assault her
at any moment. Mr. Santarelli turned around to see what
was going on as she was panicking and found Marina
distraught and Antoni perplexed.

"What is going on here?" The captain enquired. Matias
was nowhere to be found when the young lady looked
around again. She shouted and panicked, running into
the captain and crying on his arm. The man was
perplexed, so he put his hand on her back for comfort,

but he began to feel uncomfortable since they were still in the city, and people stared at them. "Perhaps we should start going quicker towards the ship." Antoni suggested as he realized the situation wasn't looking good. Marina stayed near Mr. Santarelli, even if she didn't like him because of his behavior, she still felt safer next to him, and Matias wouldn't dare to assault her then since the captain looked more intimidating than her. They came across a tavern while walking. Antoni noticed it on his left and approached his friend, pulling his sleeve, and asked him to go over to it. "Are you thinking about eating right now?" the captain inquired, puzzled. "No, I just— I thought that would be more peaceful than being on a ship." the man replied. The man remained staring at him, perplexed, and Marina jumped into the conversation with a quick "I'd love that! Please." The captain sighed and shrugged, agreeing to go eat something now rather than later. As soon as they walked in, Marina turned around and asked the captain and Antoni if they were fluent in French. "Oh, no," Mr. Santarelli answered with a chuckle. "All I know how to do is introduce myself."

"I know how to swear in French if that's something." Antoni said, placing his hands on his friend's shoulders. When they sat down, they started all looking at their menus to see what to order. Marina felt a bit bummed since all the meals were for people that ate meat, so she didn't have many options to choose from, but either way, she wasn't that hungry or in the mood to eat. When the

waiter finally approached them, he inquired what they
wanted to order. The captain assisted with all of the
orders and talked in French with the waiter. "I'll have
beef torchons with a side of mixed salad," he continued.
"Oh, and I'd like it if you could recommend any red
wines." Then it was Marina's turn. "I'd just like an
omelet with asparagus, please." she said.

"You won't order anything else?" Antoni questioned,
looking at her. Back on the ship, even she could prepare
herself an omelet. The girl hesitantly explained that she
wasn't really hungry and that a simple omelet would
suffice. The three of them started talking a lot after the
waiter wrote everything down and went to get their
dishes ready and Antoni was the loudest in the room. By
speaking with the guys and making jokes, the young lady
began to feel considerably better. The meals turned out
to be great, and the captain noticed Marina's plate and
felt awful that there wasn't much food on it, so he offered
her part of his mixed salad. Marina, flattered, grinned
awkwardly and said, "It's fine, I'm full anyways." The
captain wanted to give the lady a second chance and
didn't want to pass judgment on her too quickly because
it seemed childish. And they talked normally the entire
time, not fighting like children.

"Do you remember when we first boarded the ship and
you were so upset for the entire week?" A chuckle
escaped his friend's lips. "Yeah, you always act so

grumpy. "What is with you?" Marina snorted, adding, "Isn't it worth a try to smile? You usually appear awful and lifeless." she continued to snicker.

"Excuse me?" Asked Mr. Santarelli, completely confused.

"What? It's not as if I'm lying. You're rude and lifeless, your hair is always a mess. Would it be so hard to get it together?"

"Why would you say such a thing?"

"Goodness, don't be so sensitive. I'm just saying."
Marina inquired.

This was the final straw for the man; he was so angered by her statements that he rose, placed enough money on the table to pay for everyone's plates, and walked out, declaring, "I'm leaving, I'm done here."

"What is your problem?" the girl inquired, looking perplexed. "I just told you not to be so gloomy!" The man had already walked away when Antoni stood up and yelled, "Gabriel, wait!" He then turned back and informed Marina, sternly, "You've done it this time. I used to defend you, but not any longer." The young lady was rendered speechless. She was completely perplexed by everyone's reaction because she thought what she said was humorous and would make Antoni laugh. No one, however, found it amusing. "Why is everyone here so weird?" she sighed as she turned around to face D'Angelo. "I thought you were kind." He expressed his disappointment as he gazed at her. The girl became even more perplexed and exclaimed, "I am nice!!"

In the meantime, Antoni walked outside to see how his friend was doing. Mr. Santarelli stood outside the tavern, tears in his eyes, but he was ashamed of them and began wiping them away right away. "Come on, don't tell me you were so hurt by what she said?" his best friend pleaded, resting his hands on his shoulders. "It's not that *she* said it, it's *what* she said. I try so hard to act less upset." the distressed man remarked, looking down. "But am I ever going to be good enough? People will always judge me by my appearance." Antoni hugged him tightly after that.

"I think you're good enough to me. I adore you even more than my sister."

"Don't say that, she isn't that bad." The captain chuckled as tears streamed down his face. His friend chuckled as well and told him how he hadn't met the real side of her yet. The captain rolled his eyes, doubting it and assuming he had already met the real her.

The weather the next day was even worse than the day before. The sailors became apprehensive, thinking it would be preferable to stay in France for another day, but Mr. Santarelli refused and asked to depart as quickly as possible. Marina was miserable the entire day, due to the incident at the tavern and bothered Margherita about it. The old lady sighed, unable to bear her whining any longer, and pleaded with her to simply apologize to the man. Marina was taken aback by this and refused to apologize, claiming that she had said nothing wrong and that he should be the one to apologize for making everything appear unpleasant. "Look, I'm getting too old for this. Either you apologize or you stop whining like a child." Margherita exclaimed, squinting and pressing her fingers to her eyes. The young lady sighed and eventually agreed, wanting to show the woman that she was no longer a child and that she could act maturely if she so desired. She is, after all, eighteen, and her nineteenth birthday is approaching. She walked to the deck to sweep the floor and then rest because cleaning isn't her strong suit, and while cleaning she spotted the captain conversing with Francesca, the red-haired girl. Marina gave her a sneer since she couldn't stand her, and the unpleasant girl couldn't either. She kept sweeping the deck and waited for the girl to leave the captain so she could apologize to him alone. When she finally left, she walked downstairs and deliberately bumped her arm on Marina's shoulder, giving her a dirty look. At this time, the young girl couldn't stand her and her rage was getting the best of her, but she was able to calm herself.

Mr. Santarelli then began to walk to the main deck, and Marina quickly approached him, saying, "Mr. Santarelli. I came to say something to you." She said this while holding the broom and leaning against it. With his arms crossed, the captain gave her a dubious look and continued, "I'm listening."

"I came here to express my regret. I apologize *if* I offended you, but I'm not sure why you were so furious. It was all in good fun."

"Is this a joke?" He continued,

"No? It's not as if I offended you crazily."

LV Polcic

He chuckled bitterly, unable to believe she had given him such a poor apology. Marina was irritated when he started calling her careless, and she exclaimed, "Careless! You'll never encounter a more kind person than me! I don't eat meat because I don't like killing animals!"

"I eat meat and adore animals," he said, looking perplexed at her. "That does not, however, imply that I despise animals. Is that what you're getting at?" Marina became agitated after being thrown off by the captain. "No, I didn't mean it that way—"

"You are an immature brat who only worries about herself and never about other people's feelings. Maybe it's good you left your wedding, your poor and unfortunate fiancé." the man said calmly as he moved closer to her, making her walk backward and lean on the banister. The young lady recalled her own brother's comments to her, who had said something similar to her before he died. She began to sob uncontrollably as she held herself and pleaded with him to stop. He looked at her and inquired whether he was offending her.

"God! Yes!"

"But making fun of my appearance is fine?" He grinned in response to the girl's yell. "You're getting off the ship at the next port, Miss Marina Rivalli." Marina's heart broke when the captain stated this, and she was extremely terrified that she was ready to cry to him and beg him to stay, telling him how she'd do everything to change. A wave hit just as she was about to say something, causing the vessel to jump and the girl to fall from the ship. She screamed in terror and held out her hand as she fell. Mr. Santarelli dashed to the banister and leaned against them to check on the girl. He kept yelling at her to swim, but he had no idea that she had never learned to swim. Marina was thrown left and right by the big waves, causing her to gulp too much water and exhausting her. She began to cough and slowly gave up. After hearing the girl cry, everyone hurried to the main deck. Antoni approached him and inquired about the incident. "What!" Antoni exclaimed as the man explained the issue to his companion. "Everyone! Pull down the sails!" He yelled at the sailors, and the ship began to slow down. Margherita and Giordana tossed a long rope for the girl to grab onto. The captain began to remove his coat and boots, and Francesca inquired as to what he was doing. "I'm going to save her," he replied. "I may despise her, but I do not want her to die." The man climbed up the banister and dove into the sea, attempting to save the girl. Due to the violent sea, he had difficulty swimming.

Marina ultimately gave up trying to swim and began sinking further into the sea, gasping for air. "I deserve this," she thought to herself as her eyesight began to blur. "I deserve to die." she thought as her eyes closed slowly. She looked up to see a man reaching out to her.

The man swam up to the surface, clutching her closely, while Antoni threw a ladder for the man to climb up. He struggled to climb because he was holding the girl with one hand and climbing up with the other. Luckily she was insanely thin. He eventually made it to the top, thanks to Antoni's assistance. Marina was thrown on the floor as quickly as he could, and she appeared to be dead. Everyone, especially the captain, was terrified. His anxiety began to take hold of him, and he began to tremble. He couldn't decide what to do, so he circled the same spot ten times. He then pulled back his wet black hair away from his face, recalling reading about CPR in a medical article. He strained to recall the details, and when he did, the man got down on his knees next to her and began performing the procedure on her. He pressed his heel into her breastbone in the center of her chest.

Then he interlocked his fingers with the palm of his other hand on top of the hand on her chest. He kept pressing down for a full minute, but nothing worked. He remembered the final step as he looked at her soft lips at the moment. He felt self-conscious about pressing his lips to hers in front of everyone, as it would be perceived as inappropriate. He moved in closer to her now pale face, placed his rough hands on her soft cheeks, and whispered "Please... wake up." His tears started falling on her face and just as he was going to pinch her nose, she vomited up a lot of water and continued to take long breaths. Everyone began to applaud, and Mr. Santarelli exhaled a breath of relief before collapsing on the floor. Marina then began to cry and in a panic, held the captain tightly while continuing to thank him. Antoni dropped down to his knees and held both of them, smiling and stating how delighted he was that they were both alive.

The girl then stood up, cold and stressed, and was visibly shivering. She began to go slowly towards her modest cabin, but the captain placed his hand on her shoulder and nervously murmured, "You may, of course, remain in my cabin. My bed is larger, and everything appears to be more comfortable." He walked the young lady to his cabin after she smiled and thanked him for letting her stay in it.

The captain returned to his cabin a few hours later to check on the girl. She was sleeping in his bed with four blankets and looked peaceful. He turned around and started walking back, thinking he'd woken her up for no cause. While walking, he accidentally knocked over a vase from his work table and it shattered on the ground. "Darn, it!" He became concerned that he had accidentally woken her up and began apologizing as she rubbed her eyes. "I came to bring you something hot to eat," he remarked as he sat down next to her on the bed. "Margherita cooked up a batch of pumpkin soup. I hope you enjoy it; I mean, it's delicious." He then placed a wooden tray on the nightstand with the bowl of soup on it. "That's nice, thank you," Marina said, "but I'm not hungry—" the nervous captain stopped her and exclaimed, "God! I'm such a moron, I should've brought you hot tea... You're probably already dehydrated!" The young lady continued to snort at his worried side before resting her head on his shoulder for a little period.

Mr. Santarelli's cheeks reddened and he inquired as to what was wrong. "I'm just, such an awful person am I?" she moaned and began to explain. "It would have been better if you had just let me die. I'm so sick of living at this point." she cried as she squeezed the fold of her nightgown. The man wrapped his arm around her and looked at her with concern, saying, "Look, you aren't bad. It's simply that some of the things you say could be *damaging*. Not to mention you kind of tend to act spoiled... I try being good with you, but sometimes you make it so hard."

The girl began to cry even harder, and Mr. Santarelli panicked and tried to console her by saying, "Ah look, to be completely honest, I wasn't the best either. Because my life hasn't always been easy, I've been known to take out my frustrations on people without even realizing it..."

Marina wiped the tears from her eyes and felt a
connection to him, for she, too, has been known to strike
out at others for no reason. "I wanted to ask you," He
said. "Why did you have such a panic attack in France?"
The girl's eyes widened in fear, and she moved away
from him, requesting that the theme be changed because
she doesn't feel comfortable discussing it. The man then
had an idea and suggested that they simply talk and get
to know each other to help her relax. They ended up
laughing for an hour and conversing for a long time.

Marina was lying on her stomach, fidgeting with her legs
in the air, and snickered, "You know, I've known you for
a while now, and I never inquired about your age."

"Really?" He exclaimed, surprised all dramatically.
"How dare you! Your own captain! For your information,
Madam, I am twenty-three years old." The young lady
snickered and commented on how the dark circles under
his dark brown eyes made him appear older. The man
simply rolled his eyes and continued his questioning of
her. "Why did you come to my ship, of all places?"
Marina glanced at him anxiously and stated that she was
fleeing her wedding and needed a mode of transportation
that wouldn't get her caught by her parents. And when
she learned that he is a captain, she realized that this is
an ideal opportunity. "However, I don't entirely regret
fleeing... For the first time in my life, I was able to travel,
meet Antoni, and... meet you." She bit her lower lip as

the captain quietly smiled, pleased that someone was appreciating him.

"I feel as if, my near-death experience has opened my eyes! I'm just, starting to realize that I should stop being so whiny and for once actually be kind." She twisted her brother's ring "I've done some things in my life that I'm not particularly proud of." The man looked at her as he placed his hand on hers "That's fine. I'm honestly just happy that you're willing to acknowledge your wrongs." The young lady smiled and felt happy that he was encouraging her to be better, rather than judging her for her past.

She then stretched out her arms and began to yawn "It was nice talking to you Mr Santarelli, but it's late and I should be going to sleep." she said as she stood up. The captain looked at her nervously and asked, "You can just stay here for the night. I'm not bothered... I could either sleep with Antoni or in your cabin. It's not an issue at all. It's the least I can do."

Marina stood behind the doors, only the right side of her body being visible, and whispered, "Good night, Mr. Santarelli." and looked at him with her alluring blue eyes. He pressed his lips and wished her a good rest. The captain flopped on the bed, groaning about everything as she shut the doors. He closed his eyes and all could he think about her was her ocean-blue eyes.

Chapter VIII

August 10th, 1910.

Marina and the captain were in his cabin, sipping black coffee and chatting, some days after the incident. They decided to drink coffee together in the morning before work.

"You can't possibly be serious. You can't possibly speak so many languages!" Marina was ecstatic.

"I only speak French, English, and Italian." he says.

The girl gasped, fascinated because the only language she knows is Italian, and it would be lovely if she could speak more than one. She asked the man if he could teach her English one day, and he accepted with a warm grin. The young girl then groaned and remarked that working on a ship can be monotonous at times because you can't do much after cleaning and cooking. "I have plenty of books if you want to borrow some of mine." He said as he stood up and walked over to a large wooden casket. "Yes!" Marina exclaimed as she smiled and banged her palms on the table. "Thank you very much. I enjoy reading actually." She said. The man grinned nervously, rubbing his jawline, and felt pleased that someone else appreciates reading books as much as he does. He had a book in his hand that he thought could be of interest to her, and she approached him to take it, but as soon as the girl did, she noticed a wound on his palm. "What happened to your hand?" Marina exclaimed In a troubled tone of voice as she grabbed his arm and lifted it. The captain became nervous because he was not used to anyone touching him, so he shrugged and described how he cut his palm on glass by mistake the night before. Marina smirked and asked playfully if he wanted her to kiss his wound to make the pain go away.

The man got scarlet and didn't know what to say, so the girl snorted and told him she was joking, but then sat him in the chair and went to get a bandage and some alcohol. She cleaned his wound with alcohol and carefully wrapped it. Mr. Santarelli looked at her and couldn't look away anymore. When she was done, Marina told him to be more careful next time and he in a soft voice thanked her "Thank you. I really mean it, it feels nice that someone doesn't hate me." The young lady softly smiled at him and told him how she knows what's it like being hated, so this is the least thing she could do. "Say, that day when you fell... why didn't you swim?" Mr. Santarelli said when she was finished. After he stated those words, the girl glanced down and exclaimed, embarrassed, that she never learned to swim because it wasn't required. The man burst out laughing, unable to believe that someone had boarded his ship, knowing full well that they could not swim and would perish if an accident occurred.

"Your mockery isn't helping!" Marina exclaimed, flushed with humiliation.

"Sorry." He was ecstatic. "Hypothetically... If you want, I could teach you to swim."

The girl offered him a warm grin and expressed her delight. The ship anchored in a little town a few days later. Marina was given a swimming lesson by him, and the two of them hid on a beach where no one else could see them. Marina was at first uneasy about being in her undergarments in front of a man, but she shrugged it off and reminded herself not to get too concerned in such frivolous matters. The man removed his boots, shirt, and other belongings and put them beside her belongings. She started walking towards the sea barefoot, but she kept stopping because the rocks she trod on hurt her feet. The man kept giggling at her, and he laughed at every move and sound she made. "I hate rocky beaches." She exclaimed.

Mr. Santarelli went into the sea first, yelling at her to come in and how the sea wouldn't bite her. She kept giving him an indifferent look and was about to walk away when the captain reached out his hand and sweetly encouraged her to take his hand and they'd work it out together. Marina gently placed her hand on his, noticing how rough his hands were in comparison to her delicate and tender ones. The young lady became increasingly afraid as they progressed, and she clung to the man. "Right now, you're acting like a cat." He laughed and snickered at her, but she didn't care because she didn't want to drown because of him. He eventually threw himself into the water, urging her to get down and that he'd make sure nothing bad happens. Marina approached him and grabbed him because she was afraid. The man tried to separate her from him and urged her to try swimming because he'd hold her or be right next to her if she started to drown and he could pull her up. Marina was terrified to let go of him, but he begged her to trust him, and the girl, still clutching him, asked, "Are you sure you promise?" The man smiled sweetly and answered, "Of course, You have to learn to trust me, didn't I save you from drowning in the first place?" Marina brushed it off, finally letting go of him and attempting to swim, and the captain would be overjoyed to watch her do so, encouraging her on how well she was doing.

He softly placed his hands on her waist as she lowered her arms and began to move them. Mr. Santarelli held her the entire time as she tried to swim until he let go, sure that she would be able to swim on her own for a short while. The girl, on the other hand, sank into the sea, terrified. As she gasped for air, the man grabbed her and dragged her back up.

"I despise you."

"Miss Marina, I was simply trying to help you." he replied, smirking and placing his palm on her forehead, lifting her wet bangs from her face, which were covering her gorgeous eyes. He remained smiling at her, finding her charming, while the girl hugged him closely because she was afraid of drowning again. "If you keep holding me, you won't get anywhere." She then pushed herself away from him and yelled, "No, but I could do this." before pushing him into the water. The girl was furious with him for violating his word, and she couldn't stop laughing when he emerged from the water. His hair had fully covered his face and eyes, and the man appeared displeased. "You are very much something, aren't you?" He exclaimed as he gave her a chuckle.

Marina was laughing at him the entire time, and when she went to approach him, she tripped over a rock and fell on him. The man grabbed her right away, and they had an awkward silence. As they stared at each other's faces, their lips were almost touching. He kept staring at her big doll eyes until he coughed and snapped out of it. He asked that their swimming lesson be completed and that they go to the beach to dry off. The girl nodded and stepped away from him slowly. When they got out of the water, Marina laid down on the pebbles and completely relaxed.

"Can you tell me what you're doing?"

"Appreciating the sun. You are welcome to join me if you choose." She responded.

"You're a strange lady." He sat down next to her and carefully laid down, looking at her.

"I know."

Marina kept snorting like a pig the entire time they were taunting one other. The captain mocked her for being so clumsy all of the time, and the girl mocked him for being so concerned about everything all of the time. The young lady closed her eyes and sighed, telling him how much she needed this. And how she's starting to appreciate the fact that she's on a ship. The man looked at her strangely, as if he was surprised that someone would enjoy being on the ship, and asked her why she liked it so much, to which she said, "I suppose it's because I get to travel and feel free. There's also Antoni, who always makes me laugh, and... you. It's wonderful when you keep me company. I never realized how gorgeous your eyelashes are!" the girl exclaimed as she turned around to face him. The captain's heart continued to race and the way she complimented him made him feel loved for the first time in his life. He moaned as he remembered how badly he used to treat her. Marina was perplexed and inquired of him, "What is it?"

"The day you came," the man said, covering half of his face with his hand in embarrassment. "do you recall how rude I was to you?" The girl smiled and nodded."Well, please accept my heartfelt apologies. Everything had gotten to me, and I was sick of it. That morning, I was contemplating whether or not I should end my life. I wish I had done it; I keep wailing about how lonely I am all the time, but then I lash out at you." As he chuckled, tears began to trickle down his cheeks. He quickly realized what he had said and apologized profusely for making everything sound dismal out of nowhere. "No, I'm at fault. I was insanely rude to you. And I'm delighted you're alive," the girl said as she grabbed his hands and focused her gaze on his eyes. "My life back at home would have been a living hell if it hadn't been for you." She continued to show him how grateful she is that he feels so at ease around her that he can tell her everything that is on his mind. The man wiped away his tears out of embarrassment, and the girl exclaimed, "No no no! It's alright if you weep! It's fine with me if you do it. In addition, my father would say that if you cry a lot, you'll urinate less." When she said it, the man burst out laughing; he adored how random she could be at times.

Marina went in closer and kissed his forehead to comfort him, but suddenly panicked, exclaiming, "Ah darn, now I'm too comfortable with others." The captain touched her delicate cheek with his rough hand, looked into her eyes, and said to her how he didn't mind.

The girl became agitated and hurried away, her face flushed. Mr. Santarelli averted his gaze in embarrassment and thanked her for her kindness. They ended up falling asleep on the beach for a while, and when they awoke, Marina was frightened since her natural olive skin had become much darker. The man attempted to calm her down by telling her how well it suits her, but she was unconvinced and asked him to return to the ship. They began to dress and tossed each other their clothing and they began walking away. The girl bit her lower lip as they walked, feeling as if she should be more honest with him rather than holding so many secrets. "Mr. Santarelli...," she whispered softly as she grabbed his sleeve. "I have something to say to you.

My wedding gown was crimson on that particular day because—" As they walked, a few fishermen noticed them and commented "This new generation. No boundaries when it comes to their intimacy! Managed to ruin the beach." the girl stopped talking. The captain and the young lady looked at each other with their eyes wide open and began to feel uncomfortable by the fisherman's comment. Marina breathed a sigh of relief, concluding that it was too soon to tell people such things. Mr. Santarelli looked at Marina, puzzled, and requested her to continue. She became agitated and attempted to shift the conversation's topic by remarking, "Oh look! A lovely seashell! Have I ever mentioned how much I enjoy collecting rocks and seashells?" The man gave her a gentle chuckle and rolled his eyes.

When they boarded the ship, Antoni greeted them and inquired as to where they had been for so long. The young lady told him about how Mr. Santarelli had taken her swimming and how he should've joined them because it was so lovely. "You have no idea how great this is to me. Especially since today is a particularly difficult day for me since it is my brother's birthday."

"Aren't you a twin?" The captain enquired.

Marina cracked her knuckles and nodded. Both men were taken aback when she didn't inform them it was her birthday. The girl looked perplexed at them and explained that she no longer enjoys celebrating them because the notion of it makes her cry.

"Gabriel, look, another person who despises their birthday." Antoni added as he kicked the man's arm, causing him to gaze at them both awkwardly. D'Angelo then began pleading with the young girl to let them at least take her out for a drink tomorrow night, to which she said she'll think about it. Marina hurried to the kitchen and returned with a box of biscuits, which she handed to the two men, anxiously explaining how she baked them herself and asking whether they were any good. Mr. Santarelli devoured the entire package of biscuits as soon as he finished one. He couldn't believe she was so skilled at baking, especially considering how quickly she caught up. Marina blushed and smiled as she received compliments from both of them, and she felt very special. The girl left them after a time of conversing because she needed to change clothes and went to her cabin.

The captain began walking to his cabin with biscuits in his pockets, but his pal stopped him by placing his hand on the captain's shoulder, asking, "You're finally softening up to her?"

"It's nothing out of the ordinary."

Antoni replied, "Sure."

The captain walked to his cabin and shut the door behind him. He sat down on his bed, his hands covering his face. The man sighed, puzzled as to why he was suddenly nervous around her. He didn't know what this bizarre feeling meant, and it made him want to vomit. Mr. Santarelli closed his eyes and couldn't stop thinking about her beautiful smile and huge eyes. "Remember what Angela said," he thought to himself, as he wondered if he was revealing too much information to her all at once. "no woman wants to hear or see me sob over my issues."

Marina strolled up to her cabin, which she shared with others, in the meantime. She appeared to be happy and comfortable with everything. The young lady snatched up the garment she'd received as a gift, pressed it against her body, and twirled around in front of the mirror, daydreaming about tomorrow's night and how much fun she's had with the captain today. She then came to a halt and smiled at herself in the mirror, but her grin quickly disappeared. The girl tossed her gown to the floor, her face becoming even colder.

"You're a whore." She told herself this as she looked in the mirror. "You were just engaged to the love of your life, and you're already thinking about someone else." Marina sobbed as she clutched the wooden drawer and continued to call herself derogatory names. She felt ashamed by her own body as she placed her hand on her chest, and still felt the man's touch on her. Reminding herself of all of this caused her to have a panic attack, and she grabbed a hairbrush and threw it at the mirror, shattering one of the corners.

She slumped down on the floor and sobbed, wishing she could just move on and be happy like she used to be.

Chapter IX

The young girl finished her chores the next day and went into the kitchen to learn how to cook better. Margherita's cooking piqued her interest, especially since she'd like to impress her father with her culinary abilities one day. Marina followed the old lady's instructions, but part of it made her nervous owing to its complexity. She was attempting to learn how to make homemade pasta and was repulsed by the touch of eggs. While kneading the dough, the girl began lamenting about how much it pained her hands. The old lady encouraged her to keep going till she was finished. Marina was pleased with herself for eventually making her own homemade pasta with blood and effort. She didn't seem to mind that her face was caked in flour and her clothes were drenched in pasta sauce. Marina went to set the table, which she did very elegantly recently, even holding numerous plates at once.

She set the plate of pasta on the table for the captain and poured the pasta sauce over it. The man kindly thanked her. He complimented Margherita for cooking such a well-prepared meal as he took a bite, as he always does. "Ah, you should be praising the young girl, she did it all herself." the old lady answered. The captain who was dumbfounded, smirked at Marina "Every day, you continue to amaze me. It's delicious..." The girl flushed and smiled awkwardly. She thanked the man for the compliment and placed her hand on her cheek. After that, the young lady went outside and noticed Francesca. She dashed up to her and exclaimed that she needed to tell her something. The red-haired girl gave her an odd look and told her to hurry up. "I'm sorry if I've ever been rude to you," Marina said as she approached her and extended her hand. "I don't want to have a strained relationship with you." The girl then thought to herself that she shouldn't have apologized in the first place, but she didn't want to be on bad terms with anyone on the ship. Francesca squinted her eyes but accepted the girl's apology by shaking her hand. "I hope we can talk more." Marina replied with a smile. The other girl laughed and answered sarcastically, "Sure."

The young lady sighed and shook it off when Francesca left. She was pleased with herself for being mature and making an apology. She returned to the kitchen and took a seat at the table. Antoni was sitting at the table and patted the girl on the shoulder. Marina turned around and inquired about it. "Happy late birthday," the man said as he slid a box onto the table. "I'm hoping you enjoy it." She saw a set of lovely pearl drop earrings when she opened the box. She exclaimed and continued to smile, unable to believe that she had been given such a lovely present. But then the girl realized she didn't have her ears pierced, and she felt bad about not being able to use the gift she received from her friend. Antoni was taken aback when Marina grasped her ear and uncomfortably smirked, "Unfortunately, my ears aren't pierced. I always use clip-on earrings." He looked at the captain, who was cramming his face with food, and the man was perplexed, asking what he was smiling about. "Gabriel, prepare a needle." the man said as he stood up, grabbing the hands of both of his friends. Marina swallowed her saliva in fear.

Marina was pinned to the captain's bed by Antoni, who told her to relax and that he and Mr. Santarelli had done this previously and it had gone smoothly. The young lady couldn't help but be concerned; she had never pierced her ears for this reason. The captain sat down on his bed and placed an apple behind the girl's ear as he finished getting the needle heated. He handed his friend the needle and encouraged him to go ahead. Mr. Santarelli noticed how terrified she was and asked if she wanted to do it. "I do, I've always wanted to pierce my ears and stop wearing clip-ons." she replied. "But the pain terrifies me." She exclaimed. "You can hold my hand if it makes you feel better." the man said softly as he gently grasped her hand. Marina's heart was racing as she stared at his gentle black eyes, and she couldn't stop thinking about the pain.

Antoni went through with the needle as the captain urged her to count to ten and close her eyes. Marina screamed in agony, clutching the man's hand so tightly that she nearly broke it. Marina continued to cry uncontrollably when he finished assisting her in piercing her ears.

Everything ached, but she was ecstatic to have finally faced one of her fears. Marina rose and began to admire herself in the mirror, touching her new gleaming pearl earrings. Antoni agreed and told her how he knows how to pick the proper gifts since she couldn't stop gazing at herself and felt gorgeous. The man then pushed his hip on the captain and urged him to compliment her in the manner of a true gentleman. The man became jittery. He raised his eyes to her and gently told her that she was beautiful. The girl smiled as she gently placed her delicate fingers on her cherry-colored lips and was pleased with what the man said. Antoni then warned her to not take off her earrings for months no matter what the circumstances. She promised not to and kept smiling about her new earrings.

Antoni glanced at the clock and advised his buddies that they should start thinking about going to a pub to celebrate the lady's birthday as soon as possible. They went their separate ways to finish their chores, and Marina continued to admire herself in the mirror. She was pleased to have finally pierced her ears, and she considered it a sign of freedom. The red-haired woman halted young D'Angelo on his way to the deck. She violently gripped his shoulders and wanted to talk with him. The man was perplexed and requested her to hurry because he had responsibilities to complete.

"As your dear friend, I advise you not to speak to the new girl too much. She's an odd woman. I found her crying in the middle of the night a couple of times, and I still can't get over the fact that her wedding gown was stained with something red." Antoni groaned and rolled her eyes, asking her to stop with the nonsense and let the poor girl breathe. He requested of she be friendly for once and how he and Gabriel are going to have a drink with the girl to celebrate her nineteenth birthday, and if she wanted to perhaps join them. Francesca looked at him in annoyance and refused immediately. She couldn't stand being near her.

Marina was dressed up and waiting for the two gentlemen outdoors on the deck later that night. She was looking forward to having a drink with them and finally loosening up. Antoni kissed her hand as a joke as the two men arrived. She grinned at him, then turned to face Mr. Santarelli, who was visibly nervous. He kept biting the skin off his fingers while holding something behind his back with his other hand. The girl tried to figure out what it was, but she didn't get the chance. They walked towards the pub, and Marina wasn't expecting it to be so loud and packed with drunk old men when they arrived. She was at first uneasy, but Antoni tried to cheer her up as they sat down. The young Mr. Santarelli couldn't take his gaze away from her the entire night; she was lovely and upbeat. Her wide grin was contagious, and he continued smiling back every time she smiled at him. "I got you a present." he said anxiously as he placed the gift on the table. "I couldn't afford to get you something nicer as earrings, so I hope this will suffice." The young lady's eyes widened as she didn't realize she would be getting any more presents. She promptly unwrapped it and realized it to be a book. "Alice's Adventures in Wonderland." As she grasped the book, she said.

"Alice, she has a strong resemblance to you. I recall you saying you enjoyed reading, so I'm hoping you'll enjoy it. If you don't, I'll attempt to find something else for you." He nervously stroked the back of his head. Marina leaned against the table, swiftly grabbing his hand and smiling warmly. "No, I like it! I'm glad you mentioned how the book's protagonist reminded you of me. I couldn't have asked for a more perfect present."

"Hello? I gave you pearl earrings." Antoni replied, perplexed. "You may as well declare me the finest gift giver! You two are strange for liking to read." Marina laughed and apologized to him, sweetly expressing her admiration for his gift and promising that she would never take them off. It started with a cup of wine, then another, and another, and finally, an entire bottle while they conversed and mocked each other. The girl's cheeks had turned red from the booze, and she was laughing at everything. Antoni had never seen her so drunk before, and he was ecstatic to see her that wild that night. Mr. Santarelli and she got into a long discussion about books, which eventually morphed into him talking about writing and how much he loved it. "When I run out of ink, I usually go octopus fishing and take its ink. It's no cost to me, and I get a lot of it."

"I had no idea you were a fisherman?" She inquired.

"I do fish on an occasion, and I can sell them for a decent price if I have a good catch day. If you want, you could perhaps come fishing with me and I'll teach you?"

Marina gave him a gentle grin and expressed to him how much she'd loved that, making the captain feel all warm inside. Antoni began to feel as if he wasn't in the room with them while they talked, so he turned to his friend and was taken aback by the way he stared at the girl. He'd never seen him gaze at someone like that before. The man then decided to leave them alone to get closer and talk as much as they wanted in private. "Well, this has been fantastic, but I must depart. Instead, I'm going to go talk to a gorgeous woman here. I'll see you two on the ship." Antoni then walked away, straightening his stance as he approached a lovely lady. Marina and the captain exchanged awkward glances since they couldn't think of anything to say to each other. He apologized to her and advised her that he needed to go outdoors and do something. Anything to break the silence and calm down from anxiousness. The young girl nodded and carefully awaited his return.

"Why do I keep feeling so anxious when I'm with her." the man said as he went outside and hid among the bushes, undoing his pants, his heart racing furiously. Everything perplexed him, and while they went swimming, their lips almost touching, he continued wondering about the time. Later, he put his pants back on and strolled down to the beach to wash his hands, and while he was there, he considered bringing Marina here to view the stars and listen to the waves on the shore. He was ecstatic at the prospect of her resting on his shoulder.

He dashed to the bar, his face flushed with surprise and wrath as he walked in. Another man was already talking to her, and it appeared that they were getting along. The captain approached their table slowly and said hello to both of them. "Pleasure to meet you, Andrea Biscontini," the other man said confidently as he extended his hand to him. He then pointed to the bar counter where he worked and said, "I'm a bartender here." The captain despised him; the way he spoke irked him, and his sudden entrance had ruined his plans for the evening. Marina couldn't stop grinning at Mr. Biscontini as he spoke pleasantly to her and asked why such a lovely lady was in such a place.

"It was my birthday yesterday, so my pals wanted to join me in celebrating." She guffawed.

"Birthday? Oh, then as a gift, I'll show you my greatest beverages." As he placed his hand on the girl's shoulder, he smirked at her. Marina's cheeks flushed even more, and she followed him to the counter, abandoning her companion. The captain was irritated, and he didn't want her to be alone with a man she had just met, but he thought he was being hypocritical because they had both been strangers at one point as well. The captain remained to stare at them as he drank a whole bottle of wine by himself, and he grew increasingly irritated as he heard Marina laugh at Mr. Biscontini. The girl had a good time with the young bartender, and he offered her another drink every time she completed hers. "I believe I should come to a halt... I've already consumed far too many alcoholic beverages tonight. I don't think I've ever consumed so much alcohol in my life."

"Have one more, it's your nineteenth birthday after all," Mr. Biscontini said with a chuckle. "It's just once in a lifetime when you're nineteen." She shrugged and decided to take a few more drinks because he had a point. She eventually couldn't gaze any longer and became even more dizzy than before. Then, seemingly out of nowhere, the man placed his hand on hers and reached for a kiss; Marina, naive as she was and insanely drunk and unaware of what was going on, leaned forward and they kissed. Mr. Santarelli had had enough and stood up and walked out of the bar.

He cried the entire time he walked to the beach where he had been earlier. "I'm a walking bad luck. Just when I believed she might've had feelings for me as well, everything went wrong. When my parents kept calling me such, they were correct." As he flung pebbles into the sea, he groaned. He sat down on the ground and kept crying softly. He hated this feeling, the feeling of getting your heart broken. "I barely even know her, why do I keep having the feeling as if I'd known her forever." He kept asking himself. After a lengthy period of crying, he decided to return to his ship, and on the way, he saw his friend fixing his pants.

"How did you end up here?" The captain enquired.

"I'm returning to the ship. And where is your companion?" Antoni inquired as he continued to look around for Marina. The man averted his gaze as he explained how he had left her in the bar with the bartender. Hearing that, his friend turned pale; he couldn't believe his pal was so immature as to leave the poor girl alone in a strange environment. D'Angelo began yelling at him, causing the captain to get agitated and tremble as a result of the stress he was experiencing.

He hoped nothing had happened to her, and Antoni pressed him to explain why he had suddenly decided to abandon her. "She kissed another man. Are you pleased to hear that?" His pal averted his gaze and made the letter O with his lips. He pitied his friend, but he couldn't forgive him for still acting like a child.

Marina, on the other hand, was in the bar with a bartender who had just finished his shift. They began walking outside and he forcefully kissed her again, causing the girl's eyes to widen and her to gently push him away. Mr. Biscontini inquired as to what was wrong, and she continued to tell him that she was drunk and didn't want to do anything but go home with the captain. "Who is Mr. Santarelli?" He asked.

"He's my—"

He looked at her as he started chuckling and placing his hand on his hip "Oh he is your companion? Well, there's no one here waiting for you." Marina grew to become even more uncomfortable with him.

Because she was inebriated, the man grabbed her hand and encouraged her to go to his house and take a nap there. The girl kept moving his hand away from hers, expressing her need to be alone with the captain, whom she realized she couldn't find anyplace and she started to feel terrified. The bartender became irritated with her and abandoned her on the streets, heavily inebriated. The poor girl began to feel worried after a while. She was unable to walk, she was nauseated, her head hurt, and she was unable to locate any of her pals. She ended up sitting on the side of the road and crying because she felt so vulnerable.

Antoni and Mr. Santarelli returned to the bar to find her, hoping that she was unharmed. However, they soon realized she had departed, as had the bartender. The captain grew pale and felt sick to his stomach at that point, as he continued to imagine only the worst-case situations. D'Angelo put his hands on the captain's shoulders and told him to calm down by breathing normally. They went outside to look for her again after he calmed down, and as they walked, they heard the familiar sound of someone crying. The two men dashed off and discovered the young lady crying. They both hugged her fiercely, and Marina began crying even harder and louder as she was both relieved that they had found her and humiliated that she was drunk and vulnerable once more. They were always coming to save her, and she felt awful about it. The captain repeatedly apologized to her for leaving her alone and frightening her. She forgave him, but she demanded to know why he had abandoned her in the first place.

"I felt j— I got sick from drinking too much and needed some fresh air..." He lied his way out since he didn't want to be exposed for claiming he was envious of her adoration for someone else. Antoni paused for a moment before asking, "Say, how many drinks did you have?" The captain and Antoni both widened their eyes and stared at her in terror as the girl raised seven fingers. Even they aren't capable of consuming that much alcohol. They ultimately assisted her in standing and both held her hands as she walked so she wouldn't trip. When they got back to the ship, the girl began to trip and became unable to walk. Mr. Santarelli lifted her in bridal style without hesitation so he could gently carry her back to her cabin. "May we sit on the deck for five minutes... please." she placed her arms around his neck and begged. She sighed as he laid her down and glanced up at the stars. "I don't know whether you're interested, but you see that constellation right there?" the captain said awkwardly as he sat next to her, wanting to start a conversation so she calms down."Little Dipper is the constellation over there. The Big Dipper is the one directly beneath it. Since I generally navigate using stars, I know a lot about them." The girl raised her head and softly smiled, admiring his wisdom as she laid her head on his shoulder. "If there is no other source of guidance available, us sailors use the star Polaris to guide us in order then." He said when he caught a glimpse of her eye, in which the stars in the sky were reflected. She was glancing up when the man grinned at her stunning blue eyes. He sighed and stated, "I sometimes enjoy gazing at the stars; I find them to be very soothing. So glistening so—"

"Beautiful." She concluded his thought. At that very moment, Mr. Santarelli turned to face her and grinned, "Yes, very beautifu

Chapter X

Back to Naples a month ago. The bride's parents returned home in sorrow on the day the fiancé was murdered. They couldn't believe what they were seeing when they realized their daughter had left. Mrs. Rivalli began sobbing hysterically, feeling like a terrible mother for losing both of her children. Her spouse attempted to calm her down by tightly hugging her and urging her not to lose hope. He kept thinking about how those sailors had taken his daughter when she was in the marine. They were never up to anything good, and they could simply sell a young girl on the black market in a foreign country for a decent price. He tried to dismiss it because he didn't want to consider the possibility, but he also didn't want to believe Marina had run away or potentially abandoned them.

Both of her parents were in excruciating pain as a result of the wedding's aftermath. They were under pressure to explain everything to the guests while still avoiding making their daughter look bad. In any case, neither of them knows what happened in her room. Mr. and Mrs. Marotta, the groom's parents, paid them a visit a few days later. They appeared unconcerned with the situation as if they didn't give a damn that their oldest son had died. Marina's parents welcomed them into their home with open arms, but they had a strange sensation about them as if something horrible was about to happen.

"Ah, Mr. Rivalli, Mrs. Rivalli, It's wonderful to see you again."

"It's also a pleasure, Mr Marotta." Marina's father gave him a strange look as he shook his hand. "What brings you to our house?" He inquired.

"I believe we still have a lot to discuss, particularly regarding your daughter and our son."

Mrs. Rivalli and Mr. Rivalli exchanged puzzled looks, unsure of what would happen next. As the maid served them exquisite wine, they all sat down at the table. "You see, your daughter already has quite a poor name in this wonderful city of ours." Mr. Marotta said after taking a sip. "Making controversies at balls, your son's accident, and now the wedding." Mr. Rivalli, who was nervous, interrupted him and impatiently asked him to get to the point. "What I meant was. It would be a shame if your daughter was reported to the police. She'd be imprisoned for the rest of her life. You don't want to lose another of your children, do you? It wasn't as simple for her to get away with her brother's incident, and it won't be easy this time." Mr. Rivalli then slammed his hands on the table, pointed his finger at the man, and demanded at him not to mention his daughter or his family in general in that manner. "Be careful or else you'll lose the one child you have left." the man said, his eyes narrowing at Marina's father in annoyance. "Additionally, your miscarriage wife is unable to provide you with any more children." When Mrs. Rivalli first heard that, her eyes widened in shock. How in the world did he learn that? She started crying right away and was irrationally upset. Her husband was speechless as he saw his frightened wife. He then gave Mr. Marotta a quick glance and asked, in a raspy voice, "What do you want?"

"Money." He exclaimed. "We're sadly incredibly poor, which is hard to believe. We don't have a mansion or any clubs as we told you. Matias also never finished a reputable school nor does he speak many languages. We made up the story so that our son might con your easy daughter and trick you. Unfortunately, it turns out that our son is an imbecile, therefore we must find another way to get the money." Mrs. Rivalli became enraged at that point and yelled "No!" She wasn't going to allow herself to be so easily duped into giving them the absurd sum of money they requested. Mr. Rivalli put his hand on her chest, drew her away from the table, and gently urged her to stop, reassuring her that they would give them any sum of money they desired. She couldn't believe he was so easily defeated; she was in shock. Mr. Rivalli felt guilty for caving in, but he took out his check and requested that they note the numbers down. The parents of Matias grinned with satisfaction; at this point, they didn't even care or want to mourn their son's passing.

"Mr. Rivalli, you made a wise choice. I hope your restaurant and family name continue to prosper." Mr. Rivalli glared at him angrily and prayed for it to be over so he could lock himself in the bathroom and sob. When Matias's parents departed, Marina's father tightly grabbed his wife, who cried inconsolably into his chest, "What will happen to our daughter? What if they ultimately turn on her?" The man sighed as he looked down. "I'll give them extra money if they request it, just to keep her safe, I'll give them till they suck every last bit out of my pocket." Then his wife sniffed as he offered her his handkerchief to wipe her lovely face. After giving it some thought, she turned to face him and asked, "Husband, what if Marina isn't guilty after all? The wound that Matias had on his neck appeared to be an act of defense. His pants were also undone. Why else would Marina suddenly act in such a harsh manner?" Then he sighed and touched her cheek softly with his palm. "Despite your good intentions, I believe we should keep quiet about this. The less we discuss this, the less at risk we are. What if Marina's reputation is brought up? We are lost, however, she will be executed." She agreed and made the decision to keep her silence about it. She cried every day since she was unable to inquire about her daughter's whereabouts. She weakened more and more every day.

September 2nd , 1910.

25 days have passed since the event with Marina in the bar, which brings us to the present. Mr. Santarelli continued to be wary about getting close to her. He was afraid of being rejected and reflected that he had no time for such things. He kept lying to himself that he certainly wasn't overjoyed every time he saw her and worried that he was behaving embarrassingly in front of the lady. For weeks, D'Angelo urged him to ask her to go somewhere with him.

"You wouldn't have a problem having a simple private supper with her if all you want to do is be friends." Antoni asked.

The captain made an effort to justify anything his friend stated, "Well you see, I do not have a problem. Simply put, I'm busy." He lied. He was busy at times, but he could always find some free time for her. Antoni asked him if his hectic schedule included reading books all day. Young lady Marina entered the room with a tray of freshly brewed coffee and biscuits just as they were ready to start squabbling. She began to apologize after feeling guilty for maybe interrupting. "I'm sorry if I've disrupted your talk, gentlemen." The captain quickly altered his demeanor and told her she had been pardoned as his eyes widened and continued to gaze at every inch of her. He remained looking at the girl as she set the tray down at the table and served them coffee. At that point, Antoni rolled his eyes and became irritated. He found it difficult to understand that despite the man's repeated claims that he has no interest in the girl, he continued to gaze upon her as if it were the first time he'd never seen a woman before right upon him.

When she was finished, she made the decision to leave them alone and go make dinner. The two men were still talking and drinking coffee. Antoni was delighted by the wonderful sensation of the beverage when he took a sip. "Oh dear God, it's extremely good. Have you given it a go?" After tasting, Mr. Santarelli stated calmly that the young lady's culinary abilities had recently improved significantly. She arrived here not even knowing how to cut an onion, and now she can cook and bake a variety of foods, so he in a way felt proud of her progress. "I wanted to ask if you'd like to accompany me discreetly in my cabin to eat dinner." he said after blinking and stopping thinking of the girl. "I've heard that duck will be cooked tonight." After hearing the offer, his friend smiled and uncomfortably tapped his fingers on his coffee while saying, "Ah my apologies, I'm very busy with sewing tonight. Possibly next time. But oh! I am aware of who will be available." The captain then became frightened and attempted to put his palm over the man's lips while threatening him not to say it. Marina's name was then called out by D'Angelo, who also invited her to their table for a brief moment. As Marina began to wonder what was going on, he then put his arm around the captain's shoulder.

"Gabriel has a question for you"

"I do not—"

"He does, please explain what you asked."

"Would you... Miss Marina, like to accompany me discreetly in my cabin for dinner?" he then murmured with a sigh.

Marina was taken aback. She wasn't prepared for him to make her such a generous offer. When she realized this, she clenched her fists and told him that she was still a maid and had to prepare the dinner table in the kitchen. "It's the captain's command." He smirked as he looked down at her. Hearing him say that, Marina nervously pressed her lips and looked away. She ended up accepting the offer and the two agreed to meet up in his cabin later that night.

Later, the captain became very anxious. He desired perfection in all things that night. He even placed a single rose in a vase and lit candles. He kept thinking to himself that this would come off as a little too romantic, but Marina arrived just as he was about to change things. She asked permission to enter by knocking on the doors. Then, when he opened the doors for her, he slicked his hair and cleared his throat. The girl gasped in surprise because everything was so lovely. She then fought to hold the plates in both of her hands and almost spilled soup on the floor, and the man sprang in to assist her right away. She thanked him politely as he set them down on the table.

They had a long awkward silence after they sat down. Every time he looked at Marina, she kept grinning back at him, and each time she did the same, he pursed his lips. Then he got the courage to ask, "So, how have you been?"

"Good," Marina remarked after finishing her soup. "Since being intoxicated that night, I've tried to consume less alcohol." Mr. Santarelli then proceeded to stab the meat while nodding. "That's good. Very good actually. I should start drinking less as well." Then, turned to Marina, he questioned, "Say, how did you decide not to eat meat?" The girl responded with a delightful "Oh." after blinking and widening her eyes. "When I was around ten years old, I believe it began? My grandma has a little farm of her own, and she asked my brother and me to bring her a chicken. She chopped its neck in front of us with an axe when I believed she only wanted to pet her. Since then, I have felt bad for animals and have stopped eating meat. Even though it occasionally smells amazing, I feel awful about eating them." Hearing her brief backstory, the man couldn't help but laugh. He continued to chuckle as he imagined her terrified face upon seeing the blood all over the place. Then Marina joined in the laughter and snorted like never before. She laughed involuntarily, which caused her to apologize right away. She received a warm smile from the captain, who also encouraged her not to feel bad about her distinctive laugh and that he doesn't hate it at all. She felt very warm inside because Matias used to tell her to laugh more ladylike and hated her laugh.

Marina started crying from laughing so much and kept wiping her face with her hands. The captain then gave her a gentle grin, got to his feet, and extended a napkin to her. He removed it from his pocket and used it to tenderly wipe the tears off her face.

He made an effort to avoid looking her in the eyes as he wiped her tears because he thought it could seem strange. Marina then looked around the cabin and noticed a bunch of maps rolled up and placed securely in a box. She even noticed a harpoon hanging on the wall and an illustration of a mermaid. She was fascinated by it all. The captain noticed her gaze was fixed on the maps and inquired "Would you like to see one?" The young lady's cheeks reddened in embarrassment as she didn't intend for him to notice that she was looking at the maps. She nodded quickly and smiled. The man stood up, grabbed one of the maps, placed it on the wooden table, and spread it open. The young lady was already amazed by it and carefully looked at the map of Europe. "What kingdom is this supposed to be? It's so extremely weirdly shaped." Asked the girl as she pointed at Greece. The captain let out a chuckle "You don't know the kingdoms and continents?" Marina looked at him in worry as her lower lip quivered "Am I supposed to?" She asked in embarrassment. She didn't want the captain to find her unintelligent, especially because he was incredibly bright, and feared he might dislike unintelligent ladies. The school she went to which was only for girls, taught her only how to do basic wifely chores, never about history, geography, languages, or anything else, which she was ashamed of. "Well, it is good to know and quite interesting. I could teach you a tad of geography if you'd like?" He asked as he looked at her leaning on the table. Marina got closer to him at that moment so she can observe his talking better. He excitingly explained to her each country which she pointed at and asked what is it. "Where are we located?" She asked as she beamed with a smile while looking at the map. Mr. Santarelli thought for a moment "We are… somewhere in between Italy and Greece." "It's amazing how much you know about maps. You're incredibly intelligent." She complimented him. He let out a small grin as he scratched the back of his neck "It's nothing special I suppose…" Marina continued to praise him for being good at coordinating everything and how she envied him for being so great at math. The man felt awkward at receiving her compliments and didn't know how to respond. She continued to look at the map and ask him questions "That is Spain." He said as she pointed at the Kingdom. "And that is Norway. I've heard it's extremely cold there." Marina looked at him in confusion "Really? Colder than here during winter?" He replied "Well, it is located in the Arctic Ocean. So yes, much colder."

"Have you visited any of these countries you have mentioned?" She asked curiously. "I have, but only the Mediterranean countries. My ship only delivers cargo to them." The young lady envied him, she wished she could've visited as many countries as the captain did. She pressed her lips together as she made a disappointed face at herself for not traveling so much in her life."I envy you for getting to travel everywhere." She expressed as she looked at her elegant hands and let out a sigh. He sat down next to her at that moment "One day you'll get to travel and see the world. Maybe even with someone that you love, my advice is that you better travel with someone because traveling alone is incredibly lonely." He said as he placed his hands on his. The young lady pursed her lips. She found his words comforting and her eyes began to wonder at the old illustration of a mermaid. The man glanced at her and stood up as he took off the illustration from the wall. He handed it to her "Here, I want you to have it. A woman whose name means sea should be more than fitting for her to own a mermaid." She looked up at him bewildered and half-opened her mouth "Are you sure?" Marina asked as she held the illustration "You seem to like it by how much you keep looking at it." He let out a chuckle.

 D'Angelo then entered the cabin to seek his friend for assistance as he had just sat back down and was ready to ask the girl a question. He was advised by the captain to go because the man was still eating and that he would assist him later. The captain complained to Marina that Antoni had left the doors open and that it appeared as though he lived in the Colosseum. At that, the girl began laughing. Then, anxiously biting her bottom lip, she said, "This was extremely nice. If you'd like, we could do something similar more frequently. Simply put, I value your company greatly." The captain grinned broadly and said, "Of course. We could go on walks together perhaps?"

"I would enjoy that." She smiled at him.

Later that night, Mr. Santarelli was soundly dozing off. He grumbled in his sleep and shifted around his bed. Even as he clung to his bed covers, the man began to perspire.

He was once again alone in his cabin in his dream. Slouching in his bed. His cabin's windows were wide open, and the wind was blowing the drapes. The man kept looking at his cabin while remaining silent as he noticed a woman in it. Marina was sitting on a chair in front of him. Golden, translucent silk sheets covered her. Pearls were scattered throughout her messy locks. Her olive-skinned body glowed. She had an ethereal appearance, like a hitherto unseen deity. The young lady continued to glare at him with her enticing ocean-blue eyes. "Am I...dreaming?" questioned the captain. "Whether or not I'm real doesn't matter. What matters is that you have a strong obsession with me and have fantasies about me." The young lady replied while raising her left leg on a chair and crossing her arms. "I'm not. I am not obsessed." said Mr. Santarelli, who appeared perplexed.

He was uncertain of how to respond, and seeing her in his dream made him uneasy. He was annoyed by the fact that he was unable to determine if something was real or not. "Then why am I currently in your mind?" Marina approached him and grinned cunningly. She gently pushed him down into the bed after placing her palm on his chest. "And why am I making your heart pound faster the moment I come closer to you?" the girl asked as she climbed on top of him and laid her head on his chest, listening closely to the beat of his heart. He was the target of her mocking question. Her touch caused burns to spread throughout his body. He was having problems breathing since she had her head on his bare chest.

"Stop it." Gabriel said, but he knew that because he yearned for her, he didn't want this to end. She was his forbidden desire, and he *craved* her much as Eve craved the forbidden apple. But he was compelled to cave in, much like Adam did when he bit the apple. "You don't want that, right? You adore my *touching, staring,* and *listening* to you... You are overjoyed that someone has noticed you at last." She gently caressed his jawline as she knelt next to him, then moved her hand to his lips. In an effort to stop her, the captain wrinkled up his brows and forced his eyes shut. "Why are you doing this to me?" he demanded. "Because you want me to. I am in your mind." Marina grinned as she took his hand and put it on her exposed chest. "I am your unrequited *lust*. I'm giving in to whatever you want me to do to you." She answered. At that precise moment, the captain got to his feet and turned his back on her.

"You're making me suffer. I regret ever meeting you." He said, pressing his thin lips together as he watched the large waves of the sea outside the window. "I am aware that you are desperate to hold me and be with me." While still holding him, Marina put her hands on his back, pressed herself on him, and started lowering herself. "You're not deserving enough to be with me, though. You are aware that you are only a seaman." She grinned.

"I know." He let out a sigh. "It's a little pitiful how much you're thinking about me." He was made fun of by the girl as she sat on the edge of his bed with her legs crossed. "Perhaps you've ever wondered if I even want you. You are nothing, while I am a woman of high position."

"Marina does not care about wealth." He responded, clenching his fist and pressing his other hand against his wrist. "That is what you prefer to believe. Perhaps I told you that out of sympathy for you." The man turned around and sighed softly as Marina stated that. He couldn't help but feel a piercing pain in his chest as he stared at her, who appeared to be so ethereal. Even though she was only in his dream, his heart bled for her. He clutched the left side of his chest with his hand there. "I can tell by the way you stare at me that you are eagerly awaiting to kiss me." Sighing, Gabriel tried to ignore her, but hearing her voice was like a siren enticing men in with their singing.

Although he knew it was terrible, he couldn't help but taste her lips. She was looking up at him with her captivating ocean-blue eyes, which were the end of him. Mr. Santarelli drew closer to her. They always succeed in convincing him. As she put her hands on his chest, his face slid toward hers… but then he awoke.

Gabriel regarded his empty bed. His mind kept
wandering to her, and his heart was racing. He felt guilty
for having dreams about her since it seemed unethical.
The man made the decision to stand up and survey the
ocean. Even though it was still dark outside and he could
hardly see anything, the sight of the sea made his pulse
beat rapidly over and over again. He couldn't look at the
sea the same way anymore. As soon as he took a glance
at it, the immediate thought of *her* came to his mind.

Mar… Marina…

He felt as if he was going mad due to her name feeling
like a sin. The young lady managed to drive a captain
insane with her name despite the fact that it is unheard of
and impossible for a sailor to be unable to look at the sea.

October 21st, 1910

The young woman with auburn hair and her companion
D'Angelo were seated on the deck outside. Francesca
persisted in trying to persuade her friend that Marina is a
very dubious girl who is also quite unpleasant and is
secretly attempting to get closer to the captain. At this
point, Antoni began to chuckle at how ludicrous

everything she said had become. Since she has been bugging him about Marina for months, she has developed a fixation with the subject. "Tell you what, Antoni. I have greater knowledge because I am older than you and Gabriel. Women who steal money from other men are obvious to me when I see them." The man began to chuckle, saying, "Excuse me? Gabriel never even bought her anything. She was only ever asked to have lunch and free drinks by him and myself! Additionally, if you are upset with her for that while still receiving free drinks at pubs as a result of us two, you are being a hypocrite." Then Francesca stopped talking. She touched her pale, freckled face while resting her head on her hand. The young woman began to consider whatever wrongdoing Marina might have committed. She began to run out of explanations for the girls' inconveniences. "Yesterday I was passing by my cabin doors when I spotted Marina kneeling on the floor and kept looking at her wedding gown," she excitedly said as she then gasped and grinned. "you can't help but wonder why her wedding gown was red, can you?"

"Maybe she killed someone." her companion said while smiling and showing his dimples. Francesca excitedly pointed at him and nodded her head in agreement; she was relieved that he shared her viewpoint. But as soon as he called her insane for having such thoughts, her smile vanished from her face, and she started to get annoyed. She took her cup of coffee and started looking at the empty cup and said "You're laughing, but you're the one who will have to comfort him just like after what happened with Angela." Francesca then looked up at Antoni who then started thinking about the entire situation and not wishing for his friend to go through the same.

In the meantime, the captain was in his cabin. As usual, he was seated at his desk. He wrote in his journal while enjoying his usual glass of wine. He continued to write about his ideas, goals, and events that had occurred or may have occurred. He seemed pretty anxious today. While writing on the pages, his handwriting appeared to be rather wobbly. "Today, I anchored in Naples. I've recently been worried and lonely. This could be the result of spending so much time on the ship. I've been asked to go fishing with the lovely Miss Rivalli," he remarked aloud as he grumbled and tore the page from his journal and went to write all over again. He took a sip from the glass and then began writing again. Then someone went into his cabin, which annoyed him because all he wanted was some time to himself.

He saw it was Marina, the young girl. He invited her politely to enter after feeling ashamed that he might have mistakenly been angry at her. She approached him while he was fixing his hair and enquired, "Are you leaving or not?" Mr. Santarelli asked, "Leave? " as he stared at her bewildered. "Leaving where?" The young lady's eyes widened in perplexity. "You forgotten? For twenty minutes, I've been waiting for you outside. I thought we had already decided what we would do at 2:00 PM!" He felt awful as he hurriedly glanced at his watch. He started apologizing to her right away, acted like he had committed murder, and tried to come up with an explanation. The young girl, who was startled, calmly assured him that it was alright and that it wouldn't be a problem if she had to wait again. The captain hurried outdoors while holding his big coat. When Marina asked him about his fishing rod while he was still inside the cabin, he moaned and hurried back inside to fetch it.

After finishing up the picnic preparations, he and Marina began strolling along the sea. The whole situation caused the girl to start to worry. She felt humiliated that she had darkened her eyelashes and applied a little rogue to her lips. She clung to the basket she was holding and wondered who she was attempting to impress. The girl began to feel anxious since she didn't want it to appear that she was interested in him, which she most certainly isn't. The captain looked at her closely as she was overthinking things and softly grinned at her, saying, "I didn't get the chance to look at you better before... You look lovely with your hair down. You appear delightful." Then, Marina began to grin to herself, thanked him for the remark, and commented on how charming he looked today as well. He shivered when she stated that while laughing and putting her hand on his shoulder.

They took a seat next to the shore beneath a tree. A white blanket was spread out on the grass alongside Marina's basket of food and beverages. She took a seat to observe Gabriel fishing. The young lady was trying to read in the meantime as well a novel by Jane Austen, but in the end, she kept getting distracted by gazing at him almost every moment. The girl went to him since she too wanted to learn how to fish. She begged him to start teaching her as she sat down next to him on the ground. She was irrationally eager to learn. He gave her his fishing rod and began to explain things while placing his hands on hers. Everything fell into an awkward silence as she cast the string into the sea. Then she asked, "All right, where's the fish?" as she turned to face him. Then Mr. Santarelli smiled and said, "You're lucky if you catch it in the next ten minutes." he turned to face her. Then, out of boredom, Marina muttered, "I don't have the tolerance for this." The man sneered and rolled his eyes at her. She wouldn't have the patience necessary for fishing, he had a feeling. In the end, she returned his fishing rod, removed her shoes, and went into the sea.

The captain continued to scan the sea in an effort to spot something. The girl also looked down and noticed a large, dark object. She seized it right away and began giggling to herself unkindly. The man was startled by the object she tossed at him and collapsed to the ground on his back. He let out a little groan of pain, but Marina only kept laughing at him. The object Marina threw at him was a sea cucumber, which he grabbed. Mr.

Santarelli was immediately repulsed by it and felt sick to his stomach just touching it. He admired Marina for showing no signs of disgust. "You're completely disgusting." He informed her and began to gag once more.

He stepped up and settled down on a blanket with her after realizing she might have grown bored with his silence and constant fishing. As they began to converse, Mr. Santarelli turned his head to look at the city. Looking at his side profile, Marina nervously bit her lip as she admired his flawless lips, nose, and nearly black eyes. She hurriedly turned her head aside so she wouldn't be seen staring and appearing unpleasant. She started to feel bad for feeling this way once more when she recalled him having before mentioned his previous partner. "So, you've had a prior partner?" the girl nervously bit her lip once more and exclaimed as her curiosity overcame her. "Could you please elaborate on her?" The captain then circled back to her and smirked incredulously at her, "You're so curious, aren't you? Could I ask you a question for once?" The blush on Marina's face caused her to mumble, "Yes. only when *you* respond to mine."

"Well, Angela was my former partner," he continued, touching his chin. "she seemed cocky and assured. She may have occasionally treated me crudely, but that is behind us now." He was aware that his partner had a terrible attitude toward him, but he made an effort to overlook this and make her seem better than she actually is. The girl became angry at the mere mention of the name Angela as she began to feel guilty that someone had treated him so badly. "If I were her, I'd consider myself extremely lucky to be his lover. No! What am I telling myself at this very moment?" She questioned herself in her mind. When she arrived on his ship wearing her wedding dress, he teasingly asked her why she was wearing it. He then crossed his legs like a little child. The young woman's eyes widened, and she was afraid to speak. "I don't like talking about this."

Marina interrupted him as he was ready to apologize by stating, "But, I trust you. Given that I always ask you personal questions and that we've been acquainted for a while, I believe it is only right that I respond to you. I was going to get married that day." she said as she twisted her brother's ring and took a deep breath. "I felt such joy and such fear at the same time. My fiancé was extremely..." She halted herself when she realized she had no idea how to compliment him. He was never helpful or kind to her. She felt a chunk of apple in her throat as she spoke and her eyes began to well up with tears. She had never before shared this with anyone, and she immediately felt tremendous relief. "I loved him, I did!" she exclaimed. "But in the end, he hurt me. I didn't want to be fully committed to such a man! So I left... I realize it's a cowardly thing to do, but I had no other options!" As she started to cry hysterically, Mr.

Santarelli put his hand on hers. "It's alright. I ran away from home myself when I was sixteen years old. But my insanely abusive parents were the reason I did it. I kind of got sick of being hit on every day and hearing how I'm a disappointment and how my— alright, enough of the sad talk; it's just making us both feel upset." She quietly smiled and wiped the tears from her face as he grinned at her. He held her head on his shoulder while he stroked her hair to help her feel more at ease. Marina then turned to face the city. "Would you like to go visit my brother's grave with me?" She politely prompted him. The man felt a bit uncomfortable going to a graveyard, but he couldn't say no to her.

They visited the Naples cemetery that evening. When Marina visited her brother's grave, she did so while carrying a bouquet for him. She and the captain both picked them up when leaving from their little picnic. When she looked at his grave, the girl noticed someone already placed fresh flowers on it. She thought it might've been their parents. The girl lightly touched the tombstone as she got on her knees. "I'm sorry I didn't come to see you sooner. I was struggling with countless issues. Right now, you'd probably be making fun of me for acting so immaturely. I would then go to mother and father and cry. I wish so terribly that you could sometimes assist me." she murmured. "You were always aware of what to do. You were the intelligent one." The wind then blew in her hair, which was aggressive and quite cold that it made her gasp and shiver. As soon as the captain noticed Marina shivering from the cold, he swiftly removed his coat and put it on her. Although he was cold as well, he was more concerned with the fact that she was warmer than him.

She eventually got to her feet and moved toward the captain. She started crying a little since she missed her brother so much and he put his arm around her shoulder. Marina saw a woman standing close to them as they were departing. Amelia Mor was the one after she took a good look at her. "Marina!" The woman rushed at her while shouting. In disbelief, Marina widened her eyes and muttered, "Mia—." Amelia was ecstatic to meet her cherished old friend and was deeply concerned for her well-being and she wanted to ask her what in the world had happened to her. As Amelia drew nearer, the young lady seized the captain's hand and quickly hurried back to the ship. Amelia was left perplexed and unable to comprehend Marina's departure from her. She hadn't seen her in months and wanted so badly to talk to her and ask her how has she been lately, but unfortunately, the girl left her with a million more questions.

She ran away from her, so Mr. Santarelli questioned her why, feeling bewildered. While still in shock, Marina told him that she didn't want anyone from Naples to see her or learn that she was still alive. "I want the old me to be dead. Nothing left of her."

Chapter XI

December 6th, 1904.

Rome, fog descended and enveloped the entire city, making it difficult to see the streetlights. There were no people, dogs, or cats roaming the streets. The Santarelli family's residence was serene, much like the city. Every time someone talked, the rooms would echo with their voice. While working on his homework and reading his favorite book, Gabriel was in his room. The boy was laying in bed, kicking his legs in the air, writing on a book page. He began chewing the pencil's cap, biting too hard, and getting the eraser in his mouth. Immediately after gaging, Gabriel spat it out. He suddenly heard a scream that resembled his mother.

He became anxious about his mother and considered staying in his room or going downstairs to check on her when he felt terrified. Gabriel eventually had the confidence to sneak behind the stairway. His mother and father were yelling at one another and fighting once more. The boy didn't appreciate hearing such comments at all, and they insulted one other in every manner conceivable. He stepped on the floor and heard a sound, which made him fear that he was about to be discovered. Turning around, his mother shouted at him to stop spying and come to them as tears streamed down her cheeks. As he drew nearer to his mother, Gabriel began to tremble and saw red markings on her wrists and cheek. He had a strong hunch that his father had hurt her again. "Mother, father. I'm sorry for—," he began apologizing, but his mother smacked him across the face before he could finish.

Gabriel was in a state of shock. "All of this is your fault! All of this is a result of you telling me that your father had once more cheated on me with your teacher. You just can't stop talking, can you?" She continued to yell at him while her straight, black hair fell on her face. Alessandro Santarelli, his father, continued to maintain a stern expression as he observed them both. He couldn't believe he had tricked his mother once more and he stared at him in hatred. "You are such a disappointment of a son." Mr. Santarelli said while taking a good look at his son. "Because of how feminine you are, I'm not even able to call you my son. You can't even talk to people normally or stop reading those boring books." Gabriel simply sighed and cast a downward glance. He was sick of being made fun of every day, but he couldn't believe his father was suddenly changing the subject so that he wouldn't be held responsible.

In order to get his bottle of wine, Mr. Santarelli crossed over to the kitchen. Given that he owns it and is the heir to his family's business, it was the only wine he ever

drank. He drank the wine straight from the bottle,
making his already messy appearance worse. He didn't
even bother pouring it into a glass. Gabriel was idly
standing in the living room, unsure of what to do or say,
as his mother continued to scream, rage, and insult her
husband in any way she could. "I despise you! I want
you to die already! And as for you, I wish I had killed
you sooner!" Mrs. Santarelli cast a glance toward her
child. It wasn't the first time she had said anything like
that to him; he didn't even blink at her comments.
Gabriel detested it when his parents expressed their
desire for him to drop dead; it made him feel even more
demotivated and led him to begin thinking that he should.
Even more, his father encourages him and promises to
personally give him a rope.

The wife of Mr. Santarelli approached the entrance doors
and approached his coat that was hanging there. She
searched through its pockets for his cigar before lighting
it. She intentionally irritated her spouse by puffing close
to his face. "Don't make me hit you again. You're testing
my patience right now." As they got into another
argument, Gabriel reached into the kitchen for a glass of
water and unintentionally knocked over his father's wine,
spilling it all over the floor.

"You fool! You total moron! How could you be so
stupid!? What the hell is wrong with you??"

Gabriel pleaded with his father not to hurt him again as he began to shake. Since the boy's blood vessels were extremely sensitive, when the man grabbed him by the throat and slapped him across the face, the boy's nose began to bleed. Blood began to trickle down the floor and his white shirt, and he began to sob. Mr. Santarelli appeared wild and was breathing heavily as he continued to stare at him. Gabriel turned to his mother for assistance, but all she did was cross her arms and turn away, acting as if she hadn't even noticed anything.

He finally lost it at this point. The verbal and physical assault had become too much for him to bear. At the age of only sixteen years old, he already had the urge to end his life and couldn't handle it any longer. "I will... never be good enough for you, will I? You'll always hate me." The boy sighed as tears fell from his face. After wiping his lips clean of blood, Gabriel ran. Even though it was raining heavily outside and he could not see anything because of his watery eyes, he opened his home's doors and began sprinting as quickly as he could. He even came close to falling to the ground as he fled.

When Gabriel left, his parents exchanged glances.

"Do you believe he is permanently gone?" Mrs. Santarelli inquired, perplexed.

"He'll return. He lacks the intelligence to live on the streets. He is, after all, your son." His father responded to her while still furious about the entire evening and his wife finding out about his extramarital encounters with maids and young ladies.

Gabriel kept running despite his excruciating panting since the idea of leaving his home excited him. After a while, he became drenched in rain and felt trapped in Rome's streets. He realized he was lost when he no longer knew where to go. He didn't spend much time outside the mansion, so he wasn't familiar with the city's streets. Gabriel peered behind himself to check whether his parents were maybe following him. He briefly held out hope that they would in order to confirm their love for him. That was regrettably not the case. He knew deep down that they didn't even attempt to go outside and check on him. The boy saw a closed dry street in between two houses. He decided to sit down there and spend the night there. As he sat down and held his knees, he kept looking at the rain falling on the ground as his tears fell from his cheeks as well. He never felt this low in his life.

Gabriel was scared, he wasn't capable of surviving on his own. He didn't know anything about working for someone or how to beg for food. His nose continued to still bleed a little but at this point, he didn't care.

As he almost fell asleep from exhaustion, a strange man stood next to him with an irritated face.

"That's my spot." He said.

Gabriel panicked and immediately moved away. He started to apologize as he didn't know another person was staying here. He then noticed that the guy appeared to be his age as he looked quite young. "Is this your first night?" The boy asked him. Gabriel nodded with his eyes full of tears. "I'm D'Angelo Antoni. You?" The young man reached out his hand to him, he wanted to make friends with Gabriel.

"Gabriel Santarelli." He replied with a shaky voice. The young boy began to interrogate him about his activities on the streets, especially since, aside from his untidy wounded face and bloody clothing, he appears to be pretty wealthy. Gabriel was hesitant to share personal information with someone he had just met and didn't entirely trust, but given the nature of his nights lately, he wasn't opposed to doing so. He then began speaking quickly about his family's circumstances, including how his mother would press cigars on his arm and how often his father would slap him. Hearing him say all of that made Antoni feel terrible. He cast a quick glance at Gabriel, who was clearly upset and trembling with fear.

The boy sat nearer to him "You're not alone, you know.
My parents weren't particularly violent. But lately, my
life has been a complete wreck. Like every other day, I
was seated in the living room listening to my parents
discuss their jobs and personal lives. Then, all of a
sudden, a group of men arrived and began threatening
my father. He gambled with them and won, which left
the men upset. Father tried to work things out with them
through conversation, but they ultimately shot him in the
head. Mother was completely helpless and in shock. She
yelled at my sister and me to go away right away "He let
out a sigh "I kept my younger sister and I confined to my
bedroom. When the Carabinieri arrived, mother was
placed under arrest. My sister was also taken away, most
likely to an orphanage. I was abandoned on the streets
because they evidently thought I was old enough to live
on my own. I long for my family. However, feeling a
little bit better now that I at least have some company is
pleasant."

Gabriel grinned at that. When was the last time someone
had expressed happiness to have him as their
companion? It made him feel nice that he was being
appreciated. His stomach began to suddenly growl
because he hadn't eaten in hours as he laid his head on
Antoni's shoulder. When Antoni saw this, he reached
into his pocket and withdrew a piece of bread. Although
he had originally intended to eat it himself, Antoni didn't
mind giving it to his new friend. When he handed it to

him to eat, Gabriel began to feel bad for taking away
Antoni's meal, which he had likely worked hard to obtain.

"Well, I don't want you to starve to death over here. I'm
not coming to your funeral, I don't have anything nice to
wear." The boy inquired to him as he kept showing him
what terrible clothes he has to wear. Gabriel snickered at
that and ended up taking a bite, the bread was already
hard and not freshly baked. He didn't like the taste of it
but unfortunately, he had no other choice. The boy ended
up splitting the bread in half and gave the other half to
Antoni to eat. He got happy seeing that from Gabriel and
appreciated it.

While they were still discussing their lifestyles, Antoni
began complaining about how bad his hair had been
lately. "Ugh! It has become quite frizzy! My dear mother
always braided my hair so I look handsome; fortunately
for me, she is currently serving an unjust prison
sentence!"

"It must be great to have your mother do your hair for
you," Gabriel said gently as he turned his head the other
way. "I wish I could have experienced that. When I was
a baby and she claimed that I was a girl, she only ever
did my hair then." Gabriel had just said something
strange, and it left Antoni stunned. "I'll act as though I

didn't just hear that since that is incredibly sad and disturbing. However, you don't need to put in a lot of effort. Yes, you do... look a little bad! But it's fixable." He made notes as he combed through and pulled back the boy's hair with his hands. He was instantly showered with praise from Antoni, who told him he had gotten more attractive and that he deserved a kiss if he were a girl.

Gabriel gagged at that but ignored it because Antoni was only playing a joke on him. The rain stopped abruptly as they were conversing, and Antoni was eager to show his new friend a more pleasant area to reside. The boy showed him a house that he built out of materials he found in the streets as they passed through an empty street.

"Welcome to my home!" As he raised a curtain covering his house and mimicked the doors, the boy exclaimed.

"It's... something." Gabriel looked at it disturbed.

"Well, it's not exactly Versailles but it's good. It took me hours to make it. I even stole curtains from a poor old lady." The other boy gasped "You stole it!?" Antoni looked at him confused "We're homeless! How else do you expect to survive? Get used to it or you'll die eventually."

November 2nd , 1910

The captain awoke startled. He trembled and was dripping with sweat. He had blurry eyesight and was unable to distinguish between reality and his nightmare. He began sobbing uncontrollably as he was forced to go through his traumatic experience once more. The man began to sigh and put his hands over his eyes.

He tried to calm down by attempting to take deep breaths, but he failed. Then he stood up, made his way to his desk, and poured himself a glass of scotch. He was able to calm down after he took a drink, but he was still upset at having another dream about his parents torturing him. He frequently experienced anxiety attacks, panic attacks, and excruciatingly bad insomnia. The man was constantly glancing out of his cabin window. He listened to the waves crashing against the ship as he observed the sea. He had discovered a technique for calming himself, and it usually worked. The captain made the decision to put on his overused white shirt and proceed to the kitchen for a quick snack. "Oh, it's two in the morning," he realized as he turned to look at the clock that was set

up on his work desk. "Antoni still might be on his shift."
He briefly felt relieved that his close friend might still be
up and working.

The ship was uncomfortably empty. He never enjoyed
being by himself on the deck at that time because it
wasn't the most comfortable thing in the world to be
alone in the midst of the sea, especially when it was so
dark that you couldn't even see the sea. "He's not in
control of the helm. I hope he's still around somewhere."
Mr. Santarelli said, admitting that he was currently
longing for some company. And as he got closer to the
kitchen, he heard a resounding "No!" It was a man's
voice, and he hurried to see what had happened.

When he arrived, he observed Marina Rivalli and
D'Angelo Antoni seated at the table, appearing to be
playing cards. That evening, Marina wore a lovely light
blue nightgown and had her very long, curly, dark brown
hair loose. When he saw her, his gaze softened at her and
his heart started to beat faster. His feelings for her were
so strong and uncontrollable, especially after seeing how
happy she was that night. He felt sick to his stomach for
feeling this way.

"I won! Eat rubbish, Antoni!" She yelled.

"I'm horrified that I just lost 155,000 lire. You tricked me!"

"No, I hadn't; I just mentioned that I hadn't played cards in a while! Oh, I almost forgot to add that my father taught me how to play cards and pool since I was six years old, oops!" Antoni felt like crying for losing so terribly, but Marina remained grinning like the devil as she reached out to take all of his money. The captain never noticed this aspect of her; instead, he thought she was funny for being such a cunning trickster and an expert card player, and he even admired her. "Finally someone put down your egoism, I grew tired of you winning all the time!" he said, placing his arm on his friend's shoulder. Antoni asked him incredulously, "What! Me!? Fairly, you are truly terrible at all forms of gambling."

As Marina got up and prepared to head to her cabin, she couldn't help but giggle at the two of them "I'll let the two of you gals talk. I must return to my cabin and consider how I should use Antoni's funds for tomorrow. New shoes would be great." Mr. Santarelli took a seat next to D'Angelo, and D'Angelo just sighed. "Never engage in any sort of game with her! You will be robbed by her!" The captain, who wasn't even going to play cards with the girl, was the target of Antoni's rebuke. "I need to discuss something with you." The man noticed his pal was worn out and unhappy as he turned to face him. Since it wasn't the first time, he immediately knew what was going on.

"I've begged you repeatedly not to take your life, but I—

"For heaven's sake, not that! That feeling hasn't been mine since... since... Since Miss Rivalli arrived, oh my. Even my farewell note got tossed out." He cut Antoni off, which was a relief because he had been shocked that he hadn't felt suicidal in months. Every day for more than ten years, he has been depressed. At this point, it felt taunting, but since Marina entered his life, spending time with her has begun to improve his mood.

After a sigh of relief, Antoni enquired as to what had transpired. "My parents appeared in yet another nightmare I had. However, since you were also inside of it, this one didn't feel as terrifying. I'm just so frustrated that I keep thinking about that incident. Sometimes I long for a regular night's sleep." D'Angelo regarded him with a troubled expression; he felt guilty about seeing his friend constantly unhappy and suffering from poor health as a result of ongoing stress and trauma from which he never appears to be able to recover. Putting his hand on his "Gabriel, you need to understand that your parents can no longer abuse you. I'm sorry; what they did to you was terrible. Instead of constantly focusing on the

Judged For Mercy

past, you must also begin to consider the present and the future. If I hadn't stopped grieving about my father's death and my mother and sister being taken from me when I was sixteen, I would not have become anything." Antoni stated.

After giving it some thought, the captain realized Antoni was correct. However, there are occasions when his trauma is so overwhelming that he is easily broken. He occasionally recalls the discomfort of having cigarettes rubbed against his arm or the agony he felt when his father threw a wine bottle at his head and slashed it. He felt lifeless and irritated all the time because of those tiny things. In particular, neither his present nor his future seems to hold much promise for him. He longs to be married and have children, but is stuck working as a captain, a profession he never desired. He had always wanted to have children, become a better father than he was, and hear the simple words "I love you." from someone he would wake up to every day for the rest of his life. When the two men finished discussing it, Antoni grew intrigued and sent a glance the man's way. "Do you retain any feelings for the maid? You spend an awful deal of time with her, look at her all the time, and act strangely nervous about her. You know I'm not blind? I noticed how you before regarded her as if she were the personification of Venus, the goddess."

- 222 -

LV Polcic

The captain was at a loss for words in response to it. He was afraid of being shamed for having romantic love for his maid if he disclosed his feelings. Antoni might just keep bugging him about it if he denied it. In any case, he was reluctant to acknowledge that he finds her lovely. He was still terrified of experiencing heartbreak once more. "I'm not sure. I enjoy spending time with her since I know that nothing I say will offend her. She occasionally makes me laugh as well." Mr. Santarelli looked down as tears began to gather in his eyes; he was having trouble controlling his feelings. He only received a smile from Antoni, who then remarked, "Well, I'm glad you've found someone who makes you happy. You two would be great together. You are intelligent, a voracious reader, and oddly sensitive. Marina is shrewd, an excellent cook, and hilarious. You could give it a shot? What could possibly go wrong?"

"I would experience such severe heartbreak once more that I would feel on the verge of death to the point that I would turn to alcohol and be completely humiliated by her. Plus! She is a lady! I'm just some underpaid captain who can't even afford to buy her nice things, am I right?" He was urged by his friend to quit equating Marina with riches and to remember that material possessions aren't everything in life. "Angela might have given you the awful notion that you must buy jewelry for her whenever you see her. But I don't believe she is that way. When I sewed her a gown, she was quite gracious to me."

The captain pursed his lips and thought back to the time Marina had been very grateful for the book she received as a gift. He was unaware that she never made excessive gift requests. Even on her birthday, she resisted receiving any gifts. The captain's friend then stood up to return to the helm, turned to him as he did so, and said, "You're making a horrible mistake if you don't pursue her. Instead of doing nothing and later eating myself up with guilt, I'd prefer to try and see what happens." He left the man thinking, getting confused with his emotions and not knowing what to do anymore

Chapter XII

The weather has begun to worsen and become colder. Storms are becoming to happen more frequently and no longer catch people off guard. Each time the ship moved from left to right, it would also hop up and down, making everyone queasy. Particularly for the Neapolitan girl who wasn't accustomed to this type of weather. She was accustomed to the warmer weather, where the worst storm was usually only a light wind that would cool you off on the hottest days.

The storms began to scare Marina out, and she saw how long her hair had grown. Her hair had reached her backside when she first boarded the ship, but it has already grown past it. She came to the realization that she had to have a haircut as soon as possible to avoid turning like Rapunzel. "I think I need a haircut to de-stress." She quietly reasoned that she needed help cutting her hair, so she went to fetch Margherita.

Marina ran into Francesca once again while looking for the old woman. The girl sighed and only apologized because she had no desire to converse with her at all. Francesca yelled at Marina as she was leaving, "Wait. I need you to tell me something right away." With her lips pursed, Marina approached her carefully and asked what she wanted to know.

"You're crazy odd. Why do you keep staring at your wedding dress?" she demanded.

Being at a loss for words, Marina was unable to respond. It was none of her business why she continued looking at it, thus she wanted her life to remain private. Marina was still in mourning after her fiance's passing. She despised him and found numerous reasons to be disgusted with him. It was tough to move on, and she still felt as if he was mocking her in her thoughts when he used to visit her house and give her flowers, eat dinner with her, and spend time with her. "I suppose I just really like it." Francesca wasn't having it and started asking her difficult questions right away, "Mhm, I see. And why is it blood-stained?"

The young lady chuckled uncomfortably, "Blood? What blood? You're being quite silly right now. I told you already how it's just wine!" She was irritated that the red-haired girl didn't seem to believe her at all. Marina screamed in pain and began to get very frightened of her as she was grabbed by the arms and pinned against the wall with all of her strength. The girl couldn't believe that out of all moments, right now no sailor was on the deck to help her.

"Listen here. With your story, you might have duped Antoni, Margherita, and Gabriel. I'm not the least bit fooled by you. I've met ladies who kill men after taunting them for their money." Francesca continued to glare at her while yelling at her. She couldn't believe she was saying that, and the girl's eyes began to water. She would never defraud anyone! She continued to dispute what Francesca has been telling her while being referred to as a liar. "So, what became of your fiancé? Why did you run away from your wedding?"

"I was hurt!"

"Liar! Nobody ever hurt you! You're fabricating these tales merely to make me feel sorry for you!"

When Marina was labeled a liar about her traumatic day, she sobbed uncontrollably. She sobbed as she assured Francesca that she would never lie about such things. In that instant, Francesca grabbed her by the cheeks and threatened her "If I see you, getting close to Gabriel, I will tell everyone what you did." she said. She let go of her at that precise moment, and Marina collapsed to the ground on her knees. As Francesca went, she continued to pant for breath. The young lady was threatened by being identified for the crime she had committed and was unsure of what to do. Hope Francesca has mercy on her and no one finds out.

The hair that had landed on Marina's face was tucked behind her ears. Her hands caressed her pearl earrings as she moved and remembered Antoni. When Marina first considered seeking solace from Antoni, she was reminded that he was still asleep because of his weariness from his shift.

The girl felt sad not being able to talk to him since his jokes always made her feel better.

She then turned to face the captain's cabin and felt warmly inclined to approach him for a discussion. He constantly listened to her and offered her wise counsel, so she always enjoyed talking to him. He never made her feel uneasy or mocked her for her issues. Instantly rising, Marina approached his cabin, approached the doors, and opened them. She couldn't help but smile as she walked in and found him writing in his diary. She was delighted just to see him.

The captain grinned and said, "Ah, Miss Marina. Nice to see you here. Do you have any needs?"

"Why do you think I need anything from you?" Marina asked in shock. "I do need to chat with you though." she groaned and rubbed her arm as the captain gave her a skeptical look.

He picked a little chair and positioned it close to him while grinning at her. Again sighing, Marina took a seat. "I'm just really upset right now. I was yelled at earlier, and the person's remarks hurt me." Mr. Santarelli asked her, "Did something awful happen?" his eyes filled with anxiety. The girl gave him a pouted-lip look. "Someone intimidated me, threw me against the wall, accused me of something I've never done, and invaded my privacy!" Concerned, he inquired of her as to who had harmed her. As she explained to him that she doesn't want to mention the person's name because she doesn't want them to get into problems as a result of it, Marina's eyes were still full of tears. "I'm furious that they keep harassing me, it makes me feel so awful." She pressed the fold of her garment, saying, "I thought I changed. I worked so hard to change and was even pleased with myself." Tears dropped from her reddish cheeks.

"Miss Marina, I don't want anyone bothering you at work. You have truly changed, and you have turned into such a wonderful person!" She kept grinning at him with a subtle smirk. "Please, I beg of you, then don't do anything to anyone because of me." she moaned as she sank onto his shoulder.

"I am *your captain* after all, and it is *my* responsibility to look out for the people on *my* ship." he said, making a worried expression.

His words caused her cheeks to redden. She developed an oddly strong liking for him because of his desire to make her feel safe. She remained staring at his lips as he went on to express how much he cares for her. She was so preoccupied with his thin lips that she was unable to even remember what he had said. One kiss wouldn't harm, just one. No, she *couldn't* do it; thinking such things about her own captain was childish and unladylike of her.

She was staring at him while she was distracted, and when the man noticed this, he felt special because she was so intently focusing on him.

"*Miss Marina.*" He playfully said. but no response

"Marina Rivalli!" As soon as he yelled, Marina immediately regained consciousness and widened her large blue eyes. "What were you so focused on? You looked so lost." he continued to question her while grinning devilishly at her. The girl was so humiliated that she couldn't even think about telling him that she couldn't help but want to kiss his irresistible lips. Marina only bowed her head and said, "Oh no, that happens to me all the time! I suppose I was just thinking too much." Wishing she had said instead, "Yes my captain, lost in your wonderful dark eyes." while winking at him and acting confident. But to say that would have been foolish.

Mr. Santarelli let out a disappointed sigh. Disappointed? Why did he feel let down? Was he pleased that she was looking at him? She decided to get up and leave him because she found everything to be so confusing and so that she could get back to her work.

When she left, she took a quick peek at his cabin's glass walls. Although they were a little vague, she could see that he appeared lonely after she left, which caused her to reconsider.

In the end, Marina chose to relax in bed rather than immediately report to work. "Is he interested in me?" She grinned widely, feeling incredibly happy at the prospect of Mr. Santarelli showing romantic interest in her. Even when Matias asked for her hand in marriage, she had never experienced such heart palpitations. The young lady imagined the captain gave her a sweet kiss; it was like a dream as she placed her two fingers lightly on her lips.

Unfortunately, she came to the unfortunate realization that she might need to push him away because she was still overly wary of committed relationships, also had her heart broken too frequently to want to take the chance of doing so again, and Francesca had threatened her with getting closer to the captain. She was sorry she did it since she genuinely enjoyed his company but she also felt like she was moving on too quickly from her deceased fiancé.

It was early November morning. Being the only person in the cabin, Marina was still asleep. She continued to roll from left to right in the bed. She made a quiet moan, and then the ship suddenly moved, startling her and waking her up. The young lady experienced an unprecedented dream, which caused her to awaken in amazement and disbelief.

She had a guilt-ridden dream in which the captain was smiling and gazing at her. She was sitting on a chair and he was on his knees, putting his hands on her thighs, giving her butterflies in her stomach.

When Marina kept thinking back to her strange dream, she sighed in disgust because it made her feel that way about her *own* captain. She reprimanded herself, "I need to stop. Just thinking about him in such a way makes me feel sick." In that instant, the girl bit her finger and groaned, feeling terrible for finding him appealing in her dream.

LV Polcic

She had to slap her cheeks to bring herself together and started getting dressed for work right away. Since she arrived on the ship, she had grown to love baking and cooking and couldn't wait to get started. The young lady loved hearing compliments about her cooking because it made her so happy.

The captain's gaze was avoided by Marina the entire time she was in the kitchen and she also attempted to avoid chatting with him too much. She could not risk developing deeper affection for him. It felt like enough of a punishment that he is her captain.

Francesca walked into the kitchen which made her groan. She must now avoid him at all costs to prevent further degradation by her.

She had a fleeting memory of being harassed daily at school because of how terrified she was of her.

While walking by the table and cordially conversing with the others, Marina was holding plates in her hands.

When she saw Francesca, the girl rolled her eyes and grabbed the dirty dishes so she could wash them. She experienced such severe acute pain in her stomach as she walked that it made her ill. She dropped the dishes without even realizing it because the pain traveled down her legs and back. When everything broke, she collapsed on the ground panting.

Immediately rising to assist her, the captain and Antoni developed extreme worries for her well-being. The girl cried out in agony, "Darn it!" She yelled. Margherita handed her a wet towel so she could feel better, and both she and Giordana assisted her in standing up. The red-haired girl remained frowning, believing that Marina was deliberately stirring up trouble so that everyone would feel sorry for her.

As the girl struggled to feel better, she looked down and saw red stains on her gown. She instantly panicked and asked the two women how she needed to use the restroom right away.

She went to the Head and shut the door. The entire time, Mr. Santarelli waited by the doors, watching to see whether she might be becoming worse. He kept checking on her to see if she was alright.

"Are you feeling ill?"

"No! I'm good!" She continued to express her worry about starting her menstruation as she spoke. She has not received it in months! When the young lady learned that meant she is certainly not pregnant, she felt like a great rock had been lifted off of her chest. She continued to search for something to place underneath so that she wouldn't bleed all over the floor.

When Marina realized there was nothing in the bathroom to help her, she sighed in embarrassment. She then summoned the courage to move over to the doors and nervously pleaded with the captain, "My captain, could you please go and ask Miss Margherita for an old cloth?" Without even pausing to consider what she had said, he had set out to acquire it for her. Marina sat down on the ground and continued to think about everything, including how embarrassing it was for her to keep asking him for assistance. She felt terrible about it.

Then the man pounded on the doors while she began babbling. He was holding an old rag and some recently washed clothing and undergarments when she slowly opened the doors and peered through them. Her expression darkened with perplexity. "Given your circumstances, I felt you may benefit from taking a shower." She asked him cautiously, with a flushed face, how did he know about it since she hasn't told him how she got her menstruation, as it might seem disgusting.

"Oh, please, I'm not a moron. I know quite a lot about the female body" He said, putting his palm on his chest and giving her a smile. The girl snorted at him while grinning at him. She seized the items he had brought her and gave him a heartfelt thank you.

He left, and Marina went to clean herself up. As she scrubbed her body with the sponge, she couldn't help but think about how kindly he had earlier behaved. He didn't gag at her or react negatively to anything about her female situation. Even though it seemed like the bare least, she was grateful nonetheless. The girl then sighed and wished she had someone to treat her so well while she was married to them.

After finishing up and getting ready, she started to go to work when the captain stopped her. "What are you doing? Take a day off now. You've been working so much recently; please take some time to relax." She gave him two quick blinks before asking anxiously, "But what about the mess I caused earlier?"

"The dishes? Don't worry; Antoni and I already cleaned it up. Just rest in my cabin, please." He pointed his fingers at her and exclaimed as he did so.

The girl pressed her lips and ended up giving up and went to his cabin to sleep. He assisted her with tucking in and continued to inquire if she needed any other assistance.

"Do you require tea? I have a huge assortment of various teas, so you may essentially select whatever you want."

"I had no idea someone was into *collecting tea.* Chamomile tea would be fine, though. When my stomach ached, my mother would always make me it." Marina turned her large, blue eyes on him. Later, when he returned carrying tea, he also had an envelope in his hand, which he gave to her. "This is for you." She gasped "A letter?" Marina exclaimed, "How in the world did someone manage to write to me?" He couldn't help but snicker at her when she remarked, "It's not a letter."

"Odd, it appears there's money in it." she said as she opened the envelope and began counting the money. and gave him the cash. "No you nincompoop, it's your payment." Gabriel exclaimed, his eyes widening with a grin "Never would I unintentionally add more money."

The young lady was shocked. A payment? Did she get it solely as a result of her today's illness? She returned it after feeling so guilty about it. "I'm unable to accept this.

It's unjust." Now that she had the captain perplexed, she was questioned as to what she meant. He laughed at her when she said it felt unjust to give her more money because she was feeling sick today.

"Goodness, gracious. You deserved it, therefore I handed it to you! For the past two months, you have done an excellent job. And you worked so hard that you paid me off for letting you stay here. Unless you wish to leave." He kept chuckling at her. "No, I don't." He smiled when he heard her say that since he didn't wish of her to actually leave. "But have you ever given this type of special treatment to anyone else?" Marina nervously demanded. She thought the inquiry might have been foolish as she spoke it out. He shrugged, "No, Margherita and Giordana work excellently but their pay was always higher than everyone's so I thought a raise would be unnecessary and they wouldn't want it anyhow. In all honesty, everyone else is really lazy."

He murmured as he drew nearer to her. "Don't tell anyone I said this… However, you rank among my best staff members; everyone else is awful"

Marina snorted at him as she gasped and said "Even Antoni?"

"No, Antoni is his own man. He's like a lone wolf with his own pack. But he's also very good at his jobs like you."

Chapter XII

He pulled the curtains shut when she began to pass out so that the cabin was completely dark. She eventually fell asleep for a considerable amount of time, but when she woke up, she strangely felt uneasy about how lonesome the cabin felt. She desperately needed a company that night, but the captain was on duty.

She stood up and left the cabin while wearing her shawl to keep her warm. All the way to the lower deck, the young lady started to walk. She visited Antoni in his bedroom on the lower deck. He found an empty corner in the deck and constructed his own room since he became tired of having to share a bedroom with so many people and not having any privacy. He was jolted by Marina, who said, "Wake up." and shook him.

D'Angelo moaned and ordered her to stop talking. When the girl became irritated, she began violently shaking him. He asked her what she needed when he awoke, and if it was something foolish, he would throw her into the sea to permanently drown. She gave him a hard look "I desired company. What a terrible friend you are." The man scratched his long, curly hair while groaning "Fine! You have a five-minute speaking time."

She sat down next to him and informed him that all she wanted was his company—no need for conversation. "Please let me lie down with you."

"Yes, all the women in the world want to sleep with me", giggled Antoni. "I meant as in, *asleep.*" the girl responded while gagging in his face. She was told by the man, who rolled his eyes, that he doesn't find her attractive in that way in any case. Then he murmured that she is already the object of someone else's attention. When Marina turned to face him and inquired about what he had said because she hadn't heard it clearly, he laughed and told her to go to sleep. For the first time in a very long time, Marina slept soundly and enjoyed his company greatly.

The following morning on December 10th, she went back to the kitchen, where the captain and Antoni were conversing. "I had assumed you would be staying in my cabin." The man confusedly asked her. That night, when he went to check on her, he was perplexed to find that she wasn't in bed. The girl fidgeted with her fingers as she talked about how she had slept with Antoni because she was feeling lonely.

In his heart, the man experienced a tiny bit of jealousy. He was dying within because he knew he would never be able to sleep by her side, be blessed by waking up in the morning, and the first thing when opening his eyes she'd be the *first person to see*. He made a valiant effort yesterday to resist kissing her on the cheek as he sent her to bed in his own bed. Additionally, he was aware that Antoni would never court her and be such a terrible friend. She thanked him once again for his support and told him that she didn't want him to continue assisting her because she felt bad about it. Whether or not he was in love with her, Mr. Santarelli would have offered to help her because he valued the times she had been good to him as well.

"I'm going for a walk by the sea today, so if you'd like to join me, perhaps." he said with a clear voice. The girl nodded, saying she would be happy to spend some time outside today. Later on, the two of them started strolling to a hill with a view of the glistening Mediterranean Sea. The wind was so strong that day that Marina had to keep pressing her hat down as she sat down on the grass. Mr. Santarelli continued to glance at her and admire her side profile as he sat next to her. His heart kept fluttering at how much he praised every feature of her; she was perfect. Her beautiful sharp nose, kissable full cherry-colored lips, big ocean blue-eyes, and a freckled face. Despite the fact that he didn't believe in God, if a woman like that existed, he might. "It's an extremely lovely day today" she said while grinning. "It is. Although I much prefer rain for the weather."

LV Polcic

"Rain? Oh, it's such gloomy weather." the captain replied with a chuckle "Very fitting for me, as you once stated." That caused the young lady's cheeks to flush, but she made an awful attempt at laughing it off. "I don't think I've mentioned this before but I finished the book you gave me." She was confronted by the captain, who asked, "You have? Did you enjoy it?"

"I adored it. I love Alice and how bizarre Wonderland is." She continued to explain the story as if the captain hadn't already finished reading the book, way before her. Nonetheless, he continued to chuckle at her. One of the few people who could make him laugh was her. He let out a sigh as he looked at the sea while thinking about her. The captain then looked at her and noticed something crawling on her leg "Miss Marina, there seems to be something on your ankle." Marina looked at him confused "My ankle?" She questioned. "Yes, slightly raise your gown." The man suggested but the young lady was extremely offended and took his comment in the wrong way "Oh Mr. Santarelli! You have some nerve!" She shouted.

"What? No, Miss Marina, I believe you have a ladybug on your leg." He explained as Marina let out an "Oh." She felt embarrassed for attacking him and slightly lifted her gown and revealing her ankle. He pursed his lips as he looked at them and thought to himself how she does have very lovely legs. She put away the ladybug and then looked around and wondered. "It would be wonderful if there was a sunflower field here."

"Really? Out of all flowers you could've thought." He questioned as he let out a chuckle at her "Yes, really. They're my favorite flowers and make everything look happier." She explained as she wasn't letting him insult her favorite flower. Mr. Santarelli then crossed his legs and cracked his knuckles. He adored her happy personality.

"Miss Marina... Do you recall our first encounter?"

The girl nodded while giving him a bewildered expression. "I used to despise you. I could barely stand you"

"Oh, I hadn't noticed." Marina said with a chuckle. Gabriel didn't laugh at that and looked at her gravely. "N-no, I meant... Since then, we have grown so close that I genuinely find it difficult to envision my existence on a ship without you. In essence, we are always together. I have the utmost regard for you," he continued. "you're very charming, considerate, and helpful. You have no idea how relieved I felt when I was assured that you wouldn't judge me for feeling suicidal. You make me feel alive." The moment Marina realized how much he was liking her now, she gave him a thoughtful nod and a gentle smile.

She realized at that moment. He's interested in her. She instantly began to feel uncomfortable and wished he would stop.

Especially at this time, she didn't want any more confessions in her life. She was clearly uncomfortable, but the man didn't notice since he kept turning his head away while he spoke. The girl pursed her lips as he gave her a puppy look when he turned to face her. She was unable to resist the allure of his almost-black eyes. Mr. Santarelli then gently took her tender hands in his and held them. "I-I sincerely hope that I won't endanger our friendship at this time; I do sincerely value it greatly. What I'm attempting to express is that Miss Marina Rivalli, I think I'm..." He was interrupted by the girl as she rose and showed her anxiety.

"Please stop saying that, I beg of you!" She yelled. While still clutching her hands, he got to his feet out of confusion and asked, "What's wrong? Have I done something wrong? Im sincerely sorry. I just wanted to express my feelings for y—"

"Mr. Santarelli, please do not say it." She interrupted him once more as she put her hand up for him to halt and tears welled up in her eyes. "My sincere apologies but I cannot be with *you*... Excuse me, I must leave this instant." Her voice has gotten quiet as she was terrified to even say something to hurt him deeply.

"Marina—"

Then Marina rushed off as her hat dropped to the ground and landed directly on his shoes. She let go of his hands as he tried to grab them again, leaving him frozen, and he looked down. He began to feel guilty for having put her through so much discomfort and contempt. "I made a fool of myself." The man had thought. He collapsed to the ground on his knees as he clutched onto her hat, his scarlet cheeks streaming with tears. He had the impression that someone had just pierced his heart with all of their might. He was in such pain at that point that he was unable to tolerate it any longer.

The moment the young lady boarded the ship, she collapsed on her bed and began sobbing furiously. She continued yelling at herself while aggressively scratching her face. She then violently tossed her brother's ring across the room after grabbing it off her finger. At that time, she was extremely upset and frustrated with others and with herself.

She sobbed violently that she was unable to breathe, which pained her. He was someone Marina truly adored, and she enjoyed spending time with him, but her trauma and Francesca kept making her feel unhappy. Even though she believed she shouldn't feel that way with him, she was scared of being with anyone. That day, she sobbed for hours and resisted leaving her cabin so that she wouldn't run into the captain. She thought she might scream in misery and humiliation if she saw him today.

The captain, on the other hand, felt lifeless for even attempting to confess to her at that very moment because he felt so utterly unwanted. Then, he continued recalling the occasions when his mother would make fun of him and tell him he was ugly like his father and would never be loved, which turned out to be true. He experienced vulnerability and insecurity, but he tried to brush it off by occupying himself with work like he has been doing for the past few years.

For hours Marina kept sobbing on the ground and hating herself for breaking a man's heart. The look of betrayal in his eyes is something she'll never forgive herself. She felt as if she kept giving him false hope for weeks and all of a sudden she changed her mind and left him in the worst way possible she could've done. "Why am I like this? He must despise me now. I would despise myself as well if I were him. I truly cannot blame him."

She had to let go of Matias, even though it ached. She needed to prove to herself that she is mentally tough and ready to move on because continuing to grieve about him won't help her feel better and will only cause her more harm. "I'm sorry, I shouldn't have done that", the girl said as she stepped up, picked up her brother's ring, and put it back on her finger. She sighed and gave it a soft kiss before saying, "Thank you for always being there for me. You give me strength." In order to sleep and feel better, Marina muttered in a sleepy voice and proceeded to put on her nightgown. Instead, the exact opposite occurred; she stayed awake all night long and was going nuts from thinking about Mr. Santarelli's confession. "I despise how charming he is. His natural kindness isn't helping me much either. Agh!" Now that everyone else was asleep, she snuck out of the cabin quietly in order to get some fresh air.

"I'll go nuts if I keep thinking about him only." She thought to herself with her eyes wide open and biting her lower lip.

With nothing else in her possession but a lit candle, Marina made her way to the deck and rested against the banister while setting the candle down on one of the wooden cargo boxes. The young lady, who was starting to feel homesick, kept staring at Portofino and wanted to cry even more. She was worried about her parents and missed them dearly. She managed to ignore her love for them, so she is no longer constantly in tears over their terrible situation. "I hope they're doing better now that I'm gone. Poor mother and father."

The captain was outside on his shift and wasn't expecting anyone to be outside so late, as she murmured to herself. He panicked and began discreetly heading back as soon as he attempted to have a better look at who is it sobbing outside on the deck. Of course, that didn't work either since as soon as he stepped onto the floor, the girl lifted her head and turned around in response to the sound created by the wooden plank.

"These wooden planks are the death of me." The man told himself as he groaned.

She was overwhelmed with thousands of butterflies as she saw him. "I'm being truthful as I'm saying that I wasn't eavesdropping on you, Miss Marina I'm—I know it looks completely off right now for me, but I was just on my shift and wanted to see who it was outside so late." Marina snorted a lot as the captain stammered awkwardly through his explanation. When he was anxious, which was often, she thought he was very sweet. "Have you been crying?" He asked with concern while placing his hand gently on her face. The young lady looked up at him with an upset face and her eyes filling up with tears "I'm just, overwhelmed." He swallowed his saliva as he sighed and handed her his handkerchief for her to wipe away her tears. The girl then told him to come and talk by leaning against the banister with her back and tapping on them. She started to look up at him and flatter her eyelashes as the man talked.

"Regarding today, I apologize deeply once more. I made a mistake by doing that."

"Absolutely not. In all honesty, it was sweet and would have been better if I hadn't panicked in the middle. Ah, I'm just still a little wary of suitors and things like that." As Marina began to feel anxious, she began to play with her brother's ring. "I understand, but I simply don't want you to think less of me because of what I did today."

The girl's eyes widened, and she gave him a saddened, concerned look. "No, I never could! You are too dear to me for me to hate you!"

"You—you care about me?" The captain enquired as he cast a tender glance at her and looked down. Then the girl touched his face with her hands as she started to look down at his lips. "I do, of course. If I could turn the clock back and meet you again, I would give anything in the world to prevent our hatred from ever developing."

He continued grinning at her because he was having a difficult time believing what she was saying. She continued to stare into his drowsy dark brown eyes when he spotted her shaking from feeling extremely cold. Marina exclaimed as he quickly removed his coat and covered her. "Aren't you going to feel cold as well?"

"Your presence will keep me warm." Her eyes grew wider, she avoided eye contact with him as she kept grinning at herself and he still looked down at her. Why, oh why, even when he wasn't trying, was he so romantic? She then drew his rough hands up to her face, kissed them, and grasped them to keep him warm in some way. His cheeks were crimson, and his heart started to beat as quickly as it had ever done. She enjoyed watching him tremble and couldn't believe she had such control over him that he got nervous just being in her company. The man felt as if her eyes were seducing him and it made him insane.

Even though she wouldn't feel the same, he decided to fully confess again because he couldn't stand the pressure any longer. "You have been killing me every moment with your charms for months," he finally said. "I just adore you. I can't fathom my life without you; ever since you boarded the ship, it's as if you've managed to make me even more miserable for constantly being in your presence. " He stopped to gasp for air as anxiety began to grip him while Marina's eyes widened In disbelief. Her lip trembled "My captain, I do not understand—"

"You are a thorn in my heart! You make my guts twist just by the mere sight of you! If what I'm about to say is inconvenient in any way, please accept my sincere apology. But Miss Marina, I honestly, most sincerely, and devotedly love you." he said, taking her gentle hand and placing it on the left side of his chest. "The beat of my own heart will serve as evidence." As their faces became even near, she could hear him taking quick, low breaths.

"I hate you." She exclaimed while taking deep quick breaths "I hate you, Gabriel Santarelli." Marina kept murmuring as her breathing started to become heavy.

She grabbed onto his dark blue coat as he continued to call her name repeatedly while she could feel his heart racing wildly. Their lips were almost in touch when the young lady bit her lip.

She acknowledged how absurd this was and that she might even be caught, but she couldn't take it anymore. The man's eyes widened as she stood up and gave him a soft kiss on the lips. His hands continued to shake and tremble in the air due to the fact he wasn't sure where to put them. Incredibly in disbelief by their recent kiss, Marina pushed him back and stared at him. The captain cried out, "God, please if you tell me I'm dreaming, I'll never be happy again." and then he leaned his head on her shoulder. "You're dreaming.", Marina chuckled as she passed through his thick hair. She was given an unpleasant look by him for stating that and called her evil. "Why— why did you kiss me?" He asked with curiosity. Marina looked at him confused and chuckled saying "What do you mean? I wanted to!"

"Yes, but. In comparison to you, I am nothing. You're a lady, from a wealthy family, and everywhere you go, men are admiring you. And I'm just some captain who makes minimum money," he said as he paused to gather his breath. "I feel as if I'm just going to embarrass you, and I do not even deserve you."

"You embarrass me? I am the one who doesn't deserve you," exclaimed Marina. "I don't seek wealth, and I never have. My captain You treat me well, and I feel safe with you, so I gave you a kiss." As tears began to stream down his face, she put her hands on his cheeks. Being so adored by someone made him happy. Especially since he struggled with affection due to the fact he never received one from his parents or his previous partner.

He then grinned while burying his face in her long hair "I adore the rosemary scent you radiate. Simply said, you are perfect in every way." The young lady couldn't help but smile at his adoration towards her.

Marina chuckled as they put their foreheads against each other and appreciated each other's presence. They stayed like that for good five minutes. "I cannot believe we kissed, my goodness! My captain!" She continued to chuckle over the scenario while raising her bangs and placing her hand on her forehead. He became even more enamored with her after witnessing her spontaneous laughter. She was startled when the man knelt, tightly hugged her by her legs, and rested his head on her stomach. She shouted in a high-pitched voice. "Marina... I will do anything for you. I'd give my *life* for you. I worship the land you tread on." She was completely baffled by it because no man had ever spoken to her in such a way or, better yet, gotten down on his knees for her. She kept staring at him in confusion, as he pleaded

with her to tell him to jump into the water right away if
he had to. As she continued to snort at him, Mr.
Santarelli said.

"What's with you right now, silly!"

"I'm either too joyful right now, or I don't get enough
sleep." and pressed his face even closer against her while
beaming maniacally. She continued to gaze down at him
in awe of his charm and tenderness. She was gently
pulling him up as she desired to kiss him again. However,
when they heard someone approaching, Marina became
frightened. She gave his hands a brief kiss before telling
him that she needed to go and depart for her cabin.

Mr. Santarelli didn't care that she went so quickly at the
time because all he could focus on was the way her soft
lips felt on his. He gave her hands a gentle kiss before
she left him immediately.

Marina jumped up and down in her bed, so happy over
what had just happened earlier, that she failed to notice
Giordana snoring loudly. The young lady attempted to
sleep but failed. She kept having the impression that she
had abandoned him, which may have confused him. She
muttered to herself, "I need to go to him again. I can't
handle being here alone."

Once more rising, Marina went to his cabin. The captain
was inside, just finishing off his preparations for bed and
taking his clothes off. Naturally shocked to see her, he
asked, "What are you doing here?"

"We had already begun something, and now I can't bear
to remain in my bed by myself! *I want you.*" She looked
at him with her eyes wide open, expressing herself. The
captain was surprised. Does she desire him? He must be
having a wonderful dream right about now and would
like to stay asleep.

Marina tightly grasped him as they drew nearer to one
another, and they then kissed once more. "I love you." he
said in a raspy voice in between kisses. "My God." She
attempted to murmur, but she was unable to do so due to
how intensely they were kissing. She held his thick,
wavy, black hair as she carefully continued to slide her
hands through it. They found themselves resting next to
each other in his bed after they had finished devouring
one another.

Marina extended her arms and legs. "You have no idea
how unpleasant my bed is! Heaven is yours!" He
chuckled at her as he continued to pant and admire her.
The girl faced him, put her hand on his sharp jawline,
and felt his small facial hair pricking her fingers as she

did so. Then, as she chuckled, she slid her thumb and placed it on his lower lip. She looked at the perplexed captain. "You're telling me? I've been suffering from your presence for hours, days, weeks, and even months! And now we're both in my bed. " The girl gave him a soft smile before recalling that they shouldn't be seen together in public. "Gabriel," she said. "I need you to make a promise to me."

"You called me Gabriel?" With a broad grin on his face from joy, he lifted himself.

"Yes. And it feels odd calling you by your first name. Now, I realize that this may be killing you. But for the time being, our relationship must be kept a secret. You might find this hard to believe, but I truly don't want to be called a whore by other crew members because you are courting me." The young girl sighed as she stated, "I'm a maid after all, it's so easy to offer me incorrect judgments. It is a bit out of the ordinary for a captain and a maid to be with each other." The captain carefully caressed her beauty mark, which was located on the left side of her face next to her upper lip. "I apologize about that, but I understand. I am more interested in our current relationship right now anyways. I appreciate this moment a lot." He said, interposing his right hand's fingers with hers, and firmly gripping her hand. She was kissed by him for reassurance that he was making a promise and won't tell anyone about it. She offered him a soft kiss on the cheek as a token of her appreciation for his generosity and support. "Thank you, Gabriel." She joyfully said.

The man's eyes began to well up; he made an effort to hold back his tears, but eventually, his feelings overpowered him and tears began to fall down his cheeks. Worried, the girl inquired as to what was wrong and wiped the tears from his cheeks.

"I can't recall the last time someone treated me with such kindness before." Putting his head on her chest, she pouted and said, "I swear I'll always treat you respectfully no matter what."

Chapter XIV

December 17ᵗʰ , 1910

The following several days flew by swiftly. Every time they had the chance to be together, they ran off to a quiet place to cherish it. They were aware that there would occasionally be close calls with capture, for example.

While they were alone in the kitchen, the young lady was making coffee for the captain and her. She approached him from behind and kissed him on the head. When Antoni and the others entered, they nearly caught them getting too close to each other as they continued to be all over each other.

"We need to be more careful or else we're both doomed," Mr. Santarelli said to the girl later. She also nodded.

Then, when she went to her cabin to take a nap one time, she discovered a large arrangement of sunflowers on her bed that had been wrapped in a green bow and with a little note. While Margherita and Giordana wondered who the kind gentleman was who had given her such a lovely gift, her cheeks began to flush. On the other hand,

Francesca choked. She couldn't believe the spoiled brat was receiving such lovely presents. She only stated it once, and it was a very long time ago, so the young girl simply couldn't believe that he recalled what her favorite flower is. And she couldn't help but sigh as soon as she opened the note.

"I genuinely hope you appreciate the gift I gave you. You both exude joy, thus the flower is a good fit for you. You are to me what a sun is to the sunflower."

After reading the note the girl had received, the elderly woman felt compelled to remark, "Whoever this is, you are extraordinarily lucky."

"Yes," she sighed, "very lucky indeed." with a sweet grin as she put her fingers on her lower lip.

Fortunately, he hadn't signed the note. She didn't require anyone's signature because she was confident in knowing who the giver of the gift is. After taking a whiff of the sunflowers, Marina returned to the kitchen to grab some water so she could put the flowers in a vase. Before she went, the red-haired girl told Marina that the flowers are somewhat hideous and that whoever gave them to her is in great desperation. The only thing Marina told her was, "At least I receive gifts." and she didn't give a damn about anything else Francesca would've told her. Francesca pursed her lips but wasn't sure how to respond. It's true that no one on the ship ever gave her a present. She is only tolerated because she is Giordana's niece and for no other reason.

The girl encountered Antoni as she was exiting the cabin and moving outside. "My, my. You have a beautiful bouquet! Have they been given to you by someone?" He looked at her face and inquired with curiosity. She appeared extraordinarily content. "They were given to me by a hidden admirer! Even better, they came with a really sweet note." The girl exclaimed, flashing her dimples in a smile. It hit him when she departed after he had nodded. Not just his close friend, but someone else is interested in Marina. The captain was unable, in D'Angelo's opinion, to have given her the flowers. He would be too frightened to even approach her in the first place, he knew his friend too well.

"Gabriel!" he yelled as he hurried to his cabin.

The captain continued to rub the ink off his hands after it had been splattered on them earlier from writing a note for the young lady, grumbling as he did so. "Would you kindly quit entering my room so frequently like that! Is it that difficult to knock? Imagine, for heaven's sake, if I were *nude*!" "Even if you were, I wouldn't care," Antoni chuckled. "I've previously seen you in your underwear."

In fear, the captain widened his eyes. "Anyhow. There may be some competition for you. The gorgeous Miss Marina Rivalli is the object of desire for another crew member."

The captain's bewildered eye twitched. Only Antoni, who would never be interested in her, stands out among the group of middle-aged men who make up the rest of the crew as possible suitors of hers. "How did you learn that?" He inquired. "I saw her holding a bouquet of sunflowers, she said it's from a secret admirer." He caught the man's wink. The captain wanted to laugh out loud but refrained since it would have been too evident. He chuckled tensely. "Oh," he said, scratching his hand. "that's truly terrible." Antoni approached him and leaned in for a suspicious look. "I anticipated that the news would make you more unhappy and upset. You don't appear to be all that interested."

"Well? What should I say, exactly? I am unable to combat this unidentified individual." Mr. Santarelli made a valiant effort not to laugh. He kept picturing himself engaged in conflict with himself. D'Angelo blinked at him and said, "I suppose you're right. It's a shame you didn't engage with her more. She would have liked you, I'm sure."

The man nodded while he sighed. He presented himself as being profoundly disappointed in himself. Trying to uplift him, Antoni said, "You could still try? It makes me pleased to see you around her. I don't want of upset and

drunk Gabriel to make a sorrowful return." The captain
was truly pleased that Marina's company had increased
his sense of calm and self-assurance.

Miss Marina was approached by Mr. Santarelli, who
begged her to swiftly hide with him in the storage room
as he drew her closer to him. Since she was so clumsy,
the girl made a concerted effort to avoid accidentally
knocking things over on him. He said, "I'm sorry to have
you meet with me here. It's quite dark in here. Simply
said, I don't believe we can debate this anywhere else
right now without risk." She nodded. "I heard the flowers
I sent you were appreciated."

"Of course I did," Marina said with a smile. "I even
made Francesca jealous when I saw them on my bed."
she rubbed her palms together slyly while laughing. The
man asked her, "Francesca?" his eyes widened. "why
would she feel bitter?" As soon as she realized what she
said, Marina told him it didn't matter. She questioned
him specifically why he brought her here as she softly
placed her hand on his chest.

"Antoni believes I have competition."

"Wow, that's flattering to me." She snorted.

At her, the captain's gaze was narrowed. "We can say farewell to having a hidden relationship with each other if he learns about us. When it comes to secrets, Antoni is the biggest grandma because he tells everyone."

With an "Ah." Marina began to realize how much harder it is to conceal their intimate relationship. She began to wonder if it was worthwhile. She and he will both have their reputations destroyed once word gets out at some point. The girl was thinking to herself and lost in her thoughts as she continued staring down. She then raised her head and turned to face him. He grinned at her, comforting her. If it meant continuing to be that close to him, it was worthwhile. She then slipped as she reached out to offer him a tender kiss, landing on a shelf that shook and causing a bucket to fall across the captain's nose. "Ow—" he said out loud. Marina sighed in humiliation. "I'm sorry, but I'm unable to see anything. Oh, I'm so embarrassingly clumsy!" The man assisted her in standing up and assured her that he was unharmed and continued to check on her well-being.

The young lady gazed at him as they left the room with an expression that appeared as though she had seen a ghost. "Your face—". Confounded, the captain asked what was wrong with his face. He put his palm on his nose as Marina poked a finger at hers. His eyes widened and he stared at his hand. He sighed, "Oh bullocks." as it was covered in blood. When Marina had her monthly problem, she kept asking him if he was okay and why he was bleeding more than she was.

"I'm doing just fine. It's just that my blood vessels are really sensitive."He continued to touch his lips, unfazed by the fact that his face was fully covered in blood.

Marina began wiping his face with a piece of her clothing. "You're ruining your gown!." he said. She was ruining her clothes because of his bloody nose, and he felt terrible about it. "I'll always be able to get them cleaned, so it's alright." She gently proceeded to clean his nose while he sighed, and she later took him to his cabin to assist in stopping the bleeding from his nose.

In the meantime… Marina's parents were starting to be in a difficult marriage. Every day, her mother began to feel progressively worse. She was unable to find happiness anywhere. Losing your only children wasn't at all simple, especially when your husband exhibited stone-cold behavior.

She felt lifeless as she lay on the couch. For the first time in who knows how many months, she attempted to paint, but the effort was a total failure. She had no luck coming up with ideas. Mrs. Rivalli began to stare up at the ceiling as she continued to reflect on her life and gasped at how awful it had become. She then clung to her gown, which looked strangely filthy.

"Hello." After entering the home, her husband said in a monotone voice and removed his coat. "How was work?" She asked after glancing at him. He responded to her attempts to speak, with a simple cold "Eh." and made his way upstairs to lie down. She wanted to cry since her husband avoided her. She patiently waited for him to notice her filthy gown and inquire as to what transpired before telling him that she had gone to see him at the restaurant but was attacked with tomatoes by her neighbors who stated that her daughter was pure evil. Hearing such things said about her daughter made her feel terrible. The woman got up and carefully made her way upstairs while continuing to gaze at the photos of her family. She couldn't stop crying over how short-lived their happiness in the photos is, despite how happy their life appeared to be. Mrs. Rivalli glanced into her bedroom as she passed through the hallway and saw her husband lying on their bed. She was annoyed by the way he was sleeping soundly. She sighed and couldn't believe she had married a man who was so careless about everything.

She entered her children's bedroom. It was freezing and eerily empty. She was pretty uneasy and upset because of the loneliness. Marina's mother sighed, knelt, and grabbed hold of Rocco's bedcovers. "I miss my children. *I miss my old life*! I'm desperate to have it back! I feel unloved. My life has absolutely no meaning anymore." She started crying and was having trouble breathing. Her eyes swiftly wandered to the scissors Marina had used to murder her fiancé. She halted sobbing and continued to stare at them while pausing to reflect. She sat back down and gently picked them up before moving to the window, where she continued to gaze outside as her low ponytail was being blown by the wind.

The woman extended her arm and the scissors' blade touched her wrist. She kept second-guessing herself and wondering if she was doing the right thing. She had had enough of being upset and lifeless all the time. Because of all the crying she has done over the past year, her eye bags have fully darkened and she has even lost a lot of weight. Even her own emotionally unavailable husband was powerless to help her.

Mrs. Rivalli sighed, closed her eyes, and inhaled deeply. Her husband opened the doors and continued to stare at her with his emerald-colored eyes wide open as she was about to move her hand to end her life.

"What on earth are you doing!?" He enquired in an agitated manner.

She yelled at him "I'm attempting to kill myself. Is it not obvious enough? My life is awful! I just want my suffering to be over with already!"

"Fine," he said as he gave her a chilly stare. "I will most definitely not clean up the mess you'll make." he replied, adding, "Let me fetch you a bucket." and got a bucket for her from the bathroom. "Are you being this reckless!?" She screamed at him.

Near her, the man moved the bucket "Do it. Leave me to suffer on my own. Just as all of our children have abandoned us, leave me. Make my life miserable and pointless even worse." He caught his wife's horrified attention. She couldn't believe he was urging her to commit suicide and never once stopped to express his love for her. "Why don't you love me!?" At him, she yelled.

"What do you mean that I don't love you??"

"You never give me a look! As soon as I start crying, you're gone! I feel as though you now find me disgusting. You weren't even bothered to communicate with me earlier!"

"I'm leaving because I don't want you to watch me cry when my eyes are getting watery." He clenched his fist and said, "I went straight to our bedroom today to cry. As upset as you are, so am I. I don't want you to feel even worse and more helpless when you see how sensitive I am. You believe it's simple to contain all of my feelings and emotions?"

His wife turned to face him before glancing down at the scissors. She dropped them right away and broke down in tears. She said, "I'm very sorry, my love," while covering her face with her trembling hands. "I never want you to be by yourself."

"I'm sorry as well." He walked up to her right away and knelt before giving her a tight hug. "Instead of being so arrogant toward you, I should have spoken to you. Please understand how much I adore you." Mrs. Rivalli smiled at him as he placed his hands on her cheeks and cried. She appreciated it when he showed his actual emotions and didn't act as if nothing had happened these past few years. After that, her husband groaned and said, "I went to the Carabinieri today to see if they found any traces of her being alive." He then glanced at the scissors. When his wife asked him to tell her what he had learned, he said, "Nothing. They advised us to accept the fact that she is probably dead."

She sighed and looked down. "I sincerely hope she's not. She is intelligent and tough like you... She is extremely unlikely to die suddenly in the streets." The lips of her husband were pursed. "And I sincerely hope what you are stating is true. But if it isn't, we ought to accept the fact that she won't be returning."

When his wife nodded, tears began to stream down her face. She struggled mightily to hold onto some kind of hope that her daughter was still alive as the truth devastated her.

Chapter XV

The night was quiet and very chilly. The captain had his maid in his arms and they were both sleeping soundly in his bed. Everything was fine until Marina suddenly woke up screaming.

She struggled to breathe and began to sob furiously. Out of shock, the man woke up right away and questioned her in a loud voice about what was wrong because her shouting was making him panic hysterically. She kept crying even after he gently held her by her arms and put her head on his chest to try to quiet her down. Marina was driven wild by a nightmare in which Matias attacked her once more. She held onto his back and dug her nails deep into his skin. He made an effort not to be affected by the pain because he knew she was not doing well at the moment.

Mr. Santarelli urged her to "Listen carefully to the sound of my breathing and try to follow the rhythm" since she was still having trouble breathing. While crying, the girl continued to keep her head close to his chest and tracked the rhythm of his breathing. "Breathe in 1, 2, 3, 4, and out 1, 2, 3, 4." He said it five times. She continued to sniff as he put his hand on her hair and stroked it. When Marina did manage to speak, she started to apologize, "I'm very sorry! Right now, I'm just insanely terrified."

The man continued to softly stroke her hair, asking, "You're Terrified? What are you terrified of?"

"I just had an awful nightmare about my fiancé... I honestly don't feel at ease discussing it." He frowned and offered to make her some tea because he felt horrible that she was experiencing such frantic nightmares. "Would you like chamomile tea, mint tea, or lavender tea?"

"Whatever you believe's fine."

"I want to provide you with the greatest type of tea for calming down because you appear quite upset."

"Chamomile would be fine, thank you," swallowed Marina. "Great pick, it'll even help you sleep better." he said with a smile. He went straight to the kitchen to make her tea. The girl couldn't stop giggling at how hilarious she found his tea collection and expertise. When he returned, tea and biscuits were on a silver tray. He said, "I would've put a flower as well if we had any on the ship right now." As he set the tray on his nightstand, sat down on the bed next to her, and blew the tea for her so that it wasn't too hot, the captain remarked.

When Marina glanced at him, she sighed because she felt terrible that he was assisting her once more. "I just wish I wasn't so damaged for you to always be there for me!" the captain said as he sent a worried glance at her "Marina, I'm doing the bare minimum. If I started screaming in the middle of the night, it's not like you wouldn't quiet me down."

The girl averted her gaze and exclaimed, "Oh." She was unaware that this was regarded as the absolute least in terms of assistance.

The girl laid her head on his shoulder and said, "Thank you for being so kind to me." He grinned and assured her of his continued presence.

The ship began to appear empty the following day. Since it was Christmas Eve, everyone left to spend a few days with their families. "It's a shame we can't celebrate it all together," Antoni said as he started tightly hugging his friends. He was the last person to leave. "but it's been years since I last saw my mother, and I want to see her!"

"I honestly kind of forgot how Paola looks like," Mr. Santarelli grinned at him. "when you and I visited her in jail a few years ago, that was the last time I saw her."

"The moment I arrive," Antoni laughed, "I can bet that she'll start kissing my face and then slap my arm for not writing to her enough." Marina chuckled at that "Mothers." She exclaimed.

"Yes, but we still adore them."

"We do." The captain nervously remained mute as Marina and Antoni spoke since he didn't care for his mother at all and wanted to never see her again. He and Marina both waved at D'Angelo as he left because he had a train to catch to get to Rome. They also wished him safe travels.

The captain later questioned the girl, "Why don't you go to your family? " as she was finishing up her chores and he was assisting her. "You must miss them, I'm sure."

"I do," Marina said as she raised an eyebrow at him. "simply put, I want to avoid seeing them. And without me, you'd be lonely. You would be by yourself here!" She made a frowning face as she began to make fun of him. "Well thank you madam for keeping me company in these golly times." he rolled his eyes. Mr. Santarelli continued by telling her about Christmas and how he had read someplace about the holiday's fascinating beginnings. Marina aggressively clenched a towel as he

LV Polcic

spoke, thinking of her nightmare the entire time. After
that, the captain asked her, "Did you hear what I said?"
He noticed her mind started to wander off.

Marina gave him a look. "What? No, I'm sorry. I'm still
upset about my nightmare, but I'm sure it was quite
interesting. "You know, you can simply go and rest," the
man sighed. "In any case, you're on holiday. The rest of
the cleaning I don't mind doing myself, at all; I
genuinely like cleaning." When he stated that, the girl
grinned softly at him. She came up to him and said,
"You goddamn giraffe," The man started laughing at her,
"Bend down so I may kiss you on the cheek." He found
it hilarious to watch her struggle with her height.
Particularly given that she is 1.69 meters tall and he is
1.89 meters, almost two meters! He had always been
self-conscious about his height, but watching Marina
struggle to kiss him made him laugh out loud. He
lowered himself and the young lady got on her toes and
kissed his cheek. "When I rest we could later prepare
dinner." Marina asked him. "Cooking? With me? Oh no,
I'll burn the kitchen down. I'm terrible at cooking... I
might poison as well myself and most importantly you!"
The girl looked at him and squinted her eyes at him
"You're cooking with me whether you like it or not, Mr.
Gabriel Santarelli. If I could learn so can you." The man
felt nervous at the thought of cooking anything. Usually,
whenever he tried cooking something, it turned out so
terrible that Margherita would kick him out of the
kitchen.

"Oh, how about some authentic Italian dishes? I might perhaps across Margherita's old recipe books." When Marina realized she would be cooking dinner for just her and the captain, she exclaimed in delight. Just for the two of them, all alone, in his cozy cabin.

After a while, he joined Marina in bed because they were both fairly fatigued. He became anxious when he saw how sad she was and said, "If you want to, just go to your family. It's not like I'll be upset."

"Thank you, but I don't want to" Marina said, giving him a quick glance.

"Why not? After all, they are your parents."

"Because despite being with them, I still feel alone. All they do is speak about Rocco," the girl complained. "for heavens' sake, it seems like they've forgotten that I'm still alive. Mother then requests that we all discuss about Rocco after they even set aside an additional plate for him. Guess what, even though I adore my brother deeply, I'm over it." Just thinking about the circumstances at home made her irritated. The girl continued to clench her fists and grind her teeth to the point where her nails dug way too deeply into her skin. "Is it so hard to get their attention for once!? I'll always be in his shadow, even after my brother's gone. Is there a problem with me?" As she raised her bangs, she continued asking herself that question. The man touched her hand with his.

"Nothing is wrong with you. Yet they come off as not that great of parents." He spoke

"What? My parents have never hit me, Gabriel."

"They're not required to? They neglected you, which caused emotional harm to you. When did you first feel neglected?"

"Since... I suppose since I was seven years old." Marina maintained her denial about how terrible her parents are. She could not comprehend how abusive they are. However, as she began to reflect on her childhood, things began to make sense. "I'm messed up." the girl moaned as she fell on the captain's chest. "Then we'll be a mess together.." he said with a chuckle. "You can always talk to me if something like that bothers you since I'm kind of an expert when it comes to being neglected by my parents." The girl looked at him "I would enjoy that." She grinned at him as she experienced a strong sense of connection with him and the conviction that he is the only person in the world who fully comprehends her.

December 25th, 1910

D'Angelo, his mother, and his sister were all at home at his grandparent's place. After such a long period, he was overjoyed to see them. As soon as she saw him unlocking the doors, his mother, Mrs. Paola D'Angelo, rushed up to give him a bear embrace. "My boy! My beautiful son! I've missed you." He gave her a grin and a cheek kiss. She immediately altered her demeanor when she let go of him and poked him in the stomach. "You are too thin. Are you even being fed on that ship? You certainly have the appearance of a homeless man."

"That's because I once was, I suppose." His mother sighed as soon as he said that. She felt terrible about the pain and suffering she and her husband were causing to their children. "This is for you." He added, "I know you love perfumes." Mrs. D'Angelo's eyes widened with excitement "Perfume? For me? Oh, my dear boy, you shouldn't have!" She then looked at it and asked "Is it from France?"

"Mother I don't know. I'm pretty certain it's from here."

"Oh... not French. Well, I suppose it can *suffice*."

Valentina, his sister, approached him at that moment and made an effort to ask him questions as much as possible as she could, thus it is not odd that she inquires about Mr. Santarelli. "How are you doing?" She asked. "Good. You're still too young for him." Antoni answered her. His sister wasn't going to fool him because he knew her so well. "What!? I didn't intend to inquire about your pal." His sister insisted that her main concern was for the welfare of her beloved brother. "Valentina, don't think I don't recall you nearly fawning over Gabriel when he came to visit a year ago." Her cheeks became red as she crossed her arms and turned her head away. She then murmured, "I'm only four years away from turning eighteen..." Her brother rolled his eyes "I bought you a porcelain doll for Christmas. I cannot manage to understand how you like them. They're so disturbingly looking like you."

"Oh! She's so pretty! Thank you, Antoni! I love it so much, especially after I lost all my toys when father died." She paused as she squinted at him with a pouted lip "I'll choose to ignore what you lastly said about me."

The man then inquired as to whether his mother had received all of the letters he had written her. "Yes I have." she said. "Stop pestering your friend to write letters for you," she commanded. "his vocabulary is too sophisticated for you to have written it."

Antoni sighed, he even asked the captain not to make the letters sound complex. "I'll be sure to let him know then." He gave an eye roll.

Then Mrs. D'Angelo asked Antoni, "How is work? " as she took a seat next to him on the couch. "Have you been making any excellent money lately?" She caught his confused gaze, "Yes. With my own business growing, I believe that I am beginning to surpass Gabriel in riches. I may soon return to Rome and establish my own business there as father did." His mother loudly remarked, "How fantastic!" while grinning broadly. "I can't wait for you to move in here and live with me! Recently, being without you has been so lonely. And letters are pretty slow." she sighed. Her son shrugged. Then Antoni asked, "How are you and grandparents doing with the money?" after taking a look around the house. He noted their home doesn't appear to be as wealthy as it once did.

"Well, as you are aware, money has been tight since your father passed away. It's fine, though. I'm just relieved that both of my children are healthy." She gave him a huge kiss on the cheek after giving him a second, strong hug. Squinting, Antoni implored her to stop. "Never." she answered.

Mr. Santarelli and Marina were in the kitchen at the time. He had a terrible time learning how to cook from the girl. "Continue to knead!" She screamed. "I am! God help me, my hands are growing numb." He was struggling to knead the dough since he was getting fatigued and was thinking that it ought to have been finished by now. "Numb? Do you have any idea how much dough I worked on within a day? A lot! Step up and knead that!" The man then bowed his head and uttered "Yes, ma'am." He found the girl to be horrifyingly domineering, and he was beginning to wonder how a person like her could be so intimidating. Then he dismissed it and observed that she had always come across as a bit dictatorial.

In order to assist him in better kneading the dough because he was doing a bad job of it, the young lady then stood behind him, leaned on his back, and placed her hands on top of his. She was so near to his body that he was unable to concentrate, so he simply let her use his hands whatever she pleased. "You have to treat it gently." Marina softly spoke next to his ear. "The dough needs to be as soft as a baby's skin." He asked, beginning to wonder how she had learned all of this. "Math, physics, and history come naturally to me. But God, this is just too difficult."

"It's because you aren't putting your all into it. You continue to overthink. Baking and cooking are not scientific endeavors; they are forms of art."

"That makes sense, I think. But do you still require guidance, no?" He queried. "Both yes and no. Just use your creativity! That's why I enjoy cooking so much." As she spoke about cooking. The girl's enthusiasm for it was evident in her eyes. She caressed his face, leaving flour on it, and gave him a soft kiss on the cheek. She noticed she was missing a few ingredients when the captain laughed at her and the girls' eyes moved to the counter. "I've run out of vegetables for the focaccia." Angered, she said, "Agh, I need to go to the market!" while clenching her fists.

"Should I come with you? The captain exclaimed in excitement as he took off his pink apron. He was instantly yelled at by Marina, "No! Continue to knead! Until it becomes so soft that I hesitate to touch it, you are not leaving."

The man sighed and muttered something to himself about being tired of constantly kneading.

Then Marina removed her apron, grabbed her basket, and swiftly put his long brown coat over herself. Even though she felt silly wearing such a big coat, she made an effort to make it look well on her. It kept her cozy either way.

Since it was Christmas and nobody in their right mind would work on a holiday, she began to suspect that markets might not be open today as she was heading outdoors. She is pleased to have a week off, and others undoubtedly deserve it as well. Marina came to the market and bought the vegetables that she needed for the focaccia that she was making with Mr. Santarelli. The girl then began to calculate how much money she still had since she wanted to give the captain a Christmas present. "Oh, there are still 96,000 lire. I believe that's adequate for a book, right?" She set off for the bookstore but soon realized it was closed. Since she kept forgetting that today was a holiday and nothing worked, she felt stupid.

In dismay, Marina moaned and started to move away and feeling upset that she didn't manage to buy him anything. She noticed the captain completely covered in flour when she got onto the vessel. "I told you I couldn't do it, but you wouldn't listen." The young lady moaned before starting to mock him. She assisted him with self-cleaning. "No problem, I'll continue with it. Just take a seat, and you'll assist me in adorning the focaccia." When Mr. Santarelli looked at her, he smiled broadly and said, "I believe I have a better idea."

"Oh?" She began to wonder what it was. He quickly dashed to his cabin, came back, and set a phonograph on the table. "Which do you like better, Vissi D'Arte or Fior Che Langue?" She gasped "Goodness gracious! Is it that you have Vissi D'Arte? That one has been so long since I

last heard it! kindly make it to play." Mr. Santarelli
approached the girl from behind, put his hands on her
waist, and started to slowly dance with her as the music
began to play when he put the disc on the phonograph.
"Oh! You wanted to dance?" she exclaimed "I would
love that." he said, giving her a gentle smile. Then, as
she leaned closer to him, Marina spun. "I hope this
would be acceptable by your standards as I cannot afford
balls." He inquired.

"This is far superior to balls." The phonograph continued
to play Vissi D'Arte as the man grinned and turned to
face her. He continued to fixate on her ocean-blue eyes,
awestruck by her beauty and grace. She placed her head
on his chest and listened to the beat of his heart. "This is
the calmest and warmest Christmas I've ever had." the
captain exclaimed.

"Really? How so?" Marina inquired because she found it
difficult to imagine that someone could not enjoy a
merry Christmas. The man pursed his lips. "At
Christmastime last year, I found Angela sleeping with
another man." He remembered the incident and cast a
troubled gaze down at the ground. She had often
grumbled to him about how he was usually at sea, so he
even came early that day to see her and spend more time
with her. Only for her to break his heart in pieces when
he tried to make her happy. Because of what she had
done, he was so enraged that he quickly left her home

and celebrated Christmas alone while becoming intoxicated. As she started to feel terrible about what Angela had done to him, the young lady remarked, "I'm sorry." in a low voice. "I struggle to comprehend what it would be like to experience such a thing. I'd forever lose faith in love." He chuckled softly "I did as well. Yet you were able to restore my faith in love. And I'll forever be thankful to you for that." he said, grabbing her hands and tenderly kissing them. As he said that, Marina grinned and felt honored and special.

Chapter XVI

M r. Santarelli and Marina were spending their final night together alone. The idea of having to conceal her relationship with the captain once more made the girl unhappy. She wished she didn't have to, but she had to if it meant preserving her and his reputation. At least until she quits her job as a maid and moves out on her own.

Marina had just finished reading a chapter from *Persuasion* while sitting in the man's bed wearing his worn-out white shirt. She was waiting for the man to come into bed who was taking off his clothes. She gave him a short glance, which caused her lips to purse. He was only wearing a pair of fitted white drawers. She kept staring at his fit body, which gave her butterflies and caused her heart to beat more quickly. "What?" He asked her. He smirked and remarked that he didn't understand why she was concentrating so hard on him. "Nothing, am I forbidden from looking?" She felt ashamed for feeling this way about him and was at a loss for words. The man continued running his fingers through his hair to loosen it up and feel more at ease wearing it down. While looking at him with widened eyes, Marina continued to bite her fingernail till it snapped from the force of her bite. Marina chided herself, "You're such a mess!"

As she started to become lost in thoughts, she crossed her legs and tugged his shirt down. "Perhaps I ought to do it. I should've done it properly by now—I'm nineteen. In addition, I feel awful for consistently dissatisfying him. Although, he never truly asks me to do anything." she reflected. "I don't want him to depart because I didn't get his signals." Marina glanced at him once more as he cracked his knuckles. She bit her lip and made up her mind to get up and go over to him. She gently touched his shoulders with her hands.

By her touch, Mr. Santarelli closed his eyes and shuddered. She grinned at him and fixed him with her alluring blue eyes. Her hand was resting on his chest as she pushed him into his bed and climbed on top of him, letting her long, curly hair fall on him. "What are you doing?" He questioned, his cheeks flushed and visibly confused. "I want you badly." Although he was charmed by her comments, he began to feel as though she was rushing their relationship. "Are you sure?" he asked as he tucked her hair behind her ear nervously.

"Yes, I'm certain, Gabriel. That's what I want! This decision is mine." She yelled at him while squeezing her eyes shut in anger. Although the captain began to worry, he wanted to please her in order to make her feel better.

"Alright, I understand, darling. As long as it's your choice, I truly don't mind."

His nose was kissed by Marina as she grinned at him. She wanted to kiss him more, but he grabbed her by the waist and forced himself to get on top of her, turning her over. When he took that action, Marina shouted, "Ah!—" because she wasn't expecting it. As her cheeks turned fully red and her nose wrinkled, he grinned at her and she kept snickering at him. When the man gently took her hand and raised it above her head, the girl's lips pursed in fear. "I'm not sure how much of what your mother taught you. But the first time is always a little unpleasant and known to be a little bloody." he said. "So, if you experience any severe discomfort or spot blood, do not panic." Marina's eyes widened and she turned her head away since she didn't know that the first time hurts. "Have I ever told you how much I love your hair when it's loose?" She began to snicker at him "No, you never told me that."

Mr. Santarelli started kissing her neck, followed by her collarbone and, gradually, her chest. His hand crept beneath the shirt that she wore, and he softly gripped her leg, slowly dragging it up and pressing it against his hip. Marina continued to moan until she stared up at the ceiling and went utterly still. When she thought back to the time Matias had harmed her, her breathing became labored, and she suddenly found herself feeling repulsed

LV Polcic

by the captain's neck-kissing and could feel again Matias' touches from the day he had assaulted her. The young lady was having a panic attack and finding it difficult to breathe when she suddenly regretted wanting to have intercourse. She broke down in tears as she once more felt like a total failure.

Hearing her sob and observing her tears fall on her chest, the man shouted in terror, "Marina! Marina! What's wrong!? Did I injure you?" In a panic, he said.

As soon as he overheard her exclaim, "No!— I can't— I can't breathe!" he jumped to his feet and hurried over to the window, opening it wide. Then, to give Marina a chance to collect her breath, he took her and brought her there. She couldn't stop shaking and panting while feeling disgusted with her own body as he hugged her tightly and wanted to comfort her. "I'm sorry!" She took a deep fast breath "I feel terrible for wasting our last night together! I aimed to please you and make it seem special." Her sobs persisted.

"Satisfy me!? What are you on?"

"I feel terrible because all you've done for me for months is help me constantly, yet I can't even do one thing for you."

"For me? And you believed that you could repay a favor through... intercourse? I'm utterly confused."

"I merely wanted to establish equality in our relationship."

Mr. Santarelli smiled worriedly at her and felt terrible. "But we are on equal footing. My favorite thing about you is that you make me happy, without having it to be sexual." She said, "But— I've never even told you how I love you!" as her eyes widened and more tears started streaming down her face. "I've been afraid of being in a committed relationship once more and of you not understanding how I feel about you the entire time."

He raised a brow. "I would never treat you that way! I would sooner immediately stab myself in the heart than stab you in the back." Marina gave him a sweet grin as she felt relieved that he wasn't forcing her to confess her love for him or force herself to satisfy his needs "I still feel terrible for ruining the night by having a panic attack." the young lady said. The man sighed once more "I beg of you to stop apologizing, please. Nobody is to blame; it occurs to everyone." He softly took her hands in his and drew them up to his face. "Never apologize for such behavior. You're free to express your feelings right then and there rather than holding them inside." He kissed her on the hands that rested on his cheeks.

His words and presence made Marina feel more at ease, and she appreciated that someone had finally acknowledged her sentiments. He wiped the tears from her cheeks as she bowed her head.

"Having intercourse with someone I love used to make me so happy, but it's completely lost its appeal to me." Her wrath caused her jaw to clench as she sighed. She was placed on the bed by the captain, who continued to firmly hold her hand. "You don't have to do anything right now; do it when you're ready. I'm not going to force you to make love with me. I adore our situation as it is."

"I can't!"

"Why?—" She rose, turned to face him, and continued to bite her fingernail with her finger now bleeding while he worriedly questioned.

"Because on the day of my wedding, my fiancé hurt me!" With tears in her eyes and her hair falling across her face, Marina yelled at him.

When Mr. Santarelli understood what she meant by "Hurt." his eyes widened. He was sick to his stomach as he observed how upset and uncomfortable she seemed. "Oh my goodness, he... rape—"

The man's eyes began to well with tears, and he kept stuttering. As she cried and shook from fear of admitting her horrible day, Marina nodded. After disclosing such a difficult thing to him, she felt like she might pass out. "He...he came into my bedroom as I...I was getting ready to go to church. I initially thought he was, was just t-teasing me, but then he *smacked* me, shoved me into *my mirror*, and...and r-raped me!" As soon as he did, Gabriel drew her in and gave her a tight hug before they both fell on his bed. "I'm so sorry that ever happened to you. I regret not being able to do more for you." He kept giving her hands comforting kisses while she sobbed on his chest. "But it's m-my fault! I kept... I kept provoking him and messing with his feelings! I ought to have behaved better and tried not to make him feel t-that way."

"Marina, please refrain from blaming yourself at any time. He is at fault. He's a *monster* who deserves nothing more than to *die*." Marina sobbed. "To protect myself, I—I killed him with my scissors. I stabbed him in the neck and chest and felt good as I saw him struggle to breathe."

It suddenly made apparent why her wedding gown was coated in red. However, the fact that the man was murdered made him feel relieved. "My God, I feel horrible for what you had to endure. I'm all yours if there is anything you need from me. To help you feel more at ease, we can even end this conversation."

"—No, I want to discuss this! It's alright! The situation is fine!"

"It's not *alright*, Marina; you have a right to be upset rather than acting fine."

"Well, I'm not fine. What should I say or do? It's not like my emotions are important, to begin with. If I had told anyone what had happened, no one would have believed me. This only serves to increase the already widespread animosity I already have in Naples. Fornication."

"Oh to hell with them and old rules." sighed the captain "I'm not married, I have already had intercourse and well... I'm not entirely fine but you get my point." Marina said with her lips pursed "I suppose you're correct, but once more, as a man, you enjoy various privileges. If I went back to Naples, I feel like I'd be burned on a cross if I confessed for getting—" She swallowed her spit in disgust and frustration because she was unable to even pronounce the term "rape."

The man put his hand on her chin and gently raised her head. "Look, what matters now is that I'm very proud of you for having the courage to tell me everything because I know it must have been difficult." he said. He tried to encourage her for her bravery, whether it seemed like a little thing to say or do, he felt as though he should commend her for being this strong enough this entire time. "And I'm very glad that you confined to me the most, and I assure you that I'll always be on your side no matter what." he said.

When he said this, Marina once more burst into tears, "Thank you, that's all I needed to hear. I constantly tell myself that I'm to blame, that I wanted it, and that since he's my fiancé, it's not *rape*. I felt horrible thinking that I was in the wrong for feeling that way because he knew me the best and I should've trusted him." The man was just disgusted and kept sighing because he was so upset about this entire situation. "*Rape is rape.* He forced you against your will. You have the right to feel uncomfortable by someone forcing you to do something against your will." All she could muster was a weary nod before she started to regret having been in such a poisoned frame of mind all along. "I want to stop talking about this." she said as she leaned her head against his chest. "Please."

"Of course."

"Could you tell me about a historical or biological topic? You talking helps me to calm down."

"Would you like me to discuss the ancient world some more? I know you like hearing those from me." As soon as he said that, Marina excitedly nodded and grinned at him.

As he started speaking, he covered her with sheets and placed her on his arm. "Back in Ancient Greece, the people believed that loud, joyful noises attracted evil spirits to our world. Because the evil spirits believed that the humans were aggressive and violent, the Greeks would smash plates whenever there was a celebration." She blinked and asked, "I think you once talked about coins and death in Ancient Greece, but I cannot remember what it was." she stared up at him with wonder. When he realized what she was referring to, the man's eyes widened. "Oh! Charon's Obol! It happens when people put a coin into a dead person's mouth so they can pay Charon to cross the River Styx in the underworld." she exclaimed "What if someone couldn't bury the person with money?"

"They wouldn't receive a transport from Charon then."

"No!" She shouted out in despair for the unfortunate people who were stuck without transportation. She made the captain laugh by worrying so much for unrelated souls. The young lady started to get fatigued after a while and kept yawning. She closed her eyes and tucked her head snugly under his chin, resting her hand on his chest. "Thank you for your compassion."

"You're welcome." He answered her, kissing the top of her head. "I genuinely appreciate it." The man said, "Well thank you." with a smile. "And you make me feel safe."

"Mhm." As he proceeded to blow out the candle that had been left by his bed. "And I genuinely enjoy talking to

LV Polcic

you about my frustrations." The captain looked at her "I appreciate that, but I think you'd appreciate it more if you went to sleep and took a rest." he said as he smiled softly at her. The young lady agreed and nodded. The girl murmured "Gabriel" as she was about to nod off.

"Yes?" He asked in a worn-out voice.

She paused for a moment "I adore you."

Chapter XVII

The following day, Marina and Mr. Santarelli came to pick up D'Angelo Antoni from the train station. The girl gripped the captain's hand tightly as they made their way to the train station, starting to get lost in contemplation until she suddenly gasped. "Are you aware of what I have just realized? Matias first started courting me when I was seventeen years old." His expression showed confusion as he tried to decipher what she was trying to say. "He was twenty-six years old at the time." she said, clearing her mouth. The young lady trembled as she realized that he had courted her when she was still essentially a child in his eyes.

When the captain gagged, he inquired, "How could your parents permit you to be with him?" He was so madly perplexed by that.

"I do not know. He was even well-liked by my father. He continued complimenting me on the fantastic man I chose. To be fair, though. I do believe he was the one who chose me in all fairness?" assuming that made sense. She put her finger on her lower lip and took a moment to contemplate. He kept staring at her because he was afraid she was going to start exposing more and more of her troubling background. He pulled her in by placing his hand on her shoulder. "Well, the fact that you're now free and appear happier is what matters. To help you feel more comfortable, I wanted to take you out to dinner when we both have free time." Marina grinned at that right away "I'd adore that! That would be fantastic. Oh, I must buy a brand-new gown presently!"

She was asked why she needed a new gown just for dinner and the man chuckled at her. "Oh Gabriel, you'd understand if you were a lady." He simply rolled his eyes and kept strolling with her after that. They both went up to their pals as soon as they saw them at the train station.

"Antoni!"

"Gabriel, sweetheart!"

Hugging one other fiercely, the two men stood. "How did you spend the holidays? I hope the solitude wasn't too intense for you." Antoni questioned him. The captain spoke in response "Oh," he said, turning to face Marina. "Marina kept me company. It was lovely." He was met with an immediate glance and a smirk from Antoni. "Lovely? Did you ever tell her how you're feeling?" The captain was embarrassed and had a scarlet face. "N-no. It is not your concern." While Marina was lost in her thoughts realizing how awful more and more is Matias, Antoni started making fun of his friend for being so reserved about his feelings. Then Antoni rummaged in his luggage and pulled out a box of food. "This was brought for you by my mother. And she also told you to stop writing letters for me!" he said to him. The captain gave him a perplexed look "I was told? It was you who asked me to write on your behalf."

"And you did it voluntarily."

"You're unbelievable." He crossed his arms and rolled his eyes at Antoni. The girl couldn't help but snort as she continued to stare at the two of them.

The young lady went straight to the captain's cabin after Marina and Mr. Santarelli assisted D'Angelo with unpacking aboard the ship. They were once again compelled to conceal their love for one another because everyone boarded the ship and there was no privacy.

"Concerning that dinner you mentioned." She enquired

"Yes?"

"Have you got a particular restaurant in mind? since
many places don't offer non-meat options and I don't eat
meat. I am aware of this because my father only included
veggies and other things in his menu for me." He stroked
her hand and grinned at that. "I checked! Don't stress
over it. They serve delectable soup, grilled vegetables,
and other things! You will adore it." The girl began to
beam and bat her eyelashes in his direction as she felt
grateful that he was so considerate of her preferences. "I
can't wait to go somewhere where no one knows about
us and spend some time alone with you." The man to that
softly smiled "I wish the same."

Everyone from the ship ate dinner together one evening.
The captain and Marina had intended to go out to eat that
night, but they were unable to skip the meal that
everyone was having. For them to be the only ones gone,
it would be way too suspicious. Being nervous about
having to get ready and sneak off to the restaurant, the
maid and the captain sat down by the table with
everyone. "You haven't touched anything, Gabriel.
Surprisingly, do you not feel hungry?" Francesca asked.
"No, I'm fine."

She looked at him with distrust "Hm. Do you not want anything, Marina?"

"Water will be fine. I'm not hungry either." She answered, biting her lip. Giordana and Margherita exchanged glances as they raised their eyebrows. All afternoon, the two of them presented a weird appearance. Mr. Santarelli was irritated with himself for not being able to eat because he planned to go to a restaurant later and didn't want to be full. He looked at his watch and gasped in panic "Oh, I hope everyone has a lovely dinner, but I must get to bed soon! Goodbye!" He got to his feet and started to leave. "Already? It's hardly five o'clock in the afternoon?" Confounded, Antoni questioned. "Yes, I'm already really exhausted. For my shift, I also need to rest." Marina yawned and extended her arms as he walked away "Ah, I should also get some rest. I've put forth a lot of effort today. Goodnight!" She started moving quickly toward her cabin so she could change. "They are both odd." As he continued to chew, Antoni murmured. The red-haired girl felt unusually suspicious about it as well and made the decision to look into the matter further.

The captain and Marina met up on the deck later that night after both of them had secretly snuck out of their cabins. They were laughing at each other for being so cunning. "Will nobody realize we're both missing?" The girl asked. As he continued to tap his finger on his head and grinned at her, he said, "I'm on watch duty tonight, so no one will be outside to check on anything. Because I shall once again be the one who is ostensibly outside during the entire time. I'm two steps ahead.

"That's true. But what about me not getting caught?"

"Oh no, I forgot that you share a cabin with others!" He started to feel anxious and guilty for having already ruined their time together. Marina kept grinning evilly. "You're not the only smart one. I created the illusion that I was asleep by placing pillows beneath my bed's sheets and covering them with my nightgown." The man exclaimed, "Brilliant! I had no idea you were that shrewd."

"I learned it from the greatest," she shrugged as she eyed him. As she noticed him dressed so neatly in a black suit, the young lady bit her bottom lip. "You look quite handsome" she said, taking hold of his suit. "You dressing so elegantly for tonight was not what I had anticipated."

"Well, I reasoned, I might as well put some effort into my appearance for you since you bought a new gown just for tonight." The girl then rose to her feet and gave him a soft kiss on the chin, saying, "I love it, you look so dashing. And that suit is incredibly stylish!" She started to touch his black suit because she wanted to feel the high-quality fabric that Antoni had made it. "However, it had been gathering dust in my closet for several months because I had never worn it. I never had an occasion to dress up fancy." Marina gasped "Not even for balls?"

"I'm afraid not Marina. I do not have the luxury to go out dancing."

Looking at his face and hair, the girl grinned at him and noted that he even shaved his face for her. She immediately took his hand, and the two of them began walking in the direction of the restaurant that Mr. Santarelli had suggested they go to.

He was unable to prevent his heart from racing as they walked. He continued sneaking glances at her every thirty seconds since, in his opinion, she was breathtakingly beautiful. She didn't just look stunning tonight in the new gown; he thought she was captivating all the time. However, he felt awkward complimenting her appearance excessively lest he comes off as "obsessed." Marina noticed him looking at her before nervously looking away as he turned to stare at her once again. "Was it your gaze upon me?" She questioned while continuing to snort loudly.

"No."

"You did, and I just caught you." She said, grinning at him. "My apologies, but you just look... extremely divine. Especially with the moonlight complimenting your face so beautifully." The man's face turned scarlet from embarrassment, and he grabbed his collar. She kept laughing and said "Thank you." for his lovely remarks. "You are kind, Mr. Santarelli! You're such a gentleman!" she remarked.

They eventually arrived at the restaurant and took a seat. They both couldn't wait to order their meals because they were extremely hungry as they haven't eaten almost the entire day. The young lady commented about the restaurant while they waited for the waiter to arrive. "It does appear quite classy. I hadn't anticipated this." The captain asked, "Were you anticipating some type of tavern?" as he stared at her in confusion. She gave him a shrug and started to snicker mockingly. "Well, I did, yes."

"Oh really? You think I'm that petty to take a lady out for dinner to some ugly tavern?"

Finally, the waiter arrived just in time and saved Marina from replying to him. He gave them their menus so they could decide what they wanted to eat. He remarked as he grabbed one "I'm still waiting for your reply, just so you know."

The young lady bit her bottom lip as she nervously took the menu and continued reading it while giving Mr. Santarelli fleeting glances and remarking on how lovely he was that evening. She noticed there was nothing for her as she looked and read about the many meals they had. "Are you certain that we are in the proper establishment?" Marina enquired. "Obviously, we are. Just why do you ask?"

"Well, you said there would be food for me. There isn't any. At all. Either the meat or the soup only is on the menu. And I have no intention of drinking flavored water." When the girl mentioned this, he looked over the menu right away and widened his eyes when he saw that there were no meals for her. "What? I'm utterly lost. The last time I visited, they offered a huge variety of foods!"He then pointed his index finger upward, signaling for the waiter to approach their table.

"Is there an issue, sir?"

"Not specifically, but wasn't there risotto with vegetables? also, fish offered as well?"

"We used to have it, but the restaurant's chef changed, so the menu is now different. And also because more people consume meat than veggies, so now most of the dishes are meat." Since he had officially ruined Marina's night, the man started to sigh and hid his face with his hands. He found it incomprehensible that there were no meals at all for her. The young lady acknowledged that she was unhappy about it as well, but she didn't want to ruin their evening, so she placed her delicate hands on his wrist and stated, "It's alright. Look, if you order something and add some vegetables as a side dish, I'll eat it! Issue is resolved." As he glanced through his fingers, the man asked, "Really? Would you consider that sufficient? I don't want you to starve." She continued to assure him that she would be satisfied by it and nodded in agreement.

When the meal for the captain arrived, he put aside the vegetables and handed them to Marina, who continued to bite her lip as she realized she would probably starve to death. The captain glanced at her as they were both eating and asked, "I just wanted to ask. Have the Carabinieri received a report on you? Taking the entire circumstance into account."

"Carabinieri? I am clueless. Or else, I'm a wanted criminal. I hope not." She leaned her head against her arm as she started to think deeply about the possibility that the Carabinieri were looking for her. "I mean, I've probably had someone report me. Since I'm despised by everyone in Vomero, I wouldn't be shocked." He took a sip of the red wine he was drinking and inquired, puzzled, why everyone there seemed to despise her. "As you may already be aware, I'm not exactly a saint." She continued to smirk at him while lightly touching her lip with her finger which made him take quick glances at her lips and nervously ask "Care to elaborate?"

"It's nothing important. But this is so nice. I truly value our private time together."

"We're not entirely alone, after all. Other people are present."

"We're not surrounded by people who would judge us for being together, that's what I meant." The man exhaled a sound of an "Ah." He understood what she was saying and agreed with her. "We might then make the best of it tonight." He replied as he took her hand, removed her glove, and gently kissed her. The young lady was touched by his kiss. "But I'd still like of you to answer my question." He asked. Marina rolled her eyes "I don't think it's something to talk about in the restaurant."

"How awful is it? It's not as if you managed to commit another murder." Mr. Santarelli laughed at his joke but when he looked at her serious facial expression, he went silent immediately and realized that she was right about it not being a proper topic to talk about in the restaurant. "Even though I adore this restaurant, I genuinely would prefer if we went on a walk by the sea." She enquired "I don't mind." he said as he cast a quick glance at her. "In light of the fact that we are constantly at sea, I could use some movement."

The two of them got to their feet and went outdoors. He instantly covered her with his coat to keep her from freezing because the night was obscenely cold. Every time they let a breath out, a chilly cloud would appear in the air. "Gabriel, do you ever want a new beginning? to move somewhere where no one knows you, buy a house and lead a normal life?" Curious, she asked while holding onto the man's long coat.

"I suppose I do. I've always desired a calm lifestyle. have a wife, a job I enjoy, and other things." "A wife?" The girl asked him with a soft smile. "How strange of you." She grabbed his arm and rested her head on his shoulder.

"What makes my desire to establish a joyful marriage seem so strange?" He chuckled as he questioned. "I suppose due to the fact you're a captain. You're not really the family-oriented type of person. You're more devoted to the sea than family."

"That's true." He answered. "Which is why I despise my job." She looked up at him with curiosity "Well, do you have any specific job that you like and would like to do when you settle down?" "I would love to be a lawyer. When I went to England a couple of times, I met this one gentleman that was a lawyer. He told me about his job and how he studied at Oxford University and it sparked some kind of interest in me. People even treat him with respect while they treat me like utter garbage for being a captain." The man then sighed and cracked his knuckles "But I highly doubt I could ever even go to Oxford, I don't have the money for it." Marina, filled with guilt, pursed her lips as she kept twirling her hair curl on her finger "I'm starting to realize that sometimes I go too far with the way I shame you for being a captain."

All he did was shrug at that moment "Your words do hurt but I know you don't mean it in any bad manner. If anything I'm glad you realized your mistake. You have changed Miss Marina Rivalli." He chuckled at her as he crossed his arms. She looked down while softly smiling "Well, I do admire you for knowing what you wish to do with your life. I on the other hand have not much ideas. I thought I liked the idea of my entire life's purpose being a good obedient wife and staying at home but..."

"But?" He asked, curious.

"Being with you made me realize how I would rather slit my neck than live that godawful life. I learned that I enjoyed traveling. I enjoy living!" She grabbed his hand gently and interlocked her fingers with his "And I adore that you treat me so kindly and like a human being, not just someone to satisfy your needs."

"Well goodness Marina, I'm not a monster. Of course, I'll treat you decently." He was puzzled by her remarks as he didn't understand what was so special about the way he treated her. Mr. Santarelli wasn't realizing how his actions and words were meaningful to Marina and meant a lot to her, considering how badly Matias used to treat her.

They came across a man who appeared untrustworthy just as Marina was about to respond to him. He started to approach them.

The captain continued to watch him until he reached into his pocket and pulled out a gun. Mr. Santarelli was angrily requested to hand over his wallet as he pointed the weapon at him. "I won't say it once again." The captain became anxious since he had used all of his money on the restaurant dinner and was unsure of what to do. All he did was stand in front of the girl for protection. "Gabriel, why aren't you handing him your wallet?—" Marina demanded as her eyes grew wide. She clung to Gabriel's arm tightly and caught his worried expression as he said, with anxiety in his voice "I don't— I don't have any money left—" The robber became enraged with the two of them and violently seized the captain by his collar, yelling, "Liar!" He screamed. "I promise! I'm not carrying any money with me!" The robber gazed at both of them with malice in his eyes. He understood that he couldn't let them go right away or they would report him to the Carabinieri. The captain fell to the ground as the man pulled out his gun and hit him in the head.

With her hands covering her mouth, Marina sputtered. She was petrified and unsure of what to do to prevent harm to any of them. The captain screamed in anguish as the robber started kicking him hard in the stomach with his foot. He was being killed by savage beatings. "Halt it! Just let him be! Why are you torturing him like this!?" The young lady screamed, her face turning pale and tears streaming from her eyes. The attacker gave her a hostile look and said, "Silence or he won't be the only one hurt tonight."

"Do n-not— *touch her!*—"

The man struck the captain once more. "*Agh!*" Shouted the captain in pain. No one was nearby to aid him, who was writhing and moaning from the beating. His face began to bleed as tears began to pour from his eyes. He couldn't even defend himself or Marina at this point.

The robber's gun dropped out of his pocket as he continued to strike him. The man was preoccupied and the young lady glanced at it. She seized the opportunity right away. "Stop it!" Marina yelled as she aggressively wiped tears from her face and pointed a gun at him. "Let go of him, now!"

He gave her a glance. "Don't make me laugh. Because of the way you're holding it, you can't even shoot."

"Want to take a chance and find out for yourself?" She continued to stare at him while her eye twitched. Marina started slowly pulling the trigger, at which point the robber backed off and in a panic said, "Fine. You're lucky if he's still alive." he said while walking away from them. As he stated that, Marina's stomach dropped, and she instantly knelt and continued to touch Gabriel's damaged face while yelling, "Gabriel! Have your eyes open!" He was yelled at by her. "I'm fine—don't worry about me." he moaned as he struggled to open his eyes. "I'm just glad he spared your life."

"Please don't ever do that to me!" she pleaded while sobbing into his chest as she tightly clutched him. She was sobbing and trembling as Mr. Santarelli was surprised and widened his eyes. "I'm sorry, but it's not as if I would've let you die—" he said.

"But you'd have let yourself die horribly!? *And in front of me?*"

"For heavens' sake, I had to! I care for you Marina, I would always put my life in danger to save yours." he moaned in pain. She kept crying as she saw how bloody his face was and started to feel extremely terrible. The whole situation was upsetting her since it brought back the memory of the time her brother passed away, and she didn't want to go through that experience again.

When they returned to the ship, the young lady helped him undress so she could more readily assist him in cleaning up the wounds and sat him down on his bed. To grab some water and alcohol to clean his wounds, she hurried to the kitchen. The entire time Mr. Santarelli was waiting for her, he kept reflecting on how helpless he felt to protect her. The mugger could have easily killed her as well. He didn't want that to occur again ever.

When Miss Marina came back, she continued frantically gripping the cloth. Her poor mind was filled with anxiety as to what happened and she was anxious to see the captain injured, sitting so weak on his bed. She approached him and assisted him in cleaning his bloody face. The man moaned in anguish which startled her.

"I'm sorry, and I'll make every effort to be gentle." She continued to give him dejected looks as she softly placed her palm on his jawline.

She helped him clean his wounds for only a little while before he whispered, "Thank you, Marina." The young lady pressed her lips as they had a silent moment of looking at each other's eyes. She then placed both of her hands on his cheeks "I despise you so immensely for sacrificing yourself." Marina placed her forehead against his as he placed his hands on hers. "I love you, I'm not letting you die." The man spoke softly to her as his lips were pressed against her soft cheek. "That's very kind of you. But I don't appreciate it when you keep sacrificing yourself for me. I want you to promise to stop."

He looked up at her "I cannot promise that." Her eyes swam with tears. She began to sob as she started imagining the man she loves die in front of her. The captain begged her to not shed her tears. "I'm just incredibly tired of seeing everyone that I love, die in front of me and because of me. I watched my brother die, I killed my fiancé... I'm tired of it Gabriel. I want a normal peaceful life in which no one that I love has to die." He began to wipe the tears from her delicate cheeks as he peered up into her teary blue eyes, "I'll make every effort to not die, but recognize that I'm not letting you die either." He said.

"Please, while that man was kicking you terribly. When I saw you suffer and was powerless to do anything to ease your suffering, my heart was breaking into a million pieces." Mr. Santarelli touched her cheek as he puzzledly regarded her penetrating blue eyes. "You were the one who saved me, so thank you, sincerely for helping me! I admire you for that, and I must repent for not needing to provide protection on your behalf!" She got down on his lap and put her head on his chest "What will others say when they see you injured?" She sighed. "I'm clueless. I'll do my best to come up with a creative falsehood." Marina chuckled as her face was already buried in his ripped white shirt. "You could say that... *the Kraken* attacked you."

"I'm more shocked that you recognize that thing." She grinned menacingly at him. "My dear captain, I have a lot to surprise you with." The girl gave him flattering looks with her eyes. The captain lifted an eyebrow as he regarded her, wondering what she was trying to say. Marina moved her face closer to his before he could ask and gave him a quick, delicate kiss on the lips as the man started to groan in anguish once more. His lips were also injured, and even a light touch caused excruciating anguish. Very away, the girl started to apologize, saying, "I'm really, truly sorry!"

"It's fine. For you, I would put up with the worst suffering imaginable." As he started to stroke her curly hair, he remarked.

They spent the night sleeping in his bed. Mr. Santarelli was so worn out from everything that he dozed off right away. On the other side, Marina was incredibly worried. She started to worry about the captain's health and that someone would ultimately find out that she and the captain are having an illicit relationship. The girl forced herself to doze off by resting her head on the man's chest. She could never close her eyes without seeing the man she loved getting a vicious kick. She started to feel horrible about it because the sight of seeing him hurt was truly horrible. Mr. Santarelli nearly passing away caused Marina to start blaming herself for it. He wouldn't have been hurt if she hadn't asked him to go for a walk. Her eyes began to tear up as she sobbed quietly and felt angry with herself for repeatedly destroying people's lives as a result of her actions

Chapter XVIII

January 30th, 1911

"Good morning, dearest." The captain murmured in a
raspy tired voice. He kept looking at the young lady's
face. She hadn't slept much at all during the night due to
her excessive pondering, therefore she was still asleep.
He softly grinned at her and started to touch her soft face.
"I don't want you to sleep all day."

"Stop," Marina muttered, "I don't have to work today; it's
Sunday. Let me rest for a change." Mr. Santarelli said
with a smile as he rolled his eyes at her "I wished to
spend time with you today since I don't have any work
either." She muttered, scrunching her nose, "You're so
annoying." he leaned in and started to kiss her face. She
eventually caved and allowed him to show her all of his
affection. He kissed Marina's cheeks, chin, neck,
collarbone, chest... as she embraced him. She kept
laughing and grinning broadly at him, "I'm so enamored
by you." The captain cried out. The young lady closed
her eyes and enjoyed the present. She gave it some
thought and started thinking about how she should tell
him that she loves him too. Just when she was going to
tell him the truth, "I lo—" Francesca barged into the
captain's cabin.

"What's going on here—what is the meaning of this!?"

"Fran! How dare you enter my cabin without knocking!"
The man exclaimed as he drew nearer to Marina and
made an effort to cover her with his body and arms so
that she wouldn't appear unladylike at the moment.
While her heart was pounding out of control and she was
scared of Francesca, Marina bit her lower lip as she
clung to the sheets that she kept tugging up. "I came to
give you a brunch call. And because Marina didn't enter
the cabin the previous night, I was looking for her. Now
I can see that she has undergone prostitution."

"What!?" The girl's eyes expanded as she exclaimed.
"Gabriel I genuinely believed you were capable of more.
This is merely appalling to see. using your maid
unfairly." The captain gave her a bewildered look and
said, "I— I would never! This is absurd! I'm free to love
anyone I choose." In that instant, he strongly gripped
Marina's hand. Several crew members arrived right away
to investigate the commotion. D'Angelo covered his face
with his hand, "Oh Goodness!" he shouted. When she
watched everyone shame her for being a prostitute and
having an illicit relationship with the captain, Marina
was on the edge of sobbing. An older sailor puffed on his
pipe and chastised the young Neapolitan girl, "We did
tell that a lady should never be on the ship, but that man
never listens." A man in the crowd exclaimed "Was she
not married? Oh, how poor her spouse is." The captain

cast a glance at Marina, who was very still. She persisted in trembling while pressing the sheets against her body. He breathed deeply and stepped up, still holding her hand. "She never exploited me, and neither did I ever exploit her. You morons are wrong to even think Marina is a prostitute. Shame on you all; I could fire you all for how you treated her." He gave everyone a terrifyingly icy look as he peered around. "Then clarify for us why you are so battered?" An older sailor yelled.

"We were mugged together last night, and I'm bruised because I didn't want Marina to get harmed." He was yelled at by Francesca, "Excuse me!? You were put in jeopardy by the pinchcock! You might have died!"

"And I didn't, end of story."

"What if Venus's Curse strikes you? All thanks to her."

"Are you being serious? I'm free of any diseases!"Marina gasped, her breathing becoming labored. She grew increasingly angry at that moment for being accused of such a thing.

"I can't believe I have to say this, to start with. Marina isn't a prostitute and never was. Second of all, she won't make me sick; she isn't a random street pick that I choose for her body and self-pleasure. You are the ill one for even contemplating such a thing!" He sat down on his bed as the red-haired girl gazed her face in his direction "She doesn't love you, Gabriel. Don't you see she's merely exploiting you for money and pleasure?"

"I do care for him. I'd give my life for him. I'm tired of you harassing me all the time. I no longer need to subject you to harassment since I have had enough." The girl clenched her hand. "I might occasionally act foolish, ignorant, and impolite. But whether you like it or not, I truly and completely adore him. And nothing will alter that." Marina laid her head on his back and placed her hands on his shoulders. Francesca's eyes narrowed as she grew irritated. "Did you do that, Francesca? Did you harass her?" Giordana questioned her incredulously, unable to accept that her niece was capable of such behavior. She paused before continuing, "I didn't—I was simply warning her not to do anything foolish!"

Antoni chose to intervene. "Indeed, you have. You regularly criticize her to me, and a few times I caught you lurking on her. Do not assume that nobody can see you."Giordana and Margherita both shouted "Francesca!" as they scowled at her, saying, "How dare you do that!? What excessively rude behavior from you."

Antoni grabbed the cabin doors' doorknob and started slowly closing them as Margherita and Giordana continued shouting at Francesca. He nodded to Marina and Mr. Santarelli while grinning and letting them know that he would leave them alone. "I'm extremely sorry, this is all my fault." the man said as he grasped both of her hands.

"It isn't. In any case, people would have found out and reacted poorly. At least we are no longer required to hide.

"I suppose so. Nonetheless, I continue to worry about your reputation because I don't want to see you treated badly. Marina moaned "Gabriel, this can't get any worse than my reputation in Naples. You should not worry; I'll be alright." She gave him a sweet smile and looked into his deep eyes. Mr. Santarelli prevented her from kissing him when she tried to kiss him on the cheek and pulled her away. "Why didn't you ever tell me that Francesca had harassed you?" He questioned. "It's difficult to tell someone such a thing." she said, turning her head away from him. "And I believed that it would just make everything much worse." He sighed "I just wish I could have stopped it from occurring again."

"It's fine Gabriel. I can look after myself.

"Oh, I am sure you can." He said with a chuckle "I am certain about it. Just that it merely irritates me that you were harassed without my knowledge." She held his arm and just said, "I love you," while giving his hand a gentle kiss and placing it on her cheek. His mouth curved into a smile "I love you as well." His eyes immediately began to well up with tears, and his cheeks started to flush. Marina laughed, "Goodness, are you crying?".

"I suppose I'm just experiencing a tremendous amount of joy right now." She gave him an incredulous look and started wiping the tears from his cheeks, which he gratefully accepted.

February 10th , 1911

Along with the elderly women, Miss Marina was making breakfast in the kitchen. She hasn't talked to the red-haired girl in days, and she won't even look at her. The young lady was delighted about it because she no longer had any desire to interact with her in any way. Marina approached Margherita, who was looking through a cookbook in an effort to find a fresh recipe for once. "Is that my father's book!?" Marina exclaimed as she got a closer look at the book. Her eyes grew wider. The elderly woman turned the page and read the author's name. "Does Adriano Rivalli happen to be your father?"

LV Polcic

She inquired.

"Yes!" Marina exclaimed. She couldn't believe it at all. Marina couldn't elude her parents, not even aboard a ship. They seemed to follow her everywhere. Margherita started to laugh "Given that I like his cooking, that is a strange coincidence. He offers some excellent cooking advice as well. Even the idea of visiting his restaurant when I can, crossed my mind." The girl was very perplexed by all of that and didn't know what to say. The idea that someone she knew may hold a book that her father personally wrote disturbed her. She grabbed the cookbook from Margherita and looked through it to see what is it like. She examined the pages before stopping at one. Her father had written a recipe for pasta alla Genovese, and what she read moved her to tears.

"*This dish is devoted especially to my daughter and son, for whom this is the preferred meal.*" The girl's eyes welled up with tears because she couldn't believe her father had written that. While Marina wailed on Margherita's soft chest, the elderly woman tightly gripped her. "I cannot believe my father adores me." She cried. Margherita continued to pat her on the head while laughing as she sobbed. Mr. Santarelli entered the kitchen as soon as he completed estimating the time of arrival and looking through documents to determine how much money had been lost and gained. He rushed up to the lady when he spotted her in distress and inquired "What's the matter? What happened?"

Sniffing, Marina said "Nothing happened. Simply put, I'm a little homesick right now." "Oh." the man exclaimed. He noticed the tears on her face "Would you be interested in walking with me later? That might improve your mood." Margherita remained to stare at them, finding it hard to picture the captain pursuing the girl. "Thank you, Gabriel, it would." As he assisted her to tuck her lank hair behind her ears, he grinned at her. "Avoid crying. Seeing you in such distress hurts." He gently wiped a tear away from the young lady's face with a napkin he kept in his pocket as she grinned at him.

"Are you aware that I and other people are still in the same room as you, my two children?" Margherita asked, crossing her arms. "Gabriel, even though everyone knows you're courting her, there are still some things you should keep private." As soon as they realized that others were staring at them, the captain and the maid to that apologized. "We presumably were just caught up in the moment." Marina mused.

Around seven o'clock that evening, Marina and Mr. Santarelli went for a stroll through Portofino. They talked about one other's lives as they strolled through the

town, taking in its unique beauty as they did so.
"Goodness, this is honestly one of the prettiest towns I've
ever seen," Marina said, continuing to glance around and
gasp. Mr. Santarelli had been to Portofino many times
previously, so he continued to remark on Miss Marina's
elegance instead and to smile softly at her. "Yes, it is
quite nice. I just couldn't see me ever relocating to such
rural areas." Marina furthered that "Really? I prefer
smaller towns to large, hectic cities that are clogged with
carriages and brand-new vehicles. Also, the stench of
industries is unpleasant to smell. It ruins the atmosphere
completely."

"For a larger city, Rome is fairly pleasant. A very little
bit, I miss living there. Since I didn't always have the
luxury of a calm environment at home where I could
focus, I knew to go to the Colosseum every day after
school and finish my schoolwork there. To see Rome
and witness the Roman ruins once more, I would do
anything." The man remembered his hometown and
sighed. It was one of the few occasions in his life when
he had tranquillity, thus the remembrance touched him.
"Maybe you could take me to Rome for a day and show
me how gorgeous it truly is."

"It would be my pleasure." She was given a hand kiss by
Mr. Santarelli. Sadly, their joy was fleeting since trouble
returned. "Marina Rivalli!" A Man shouted. The captain
was baffled and questioned whether Marina knew

Judged For Mercy

anyone in Portofino. Particularly considering that she had never been in it before. It turned out to be Mr. Andrea Biscontini, the bartender she had first met months earlier. By catching a glimpse of him, Marina pursed her lips. She couldn't put her finger on why she felt uncomfortable around him, but it was for some odd reason. "Mr. Biscontini, ah. I didn't expect to run across you in this charming little town."

"Well, I also hadn't anticipated it. However, it's fantastic to see you. You continue to be as stunning as when I last saw you." Mr. Santarelli's hand tightened into a fist. He had never liked the bartender and couldn't bear to face him for another second or minute. "So, how are you doing?" Mr. Biscontini asked. Before responding, Marina paused and said, "I've been fine, I suppose. I'm assuming that you are doing well.

"Oh yes, I have. But, it would have been preferable if I had heard from you again.

"Oh? I'm sorry, but I honestly can't say that I remember you all that well." The man became angry at that point when he realized the girl had no interest in him and barely remembered him at all. And he became enraged at the sight of the captain standing near to her. "What do you mean? I believed we had a unique situation. I mean, for heaven's sake, we kissed!" At that moment Marina went completely pale. Her breathing got more labored as everything began to whirl. "What?" Because she was still in disbelief after what he had said, she questioned in a monotone voice, "Y—you kissed me?"

"Yes? Do you not remember?"

"No!?" The girl shouted. "Oh my goodness, you got me drunk!" Everything from the memories of her birthday began to return to her as she covered her lips with her palm. The man taking advantage of her made her feel abhorrently repulsed. The captain was furious upon seeing what was taking place and wished to break the bartender's all 206 bones. Since she didn't want any disturbance in the middle of the street, Marina stopped him before he could do anything. "Gabriel, this is not your business. Don't take any action." He stepped back in frustration while looking at the young lady and Mr. Biscontini arguing. "I did not make you intoxicated! You desired a beverage! And confess it—I know you do— that you like me as well. I observed your gaze on me that evening."

"Looked at you!?" Marina gasped, "I was so intoxicated that I could hardly look! You are so unfamiliar to me that I hardly even find you interesting." She started ranting and the bartender started to feel embarrassed. He pursed his lips as he continued to look at her and the captain, who was stinging his eye.

In that instant, Mr. Biscontini turned to face Marina. "Is it because of him? The young lady asked with confusion, "What?" She inquired. "Do you now suddenly not love me because of this, peasant?" The captain glared at him angrily and exclaimed, "Peasant!" He was incensed by Mr. Biscontini's comments and was unable to endure listening to him any longer. As well, he could feel that Marina was losing her patience with him. She was growing weary of fighting with him and also terrified of being taken advantage of once more. Because she had allowed herself to be in this predicament, she felt disgusted with herself. The young lady was ill to her stomach every time she caught sight of the bartender because of what he had done to her.

"Marina, I've been thinking of you for a very long time. I have yearned to see you once more, and now that I have, I must claim you as mine." The young lady's eyes widened in perplexity. She stepped back and began to believe that he had entirely lost his mind. "Pardon me? Make me yours?" She questioned as she started to tightly grasp a gown fold. "You're ideal! You're the perfect wife a man could ask for! I can just about picture the two of us living contentedly. I would go about my business as usual, and you would be content at home with our six

LV Polcic

children and perhaps a dog for company. We would all
eat dinner together when I got home. Just perfect."

"But I don't wish to stay at home all day... I'm terrified
just thinking about it." She felt shivers down her spine.

"Oh, stop being absurd! What woman's life isn't made
happy by the notion of caring for her spouse and
children?"

Mr. Biscontini knelt and grabbed Marina's hand firmly
as she bit her lower lip. "Do me a favor and marry me.
Be with me!" Mr. Santarelli continued to glance at the
bartender while gazing at the young lady who was
remaining mute. The idea that Marina would leave him
for Mr. Biscontini so swiftly made his face burn and
growing chest pain appeared after thinking Particularly
at how much more in life Mr. Biscontini can provide her
than he ever could. He honestly wouldn't be astonished if
the young lady left him as a result of that. The captain
averted his eyes while pursing his lips.

"No!" she finally said, "You're insane. I won't essentially
serve as your housekeeper! What makes you think that I
would want such a life?"

"You're a woman! What more do you require?"

"To live?To be able to decide for myself what I want in life! You have no right to even consider that I could want to spend time with you. I hardly ever even consider you! You disgust me!" She clenched her fist and shouted at him so fiercely that her voice became hoarse and her throat started to sting.

"Do you not feel anything towards me!?" He questioned.

"I feel sorry for you."

Marina clenched her jaw as Mr. Biscontini began to come closer to her and glared at her with frustration in his eyes. The captain moved to assist the young lady because he could no longer stand by and say nothing. "If I ever see you near her again, I'll hit you so fiercely that you won't be able to stand up." He turned to stare at the bartender, his eyes frigid. So icy that everyone who caught his eye would shudder from fear of him. They went from being dark brown to completely black at that moment. Marina had never seen him so furious before and she found it fascinating. She remained behind him the entire time as he continued to argue with Mr. Biscontini.

"Is that a threat?"

"If you wish to play with your life, it will be a promise."

"It's nothing but amusing to see such a worthless person pretending to be so stern and authoritative while being nothing compared with what you deserve Marina." said the bartender. "Seeing you with him makes me laugh and cry at the same time" When Mr. Santarelli was told that he wasn't worthy enough for the young lady, he glared aside in annoyance and sighed as he began to feel insecure. He pursed his lips and stopped clenching his fist. Marina screamed as the aggressive bartender grabbed her wrist and pulled her in at that precise moment.

"Go away from me!" She urged. He started to say, "Stop screaming—" but the captain punched him in the face with his knuckles before he could finish. "What's wrong with you!?" He shouted. Mr. Santarelli began shaking his hand after hitting him so hard that his knuckles were excruciatingly painful. The bartender was on the edge of tears as blood started to stream from his nose and he carefully grasped it. "I warned you to stay away from her, but you chose not to heed my advice. Dare to underestimate me once more. You won't open your eyes next time." The captain took a long, sharp breath before adjusting his hair. As she approached the bartender, Miss Rivalli bit her lower lip. "Are you alright?" She cast him a worried glance. The captain stared at Marina with his eyes wide open, unable to believe that she had gone to see if the man had been seriously hurt.

"I'm decent. Just that my nose—" He received a crotch kick after she raised her knee and kicked him fiercely with all of her force. Mr. Biscontini collapsed to the ground and felt like throwing up. "Considering what you have done to me, be thankful that I did not handle you much worse." Marina kicking the man caused Mr. Santarelli to burst out laughing and grinning broadly. In that instant, he was irrationally ecstatic about her.

"Whore!" Mr. Biscontini shouted, clutching at his stomach while the captain's hit had left his mouth to be fully covered by the blood. "Tell me something I haven't heard before." She responded to him without giving him a second glance. She was genuinely pleased that she would never go back to Portofino so she didn't have to see his face again.

Mr. Biscontini continued to writhe in agony as they left, grumbling to himself about how much he detested the girl. Marina continued to move quickly the entire time, her head spinning with thoughts. She didn't move her head for the entire two minutes. Because of all that had happened in her life, the girl remained clinging as firmly as she could to the captain's hand. As Mr. Santarelli caught a glimpse of her and noticed how afraid she appeared, he put his arms on her shoulders and commanded her to stop moving. "Please let me know if you don't feel well." While lowering her gaze, Marina pursed her lips. She averted her eyes from him and cocked her head to the left. "Speak with me." He asked. A single tear then fell from Marina's cheek as she clenched her fist "I'm mad." She exhaled sharply and deeply, "I hate him! He got me intoxicated! Then had the gall to approach me, make a proposal, and grab me forcefully." In that instant, the young lady started to shiver from her sense of overwhelm. Her recollections of Matias raping her on their wedding day were brought back by the bartender's actions. "I wish him nothing but the absolute worst!! May his life be a living hell from this day on!"

"Alright... The deaths, in my opinion, should be calmed down from you." The captain watched as her countenance darkened and he grinned awkwardly. "I understand that you're upset right now, and I'm just as irritated as you are. So you ought to just try to forget about him. When your mind is so tainted with bad beliefs, your life will only get worse."

"But Gabriel—"

"No. Let me speak if you will. I desire that you be well and happy. It aches to see you in this condition." Then, as he pulled her hands closer to his face and gave them a tender kiss he said, "Please..." Marina then started crying and gave the captain a tight embrace. "I detest him so much." she wailed, sobbing hysterically on his chest. "I detest him! I no longer feel secure." He gave her a hug and laid his head on hers "It's alright, I am all yours. Nobody will ever again harm you." Marina kept gripping him even tighter and digging her nails into his skin as she sobbed on his chest. "Thank you." Her voice became brittle, and she murmured. "I want to go home."

"Ah well. If you would like, I can always depart for Naples."

"I intended... to go to your cabin." Marina considered the captain's cabin as her home since she felt the safest and most content there. Especially by the fact that Mr. Santarelli always warmed her heart and she wouldn't want to be anywhere but in his presence only. When Mr. Santarelli understood what she was saying, he let out an "Oh." He was somewhat relieved to hear her say that because he didn't want her to leave. He would be too heartbroken by it. "I'm glad to hear that. If you left me so quickly, I would be lonely." He caught Marina's chuckle. "I wouldn't abandon you!"

"Never?" He inquired.

"Never at all."

Chapter XIX

The sun's rays softly landed on Mr. Santarelli's face as he slept. Silently announcing to him that the morning already arrived. The man moaned out of annoyance since his deep sleep was disturbed by this. While opening his dark-brown eyes, he looked at Marina who was sound asleep. He continued to admire her beauty as he gripped her firmly around the torso. On his bed, Marina's hair was fully loose and dispersed. Her lovely, crimson lips caught his sight while her nightgown started to sag off her shoulder. Even a few hairs of her curly hair barely covered her exhausted face. The captain considered her sight a blessing for his eyes. He mused to himself that he was the luckiest man alive at this very moment as if Venus were in his bed. He then attempted to rest again while placing his head on her stomach. "I feel at peace when with you." She received a tender chest kiss from him as he said, "You gave my life meaning. God, I loathe you for being so captivating even while you're asleep." Marina muttered, "Very thoughtful of you to say this early in the morning."

"Oh, good to see you awake."

"Your devotion has awoken me." She replied as she yawned and spread her arms wide. "Did you sleep well?" he asked, grinning at her. The girl raised an eyebrow and

stared at him. "It was fine up until you started snoring."
The man gasped as he continued to claim that he never
snores. On the other hand, Marina was aware of what she
would hear from him in the wee hours. Extreme loud
snoring. The girl continued to yawn while resting her
head on his shoulder. Every time she attempted to fix her
nightgown, it slipped off her shoulder and nearly
exposed her breast. "Should I go make coffee for us
two?" the captain questioned. "It's alright, I can make it
since my shift starts soon." Marina retorted. He took a
glance at the time. "Is it seven o'clock already? It's
unfortunate. I wished we had more time to discuss."

"Talk to me right now while there is still time. You can
also assist me in getting ready. For instance, since it
takes a lot of time for me to fix my hair alone, you might
assist me."

"Yes, but remember that I do not know how to do
hairstyles for women because my hair isn't as beautiful
as yours is." Marina chuckled at him "It's only a bun, it's
not science." He sat down on a wooden chair behind her
and continued to think of ways to assist her with her long,
curly hair while she crossed her knees and handed him
her hairpin. He persisted in twisting her hair while he
looked at it. "Why is this so difficult? I can write the
coordinates of where my ship is by myself, but I cannot
do your hair." She rolled her eyes "Because there's no
need to give it any thought. Simply twist it, roll it up,

and pin it to hold it in place." Mr. Santarelli, who had just succeeded in giving her a bun, was incredibly proud of himself when she stated that. More impressed than any mathematical puzzle he could crack. "See, I knew you could do it," Marina exclaimed as she turned to face him. "I could potentially employ you as my hairstylist permanently."

"No, please do not. This was already torturous. especially in light of how outrageously long your hair is."

After turning around, the young lady grabbed him by the chin. She gave him a heartfelt kiss on the lips and stated, "You did a terrific job." He smiled softly and put his hand behind her ear. "Gabriel!" Their moment of appreciation was cut short due to D'Angelo shouting as he hurried into the cabin without knocking on the doors. "The doors, Antoni! The doors! I urged you to knock."

"Then lock that darn thing!" He took a deep breath and yelled at him in anger. "What is it? Has something occurred?" asked Mr. Santarelli, gazing at Antoni, who was wearing a worried look. "The mast broke. It was likely torn down by the wind. I tried everything to fix it this morning, but I'm at a loss on what to do." In a panic, the captain leaped to his feet and circled his cabin looking for a solution. The tension of being unsure of what to do caused his heart to start beating more quickly. He felt as if his heart was going to jump out of his chest.

They can't sail without a mast, and he will lose money. While watching him become uneasy, Marina bit her bottom lip. She was upset to see him under such pressure and wanted to assist him. The young lady got up and asked Antoni, "Exactly where are we?"

"Liso di Ostia isn't that far distant from us. possibly an hour away." Answered Antoni. "Alright... They have a harbor large enough for larger ships, judging by a trip I've taken there a couple of years ago. You should make a complete 180-degree turn and head in that direction."

"Wait, what? What direction?" Mr. Santarelli enquired in confusion. "What are you referring to?" Stress caused him to cross his arms and start biting the skin off of his fingernails. "Well, Liso di Ostia isn't that far away from the position of our ship," Marina said, turning her head away and cracking her knuckles. "even though we lack a mast, we could still sail to that port and have the ship fixed there. Additionally, it's close to Rome, so if no one in the town is available to fix the mast, we may hire

someone from Rome to come. Probably, you've got
something better in mind."

He carefully followed whatever she said. He couldn't
believe she had come up with such a brilliant idea. She
handled everything with such poise and composure. "I
must hear what you have to say, though. You are in
charge." As he nervously awaited the order, Antoni
questioned what he should do. Mr. Santarelli turned to
face D'Angelo before returning his gaze to the young
lady. "Set the course of the ship for Liso di Ostia."
Marina gazed up at the captain with widening eyes. She
was flattered that he admired her approach to the
problem. "How extensive is the harm, though?" asked
the captain, who was a little wary about what he was
about to see. The captain and the maid were invited to
come to witness the damage for themselves as Antoni
sighed. Marina quickly covered herself in Mr.
Santarelli's dark blue coat so she wouldn't appear
indecent and hurried outside to take a look at the issue.
She and Mr. Santarelli both became pale as their eyes
dilated at the devastation. He hid his face in his hands
and stifled a dejected groan. "It's going to be dreadful to
fix this."

Mr. Santarelli was becoming overly anxious due to the
circumstance. Margherita, an elderly woman, came up to
him at that same moment and put her hand on his
shoulder, asking, "How can you resolve this? The mast

broke down, how in the world did you ever manage that?" She inquired, perplexed by the circumstance. "I did not damage it. The mast snapped even before my shift. And I'll look for someone to repair it. I'll spend a fortune on it, God." The man started to sigh at the idea of giving up so much money in order to fix the ship.

As soon as they had anchored in the town the captain hurried to Marina, who was assisting in cleaning up the mess on the deck, and asked, "Will you please accompany me by going out for a walk to help me calm down?" She gasped and asked, "Now?" Work needs to be done. Such a mess was produced by the mast."

"Marina, I'm about to use the gun to shoot myself in the head from how frustrated I am at this very moment. Either accompany me or go later and aid Antoni in planning my funeral." As she walked alongside him in the town by the sea, she swallowed her spit as she stared at him bewildered. "The mast has taken a toll on you." When she chuckled at him, Mr. Santarelli gave her a glance and said, "Laugh all you want Marina, but you won't when you'll have to eat nothing but cabbage for breakfast, lunch, and dinner every day."

The young lady's eye twitched as she realized how pricey replacing the mast would be. As a means of calming himself down, she witnessed him clenching his fist or snapping his fingers. "It's going to be okay." she said as she glanced up at him and softly held his hand. "I'll assist you, however I can." The feeling of her gentle hand instantly made the captain feel calmer, and he grinned at her as he did so, asking, "What would I do without you?" He queried.

"Probably keep worrying?" She chuckled.

"I detest how draining this entire situation will be." the man said as he slumped down on a bench and covered his face with his hands. "To be with you after my lengthy shift was over was all I wanted." He continued to pout as Marina took a seat next to him. "I understand," she said as she put her hands on his shoulders. "however, you should put us to the side right now and concentrate on your work."

"My work But!—"

"Look, I understand that you have trouble managing stress and that this is difficult. We may take the train to Rome since we're not far away from it, explore the city for a day, and then return here if you want to take a break." As she said that, Mr. Santarelli continued to think to himself. Considering whether or not taking a day

off will be worthwhile, especially if going to Rome. He
put his hands down and turned to face the girl, saying,
"I'd love that, but what would others think? Furthermore,
we'll probably miss the train."

"Then let's go!" Marina exclaimed as she seized his hand
and dragged him to stand up. To catch a train to Rome,
they both started running to the closest train station.
Even though Marina could hardly move in her shoes, the
captain was able to catch her each time she nearly fell.
She even grabbed a fold of her dress and pulled it up so
she wouldn't trip and fall while running. People gave
them strange looks when they saw two idling strangers
laughing madly and sprinting around the small town.

They both started shouting at the conductor as soon as
they arrived at the railway station, "Wait! Wait for us!"
They ran out of breath, halted, and started to pant. "Is
there a train heading to Rome today?" the young lady
asked the conductor after taking a big breath.

"Yes, it will depart in five minutes. You folks better
move quickly." Answered the conductor.

"What!? five minutes!?" She yelled loudly. She and Mr. Santarelli hurried as quickly as they could to the ticket counter to purchase two tickets to Rome. "Hello, how may I help you?" When the booking clerk saw them, she was astonished because the captain and the young lady both appeared to be a mess. "Yes, Hello. We would like to buy two tickets for the train leaving now for Rome." questioned Mr. Santarelli as he was withdrawing cash to pay for the tickets. The reservationist wrinkled her brow and inquired, "The train departs in four minutes. Next time, you should make a better travel plan."

"And the next time, you ought to mind your own business." Marina yelled as she repeatedly tapped her finger on the counter to get the tickets. The woman rolled her eyes and handed them their tickets, but as the young lady and the captain hurried to their train, she snatched them from her hands. They sprinted inside the train, with no luggage or anything. Just them and their two tickets. They started laughing as soon as they sat down because they were so incredibly joyful. "The next time, you ought to mind your own business. Jesus, you're so stern and aggressive." Mr. Santarelli said, turning to face Marina. "Yes, she won't dictate how I should organize my travels. I'll handle the rest; just let her give me my ticket."The stress he was feeling over the mast was forgotten as he continued to laugh at her.

He firmly gripped Marina's hand as she put her head on his shoulder and expressed her disbelief that she was with him alone on the way to Rome. She was so ecstatic to see him truly smiling that she couldn't take her eyes off him. "I'm eager for us to visit the city. I'll show you around all of my favorite locations." Mr. Santarelli said, gazing at his watch. "I even know a fantastic restaurant there."

"Oh, right. Similar to the fantastic restaurant you took me to, where there were many options without meat?" The young lady smirked at him. "Hey! It wasn't my fault, so that's unfair! I was unaware that the menu had been altered." Mr. Santarelli started to defend himself as Marina continued to glare at him with her arms crossed. Later, she put her hand on his chest and inquired about his emotions. "Do you feel less stressed right now?" The captain's lips were pursed. "I do a little... It is pleasant to be moving along on land. A year has passed since I last rode a train. A man forgets what it's like to ride in a vehicle that isn't battered by waves all the time." He let out a contented sigh and peered out the window at the towns and forests they were driving by. It was a peaceful moment that he and the girl were having. They sat there together utterly in silence, just appreciating each other's presence for a whole hour and a half while resting on each other.

"Marina, get up." As he gently shook the girl, Mr. Santarelli spoke softly to her. Due to how peaceful the entire travel had been, Marina dozed off on the way to their destination. "We're here already?" prompted Marina. He took a strand of her loose hair and tucked it behind her ear while nodding. The young lady yawned as she stood up and stretched out her arms "I cannot believe I'm saying this but I've gotten so low when it comes to life, that sleeping here on the train was the best sleep I've had in months." She put her hands on her hips as she felt ashamed of how low-class she had become. "Welcome to life as a peasant. We had been eager to meet you." As he stood up and giggled at himself, Mr. Santarelli replied sarcastically, his bones aching from sitting in the same posture for so long. The young lady had trouble believing she was in Rome as they made their way outdoors.

As carriages continued to pass extremely close to her, some even nearly collided with her since she was so preoccupied with looking everywhere. She kept being amazed by all the sights her eye could see. Even though Mr. Santarelli had already seen the entire city thousands of times, she would point out anything new that she had noticed. The man remarked as he walked around the streets, "Truly *nothing* had changed after all these years."

"It's a wonderful city. Being in such a massive city, as opposed to Naples, which isn't so big, feels strange." As she continued to gasp at the Roman ruins, the young lady exclaimed. With her eyes wide open, she fiercely grasped the captain's hand and started to go quickly in the direction of the Colosseum. "Look! Isn't it lovely? I could just stare at that all day."

"We don't have much time to spend here." He said while placing his hand on her waist.

"We still have a few hours until we must return to the ship." Marina sighed in response. She had only a few hours to spend in one of Europe's most stunning cities when she finally arrived there. She repeatedly begged to stay for a few more days, but he declined, saying, "I have a job to do, I'm not on vacation."

"Alright, fine. Let's move on from the pointless ship and go visit some other things. I'm attempting to flee from it rather than endure its constant taunts." When Marina murmured, Mr. Santarelli laughed and covered his mouth with his fist. On that particular day, several men gave the young lady many admiring glances. And who wouldn't glance at her? She wore a white dress, gloves, and a large hat that was wrapped in a blue bow around her neck. She looked stunning that day. When one of the men passed by and gave her an inappropriately lengthy look, the captain tightened his hold on her hand. "You're going to rip my hand off." Marina laughed as she offered him a sly smirk about his jealousy. His lips were tightened and eyes narrowed as he felt bitter over so many men in Rome gazing at her. He felt ashamed of this emotion but his feelings were too strong and made him feel anxious. Particularly considering that one man had the nerve to even whistle at her! When Marina responded, she turned around and whistled back at him, confusing him by doing so. Her manners occasionally left Mr. Santarelli speechless and unable to believe her. "Where in the world did you learn how to whistle with your fingers?" He inquired. "My father taught me many tricks. When I went to a horse race, it was useful. made the anticipation of winning better." She was addressed by the captain, who grinned and rolled his eyes at her. "I'm intrigued by you more and more as I discover more about you."

After spending a few hours doing nothing but roaming around the city and admiring the architecture and numerous historical landmarks that never ceased to amaze the captain, they sat down by the fountain in Piazza Navona to unwind for a while. Even if Marina wasn't particularly interested in history or even know about it, she was more than willing to listen to him talk and he seized every opportunity to provide a historical fascinating tidbit about a certain monument whenever they passed by it. Not even monuments, but streets as well! "We should go see the gardens at Villa Borghese later. I think you'd enjoy seeing it and how it first started as a little vineyard. It's lovely and soothing." The captain offered earlier Marina a daisy as they walked, and Marina nodded as she picked out its petals while quietly grinning, looking down, and fiddling with her legs.

"Ah, I appreciate you persuading me to come here. I didn't realize I needed this quick trip until I arrived." The captain spoke to the young lady while gazing up at the sky and closing his eyes. While he did so, Marina turned her head to the side when she heard a man and a woman speaking loudly to each other. She observed that a mother and her sons were being photographed by a street photographer. She grabbed Mr. Santarelli's sleeve "Look!" She shouted while pointing at the elderly man who was taking pictures of anyone who requested one. "A street photographer?" The captain looked at Marina and questioned. "Yes! There ought to be a picture of the two of us! to preserve a physical form of our time spent in Rome! It would be lovely!"

"I'm not sure. I've never been one for taking pictures. I'm not the best at posing, unfortunately." He clarified. "It's simple." Marina chuckled. "I enjoy being captured in pictures." She jokingly struck a position to demonstrate her photogenic qualities as she stated. He rolled his eyes at her and laughed as he agreed to her suggestion. He was pulled over to the photographer by Marina, who

graciously allowed them to snap a shot of the two of
them. Marina and Mr. Santarelli were attempting to
strike the ideal position as the photographer adjusted his
camera and ducked under the camera's black covering.
With the exception of the captain, who was repositioning
himself and moaning at every second, the young lady
was immediately happy with her choice of position. "Just
stand where you feel most comfortable... like me!" Mr.
Santarelli said, "I'm trying." while she continued to smile
at the camera. "However, nothing is correct." She looked
in his direction to see how he was standing and gave him
a bewildered look on her face. The photographer yelled
"Smile!" to them two as she looked at the man. In her
haste, Marina turned her head in the direction of the
camera, but she was unprepared for the flash, which
caused her to look bewildered.

She became irritated with herself for making a weird
look, and she realized that this was the only chance for
them to take a photo together. The captain put his hand
on Marina's shoulder and told her the picture will turn
out alright as Marina hid her face in misery. The girl's
mouth and eyes were wide open after they got their
picture. For the first time, she was appalled by how
awful she appeared in a photo. "Why do I appear that
way when you appear so composed and well-posed?"
The image made Mr. Santarelli laugh uncontrollably,
and he had to sit down on a seat to collect his breath.
"You look hilarious and completely bewildered!
Hahahah!"

"Stop laughing, now! I appear absurd! It is distressing!"

"Hahahaha!" He continued laughing at the picture. The captain retained the photo in his hand and held it above his head, preventing Marina from reaching it when she wanted to toss it in the garbage right away. He was starting to aggravate her, and she became so angry with him that she crossed her arms and said, "You're cruel!" She pointed at him, scrunching her nose, and having a sour facial expression. "Calm down, you look radiant no matter what." Mr. Santarelli said as he drew her in closer to him and kissed her close to her eye. "I adore the picture. It has greater charm because it's humorous." To ensure that the photo will always be with him, he carefully folded it and placed it inside his wallet. After hearing what he said, Marina's lip curved into a smile, and bit her bottom lip.

Later, Mr. Santarelli took her to the Trevi Fountain where they had freshly baked chocolate croissants that they had purchased from a local bakery. The young lady couldn't finish hers since she was full and the captain went to take hers since he could always eat. Marina immediately snatched her croissant from his hand because she wanted to feed the pigeons with it. He glared at her for not letting him eat the croissant. Marina continued looking at the water while leaning on the wall.

While the captain was tying his necktie, she gently extended her hand and went through the fountain's water while humming. He sat down next to the girl on a seat and listened to the fountain and her humming. Hearing the sound of cascading water was quite calming that he ultimately forgot about all worries he had collected in his head. "Did you know the word Trevi means three roads?" he let out a breath. "Because the fountain was built at the crossroads of three of Rome's main thoroughfares, it was given that name." In response, Marina gave a nod and said, "Interesting. Do you perhaps recognize the figures on the fountain?"

"In the center, it's God Oceanus and he's being pulled by his two sea horses who represent two different moods of the sea. One is docile and the other one is insane like you" the captain said, placing his palm on his chin and cackling. While he was speaking, she spun around and sprayed him in the face with the small amount of water she had in her hand. The man laughed at her while squinting his eyes. "I'll miss Rome." the young lady sighed as she laid her head on his shoulder. "I hope I could settle down here and open a bakery close to this fountain."

"Throw a coin in the fountain and your wish might come true." he said as he softly smiled at her.

She gasped as Mr. Santarelli gave her a gold coin. The young lady took it right away. Before tossing the coin into the fountain, she kissed it and pondered her desire. She maintained her smile while putting her palms together next to her lips. Then it dawned on Marina that Gabriel was from Rome and probably had family in the area who he would love to meet. "Gabriel, don't your parents reside in Rome?" She questioned.

"Why do you ask, exactly?"

"Don't you want to see them, though? After all, they are your parents." She said and Mr. Santarelli got to his feet. "Uhm... no. I don't remember my father ever treating me well, and I can't think of anything I might say to be complimentary of him." Marina continued to persuade him "Gabriel, come on, he's your father." She said as she stared at him bewildered. "He must be sorry since he must have missed you when you ran away from home years ago! Every parent adores their child."

"Marina, you've never met my parents. So please refrain."At that very moment, Marina interrupted him and shouted, "Well yes, I haven't met them! I would love to eventually meet your parents or perhaps grandparents! They are members of your family, and families always need to forgive one another." She said that which made

Mr. Santarelli felt his chest getting heavy. He believed she was correct that he should forget his father's abuse of him, which left him permanently scarred. After six years of not seeing his parents, he made the decision to go see them since he felt horrible for never having written to them.

It was already five in the afternoon when Marina and the captain had walked to his parent's mansion. The young lady initially believed they were in the wrong place because it didn't make sense to her that Mr. Santarelli's parents would have owned a mansion. However, it was his childhood home. She opened the mansion's gates and entered the grounds, giving him a series of bewildered stares. "Are you certain that we are in the proper location?" She kept wondering why Gabriel kept telling her how impoverished and broke he was. However, he did reside here. She caught his perplexed gaze, "Yes? I am aware of my former residence, Marina." Looking around, Marina pressed her lips together as she noted the neglected fountains and an overgrown garden. "Jesus, your parents don't bother taking care of the mansion." When she mentioned that, the captain realized she was correct and that this was an odd observation. Typically, the garden was aesthetically pleasing and the fountains were constantly releasing water. Then he realized how much his house had changed since he had last seen it.

As they approached the front doors, Mr. Santarelli continued to observe them. He raised his hand, but it started to tremble. He was terrified of knocking on the doors and seeing his disappointed-looking father inside. Then, he forced himself to swallow his spit since he didn't want even Marina to be displeased with him for being so overly anxious. The young lady seized his other hand in search of comfort for him. He inhaled deeply before closing his eyes and knocking three times on the doors. He kept waiting, but no one appeared to open. "He's probably drunk or went to ruin someone else's marriage." Marina gave him a look. "You are unable to know that. Perhaps he's simply busy?" She made an effort to remain optimistic in this circumstance, but it was getting harder as the captain's expression changed from paranoid to dissatisfied. They could hear someone walking inside and approaching the doors as she was saying that. Opening them, Mr. Santarelli's father asked angrily, "What is it? What are you two seeking? If the church sent you again to try to convince me, I've already told you several times that I won't be donating to the orphans. I'd sooner be crucified than give money to bastard children. Leave instantly or I'm getting my gun!" In a state of fear, Marina ran behind the captain, grabbing hold of his clothing and yelling, "Excuse me!? Gabriel tell him to calm down!" Mr. Santarelli groaned and said, "The church didn't send us. I came to see you." Alessandro Santarelli, his father, then raised his head to have a better look at the man in front of him. "Couldn't be... Gabriel?"

"Father."

"It appears you're alive."

"It appears I am." They both exchanged cold-eyed looks and remained silent for at least a minute. As she stared at the two, the young lady placed her index finger on her lower lip. The two men resembled each other, she could see it. Although Gabriel's nose is straight and perfect like his mother's, however, the captain's father's nose is hooked. He's much older, a little bit shorter than him...Additionally, the captain's father's face is covered in a thick black beard. He appeared worn out, almost like a corpse that had just awoken from the dead and was standing. "Hello, my name is Marina Carla Rivalli. It's nice to meet you." She smiled and extended her hand to his father, but he just responded with a sour look and a grunt. Marina put her hand down after being perplexed by the rejection of her handshake. Mr. Santarelli gave his father a slow headshake as he expressed dissatisfaction. "Boy, what do you want? You vanished for six years, and now you've returned with a worse appearance than of a rat who ate poison." The captain exclaimed, "Hah! I appreciate that; that was the kindest thing you've ever said to me, father!" His father shouted at him "I don't want to hear it from you, so listen. You have no business speaking to me in this manner." Then Marina cut him off by saying, "How about we go inside and have some tea." The father of Mr. Santarelli groaned and made room for them to enter. "What are you doing?" the captain muttered as he cast a bewildered glance at the young lady. "I'm wasting my time doing this." He was asked to enter the house by Marina since she didn't want to listen to him.

The young lady was in awe at the mansion's interior when they sat down on the couch in the living room. "Gabriel, Didn't you say you were poor to me?" She inquired. "I'm indeed. All my money and possessions belong to my parents. Nothing that is mine nor do I desire to possess." He responded, crossing his arms. They were given tea by a maid who approached them. The young lady thanked the maid for giving her a beverage and grabbed the cup and plate. Given Marina's statement, the maid was taken aback and remarked, "Goodness, haven't heard a simple thank you in this house for years." and walked away. The captain and the young lady exchanged bewildered looks as they both asked, "For years? Has my father become that much crueler?" He questioned. At that very moment, Mr. Alessandro Santarelli entered the room and sat down on the couch across from the two.

He poured himself a glass of wine, to which his son sighed in disappointment as he wished he would already cease drinking because he is still a big drinker. He was utterly repulsed by the sight of empty wine bottles everywhere. "Father, you appear sick. Are you alright?"

"You should mind your own business." His father answered back in anger. The captain remained silent for a moment, he merely wanted to know how his single father's health was.

Gabriel questioned "Where is mother?" as he observed that the home was both deserted and excessively silent. "What do you think?" his father scowled at him. "She left the instant you fled the house. snatched her jewels and left the scene. I hope she's dead." His son exclaimed, "Left? What do you mean by left? What happened to her?"

"Son, I don't even care or know. I'm just relieved that her female hysteria isn't bothering me anymore." At that same moment, Marina gave the captain's father a disgusted stare. The phrase "Female Hysteria" infuriated her and always made her feel sick. "You are aware of how she was. She was alright for a split second before suddenly erupting into one of her crazy fits during which she screamed, sobbed, and broke everything. That whore destroyed my pricey painting." Mr. Santarelli has vivid memories of his mother's lifestyle. He despised when she would suddenly become angry because she would always vent her rage at him.

Then Marina inquired, "Mr. Santarelli, may I inquire as to what you do for a living?"

"My family has owned a wine business for a century," he responded. "As the eldest son, I am the rightful heir. Several vineyards in the kingdom are owned by us." As he leaned in closer to Marina, the captain boasted, "Father's wine is also King Umberto's favorite. I've heard it's also common in Austria-Hungary." The young lady chuckled at it and showed great admiration. His father squinted his eyes and stared at him. "What happened to you? Do you even work?"

"Of course I work." Mr. Santarelli said as he stared at him bewildered. "For the past three years, I have been the cargo ship's captain."

"Captain? Have you lost your mind? Are you attempting to make me and your family look embarrassed? You moron, you couldn't even find a decent enough job. You chose to become a seaman, the dirtiest job imaginable!?"The captain's father violently set down his glass of wine and started yelling at him. With his hand on his chest, Gabriel widened his eyes. "What else was I supposed to do? I didn't finish school, I had no money for better education and I had no connections in any other businesses. You should be proud of me for even succeeding given the way you raised me; this was the best I could have done."

"Raised you!? Your mother did all of the job. I'm not to fault, you bastard." As Marina became enraged with Alessandro for yelling at his son and insulting him, she interjected into their disagreement. "Sir, you need to be ashamed of yourself! Gabriel is a wonderful son, and every parent should be proud to have him! Gabriel has accomplished something on his own even if you and his mother were hardly ever in his life! Indeed, being the captain of a cargo ship isn't the most glamorous position and it's to cry about—" Mr. Santarelli cut her off. "Marina, where are you going with this?"

"I'm trying to say is that, despite all of that, your son has built himself a career on his own," she added. "He's really smart; in fact, I'd say he's one of the smartest persons I've ever met or heard of. Unlike you, he is gentle and caring." In that instant, his father got to his feet and said, "Who are you to talk to me that way, young lady?" The captain begged her to sit down as she got up and glared at him angrily, saying, "I'm someone who truly cares about your son. If I ever mentioned that you were my father or had even a bit of the same blood as you, I'd feel ashamed." Her arms were crossed.

The manner in which she kept defending him made Mr. Santarelli feel flattered. Never in his life has someone cared so much about him that they would defend him. He maintained giving the girl the highest possible regard as he kept looking up at her, his Angel. Due to the woman talking back at him, his father's breathing became labored. He made a fist out of his hand and moved to strike the girl. The captain quickly rose and struck his father in the face with as much force as he could as Marina screamed in panic and covered her face with her arms. Alessandro fell on his table and broke it.

"Leave her alone!" As he took short, sharp breaths, he yelled. When Alessandro realized he had broken his wine bottle and was covered in wine, he moaned in frustration. "I won't allow you to harm her the way you harmed me all those years ago! You must not even dare to touch her."Marina couldn't move since she was so shocked by what had happened, so Mr. Santarelli grasped her arm firmly. "I tried to get along with you, I even tried to forgive you for everything! But you're just so difficult to get along with! No wonder mother left you."

Mr. Alessandro Santarelli started to chuckle, acting as though he was going crazy. The captain and Marina were left perplexed: "You think you've done something by punching me? When you left these doors six years ago, you were still the same insecure, useless child. You've

accomplished nothing with your life. You're nothing."
Marina glanced at her love and put her hand on his
shoulder while saying, "No Gabriel, it's not true." and
giving him a troubled expression as Gabriel stared at him
with fear in his eyes. Mr. Santarelli held Marina closely
in his arms as he went out of the mansion while taking a
deep breath. While rushing towards the doors, the young
lady saw an unused wine bottle and quickly snatched it.
She saw an opportunity to drink the finest wine in the
kingdom and she didn't want to miss her chance of
stealing it from the captain's father.

The maid complimented the two of them for having the
courage to challenge Alessandro as they were leaving. "I
hope you two have a good life." As she moaned at the
mess she would have to clean up, the maid murmured.

The captain and Marina made their way to the train
station where they boarded the first train back to the ship.
Marina felt horrible for ruining the trip as they traveled
to their destination. "I'm so sorry, I should have listened
to you." she murmured as she rested her head on her
hand and looked out the window. "I never should have
persuaded you to visit your horrible father. It's all my
fault... We could have stayed in the city longer, but I
wrecked everything instead."

He sighed "It's alright; the damage has been done." She
sobbed, "It's not alright! I had to witness your father

insulting you." Mr. Santarelli said quietly as he firmly held her hand "You didn't know him. Although I wish you had listened to me when I warned you not to visit him. Having flaws is what makes us human." As he cleaned her cheeks from her tears, he sighed. "Dearest please, hold back your tears, or I'll start crying too." While trying to wipe her face, Marina sniffed and grinned at him while furrowing her brows. The man sighed at that precise moment. "I ought to have informed you about him so you were aware of the circumstance... I and my mother would be smacked for any slight irritation of his. He had affairs with our housekeepers, which drove my mother crazy. Even when I was nine years old, he had an affair with my teacher. I was filled with bruise marks because of him hitting me. He called me feminine all the time because of my delicate demeanor, which made me feel uncertain about my masculinity. The worst thing he has ever done to me was this." A large scar on his scalp was visible as he lowered his head and separated his long black hair.

"What—"

"Years ago, he tossed a wine bottle at me. It shattered, while seriously injuring me. He did not attempt to assist me with my injury. He kept screaming at me while my face was covered in blood." Marina covered her lips with her hands as she gasped in that instant. She broke down in tears as she felt terrible about how his father had treated him. She was unable to picture her papà ever subjecting her to such treatment. She tenderly took the man in her arms and embraced him close to her chest. He began to cry at her consolation. He felt like a small child who merely needed reassurance In the moments when his life at home was difficult.

Chapter XX

April 5th, 1911

I t was the middle of the night. Marina allowed Mr. Santarelli to braid her long, curly hair while she prepared for bed in his cabin. As his hand touched her cheek, she placed her hand on his and asked "Is your hand alright?" His knuckles got bruised from when he hit his father. That day as soon as they came back to the ship, Marina bandaged it. "It could be worse. It's fine now, you don't have to worry about it." The captain replied. He got silent for a moment and asked her, "Listen, we're going to stop at Naples tomorrow." at that precise moment. "So, if you'd like, we can go visit your brother." After giving it some thinking, the young lady replied, "That would be lovely actually." She then recalled the moment she last visited her brother's cemetery and encountered Amelia. not only encountered but also fled from her. She started to feel bad about it and wanted to go see her beloved old friend and make amends for leaving her without giving any reason. "On the other hand, I have a better idea. We could go and visit my friend for a change."

"Your friend? You never mentioned your friend to me, right?" The captain questioned. "Yes. Mia is a close friend. She and my brother Rocco once shared a romantic relationship. But I've known her since I was just a kid." Marina answered. After some consideration, he decided to agree. Due to his discomfort in meeting new people, he didn't want to get in the way of her relationships with others. She let out a breath as she lay down on the bed. "I genuinely miss her. We even attended ballet lessons together. Up until I was expelled from it because I knocked a girl off the stage, causing her to break her leg."Gabriel questioned her as he regarded her. "Excuse me? What did you do?"

"Well, I was envious of her for getting to play the White Swan. Because the teacher claimed that I couldn't manage my temper or anything, I was made to play the Black Swan." As she thought back to the incident, Marina sighed. "I see, and pushing the girl off the stage showed how calm you are?" He added in a mocking tone. The young lady threw a pillow at him and ordered him not to use sarcasm on her because she doesn't like it. He immediately tossed the pillow aside, leaped on top of her, and started grappling with her. "You ordered me? Sorry, Your Majesty Queen Margherita of Savoy, I didn't recognize you." Marina snickered and laughed madly as she pushed him away with her legs and begged him to stop. "I apologize! I give up!" She cried out as she struggled to free herself from his heavy body. She attempted to catch her breath as the man chuckled and sat down next to her. "You're unbelievable, you ruined my braid." She said as she cast a glance his way, he continued to snicker while looking out the window. By the time he turned his head around, Marina was already deep asleep. He leaned closer to her and tenderly pressed his lips onto her forehead as he moved away the bangs from her face. Gabriel stood up to undress and go to bed. He looked at his work table on which there was a bottle of wine. He kept looking at it in utter silence. He hasn't drunk anything in a while and suddenly the wine began to call him. He walked closer to it and bit the skin around his fingernails from overthinking his actions "I shouldn't. I should go to bed instead." He reached his hand out to put the bottle away but when he looked at his bruised hand, it began to tremble.

Suddenly the memories came back of his father abusing him as a child and once again when he decided to apologize to him. The thought of his father upset him, it angered him. He wanted to scream and keep hitting him to lash out all of his anger. But he knew that would be unethical to do. The captain squeezed his fist and let out a deep sharp breath. He regretted this decision entirely and would never forgive himself. He ended up sitting down and drinking his problems away as he looked at the young lady who was asleep and felt ashamed of himself and was thankful she couldn't see him in this condition.

The following evening, Miss Marina was in the kitchen getting ready to bring a basket to her dear friend. She offered her treats and flowers as an affectionate gift in an effort to make her feel happy to see her. However, she couldn't find a wine bottle she had put in the captain's cabin and thought she must've placed it somewhere else and forgot where exactly. She rushed outside to the captain who was waiting for her and handed her her shawl to cover herself with as it was still a little chilly, outside after wrapping the basket with a ribbon. They began making their way through Naples' streets. No one was seen on any of the city's streets. On rare occasions, you could have noticed a cat or perhaps a dog running around, or you might hear a child screaming inside a house. When Marina realized that the street she was on now was the same one she walked on to flee from her parents and the consequences of killing Matias Marotta, she clung to the basket. Her lip began to tremble, and Mr. Santarelli noticed that she was oddly too quiet. He worriedly put his hand on her shoulder and enquired as to what might be wrong. "I'm fine. I suddenly had a memory of the time I fled my wedding." Marina spoke while struggling to contain her tears as her voice grew harsh. Mr. Santarelli gently took her hand, brought it up to his face, kissed her soft hand, and continued to reassure her.

Eventually, they arrived at Amelia's home. "This is it. This is her residence." The young girl said as her eyes widened and she started to wonder if she should knock. She gave the doors two knocks while she waited for an answer. A split second later, Amelia Mor unlocked the doors while wrapping her husband's robe over her. "Who is it at this hour of the night?" Amelia inquired. She stopped abruptly when she realized Marina was at her door and gasped. "Marina Rivalli." Discreetly asking, "What are you doing here?" She inquired. "I wanted to come and see you," Marina retorted "We haven't seen one another in months."

"Yes, because you kicked me out of your wedding." She crossed her arms. Mr. Santarelli placed his hand on his hip and raised a brow while glancing at the young lady. Marina pursed her lips to that "It's been a long time since that event! Here! I brought you a gift basket!" Amelia looked at it and sighed "Come inside and we'll talk." Marina smiled at her and revealed both of her dimples. As they walked inside of Amelia's house she told Marina to put the basket down on the table in the kitchen. Marina and the captain sat down at the table while Amelia went to make coffee for them three. "You have a lovely home." Complimented Mr. Santarelli "Marina, who is this man in my house?" Exclaimed Amelia Mor.

"Oh, this is Gabriel." Answered Marina as she completely forgot to introduce the captain to her friend "Yes, I apologize for not introducing myself earlier. I'm Gabriel Santarelli, captain of a ship. It's a pleasure to meet you Miss Amelia." Amelia paused as she looked at the captain and then at her friend. It immediately clicked to her that Marina and Mr. Santarelli have something going on together. Especially because it's quite odd for a woman to be all alone together with a man so late at night, without it meaning anything. Amelia awkwardly cackled and turned around to continue making coffee. She couldn't believe that in just a few months, Marina managed to get engaged to another man. She hoped that at least this time she found someone who won't have affairs or control her. But knowing Marina, that was impossible.

Amelia placed down cups with coffee, a pot of milk, and sugar aside. She sat down and sighed. Amelia grabbed Marina's hands and smiled at her "I missed you..." the young lady's eyes started to fill up with tears "I missed you as well."

"I'm still hurt over you telling me not to come to your wedding." Mia said harshly as she pressed her full lips and looked at Marina straight in the eyes "Why would you be hurt? I told you to not come because you lied to me about Matias."

"Are you serious?" Asked Amelia "After all those months, you still think he hasn't had an affair with another woman!?" Mr. Santarelli looked at Marina confused and shocked by the new information "He slept with another woman? Goodness..." Marina's mouth set in a hard line while glaring at her friend with anger and letting go of her hands "He did not have an affair." "Marina I saw it! I'm not blind unlike you who was blinded by his fake love towards you!"

Amelia and Marina persisted in debating who was right and wrong. The more Mia spoke, the more she started to realize that she was to blame but didn't want to accept it, so Marina persisted in insisting that she was the one in the right.

"Matias was terrible; what don't you get? He never even tried to help you achieve your goals. He often demanded that you keep quiet in public. Why does he having an affair surprise you so much?" Amelia yelled and pounded the table with her fists. The girl pursed her lips and furrowed her brows. "Because I loved him. Why do you think it's so simple to believe that the person you loved was a terrible person?" "I know! because you are one too!" Marina's mouth gaped open in shock at Mia's exclamation. "Tell me one thing I did that was terrible and characterizes me as a terrible person!"

"You advised me not to attend your wedding, and following Rocco's passing, you never made an effort to get in touch with me. Once you became engaged to Matias, you would disregard me. When I wanted to spend some time alone with Rocco, you would be envious. Not to mention that—" Marina interrupted

Amelia at that very moment. "Alright, I get it! Why do
you keep judging me for my past!? Why cannot you
accept that I have changed? I've worked so hard to be a
better person and yet you still keep throwing my past in
my face!" She wanted to put a stop to the talk since she
felt extremely embarrassed of all the bad things she had
done in the past and didn't want Mr. Santarelli to know
about them. "Do you believe that you can just decide to
forget about your past one day when you wake up? Your
actions have consequences! Whether you like it or not,
you hurt other people. And I am aware that you are to
blame for Rocco's demise. When riding his horse, Rocco
would never have gone in the wrong direction." The
young lady regarded her incredulously and sought to
justify herself by saying, "I haven't!—"

"No! Silence! I won't put up with your actions any
longer! Either you eventually grow up or you keep
acting like the pampered, hateful brat you always were.
Seriously, is it so difficult for you to say you're sorry?"
Marina made a pause. She looked down in shame and
resolves to remain mute while Mr. Santarelli keeps
staring at her and wishes she would admit her errors.
"Answer me." argued Amelia. "No, it is not challenging.
I won't accept responsibility for anything I didn't
blatantly do." "Lord, give me strength." Amelia groaned
as the young lady yelled, "You're the one to argue when
you have gotten married to another man so quickly and
completely forgot about my brother!" and slapped her
hands on the table.

"How dare you! How could you say such a thing? He had never been respected in his life outside of me. And I'm entitled to move forward and find happiness." Amelia clasped her hands to her head and moaned in response to the abrupt creaking on the upper wooden floor. "Nicolas, Louis. Get downstairs right away." The two little boys hurried to their mother right away and were puzzled as to how she could have heard them. "I've urged you numerous times not to eavesdrop! That is extremely rude." They observed her yell, "Sorry, mommy." Louis said, adjusting his glasses, "We just wanted to see why you were yelling." Nicolas explained.

"I'm very sorry. I apologize for waking up the two of you."Amelia tickled each of her sons beneath the neck and gave them cheek kisses. "You have children?" Marina kept asking as she continued to stare at them. "They are two years old, yes." "They're extremely cute." the young lady chuckled "Brings to remember Rocco and I when we were in their age."

"Perhaps it's because you're related to them?" Asked Amelia while her son Louis sat in her lap "What? Wait, excuse me? They're my nephews, right?" As she gazed at the boys, she couldn't believe what she was seeing. She is an aunt, but how is that possible? Unless Amelia became pregnant before Rocco's passing. Marina covered her mouth with her hands as she continued to stare perplexed at her nephews. She could see more and more of Rocco in them the longer she stared at them. They resembled their mother in terms of appearance— black, curling hair, and dark skin just that theirs was lighter than their mothers. And they had her adorable, rounded nose, too. In contrast, they shared Rocco's face shape, lips, and expressions, which made her heart swell with happiness. "I wish I had known about you two so much sooner." Marina said as she bent down to kiss both boys on the cheek. "God, you two are so adorable. " The twins were completely perplexed as the woman cuddling them said, "I'm your aunt! Aunt Marina! Your father's sister! We were twins as well actually." Amelia smiled at them while Mr. Santarelli tried to comprehend so much information thrown at once about Marina and her life.

He remained completely silent the entire time because he didn't want to get between Marina and her dear friend and further detract from the mood. But seeing the young lady so content with her nephews caused a smile to form on his lips. He suddenly had a mental picture of her loving their children so deeply, and it caused him to daydream and become lost in his thoughts. He was the happiest when he imagined them living in their own house they could call home, getting married, and having their own children. "Who is that large man, mommy?"Louis, who was trying to push his aunt away from him because she was still kissing his entire face, asked.

"That's... Marina, could you help me?" asked Amelia, who was unsure of how to address the captain.

"That is Gabriel. He is my lover—" She was abruptly cut off by the captain, who said, "I'm the captain of a big and strong ship!" To amuse the kids, he rose dramatically and put his hand on his chest.

"Woah! Do you have any experience with monsters, sir?

"Sure, that. I've witnessed a lot of them, including the Kraken. frightful sirens that with their mystical voices nearly killed me! I even came across a stunning mermaid with gorgeous curly hair that completely captured my heart." The boys enjoyed the speech and cracked up. "That's aunt Marina!" When Marina discovered it was, in fact, her, the captain denied it, saying he had truly encountered a mermaid who had caused him to fall madly in love with her. The boys started leaping on him and forcing him to carry them around when he went to the couch to play with them. Marina and Amelia couldn't stop grinning as the boys played and tormented Gabriel. "Why didn't you ever tell me I was an aunt? They're such sweet kids."

"Because I didn't want you to mention them to Adriano and Annabella. They might negatively affect my children, I feared. Rocco and I discussed how to live together on our own while avoiding having a negative effect from the presence of your parents. You and your brother have experienced the worst parenting ever from them."Amelia's statement caught Marina off guard, causing her to blink three times. She was perplexed and in denial. "They raised Rocco and me well."

"Marina, every time you caused trouble, they let you go. To brag about their son to others, they overworked Rocco with extra activities." Amelia worriedly regarded her pal. "For not being as great as your brother, they constantly insulted you. They probably even put a lot of pressure on you regarding the wedding, I bet." Amelia had once more been correct, Marina reflected as she bit her lower lip. "But let's not talk about that, I'm tired. I want to talk about you and the captain." Amelia grinned smugly at Marina as she continued to anxiously twist a hair strand. "What specifically do you want to know?"

"How did that take place? How on earth did you and the captain of a ship get together, anyway? I wonder what will your parents have to say about that! *Hah*!"

"It's a long story, but he helped me escape my wedding and saved my life. I don't know where I would be right now if it weren't for him." She looked at her beloved and grinned warmly at him as she sighed. "Yes, your wedding. Whatever did happen to Matias?" As soon as Mia learned Matias was no longer in the picture, she inquired about what had happened to him.

When Marina heard her friends' inquiry, she was sipping coffee while holding the cup and plate, and her hands began to shake. She even managed to spill some coffee on herself, but she was so preoccupied with recalling what had occurred to her on her wedding day that she didn't even notice. "I was getting ready in my bedroom when he entered and started pressuring me into having intercourse with him." Amelia held Marina's hand tightly as her anxiety increased and she furrowed her brow in dread. "I tried to get him off of me, but he overpowered me and... raped me." She started breathing deeply and closed her eyes to calm herself down. She was still uncomfortable talking about this subject, and it required all of her willpower to do so. Amelia's bottom lip quivered and her eyes widened.

Although she was aware of Matias's cruelty and his abject horribleness, the idea that he would harm Marina in such a way was beyond her comprehension. Amelia got to her feet right away and proceeded to give her friend a bear embrace. The girl's eyes began to cry, and the droplet landed on Amelia's dark brown skin. "I'm sorry you ever experienced it. I wish I had been there for you more."

"It's fine, I should have paid attention when you warned me about him, I suppose." She sobbed. She received a napkin from Amelia to use to wipe her face. "I was hoping to speak to you like the good old days, but now I'm over here crying." Marina laughed as she wiped her tears from her face. "Sure, as if you haven't shed a lot of tears in those good old days." her companion chuckled at that. "But look." Amelia gestured with her head toward Mr. Santarelli, who was dozing off on the couch. He had Louis and Nicolas on his lap and chest while they slept. They were exhausted from playing and it was already very late. The sight of him sleeping with her nephews made Marina incredibly happy, and it was a lovely sight to behold.

"Please don't mess it up. He appears to be quite concerned about you. For God's sake, he's sleeping with my boys, whom he just met."

"He is wonderful, yes. He is too patient with me, and I feel bad saying it, but sometimes I feel like I don't deserve him. I keep thinking about him in that way, Mia, and I'm dying. Every time he takes off his uniform, my heart almost jumps out of my chest." When Marina told her that with the most aggressive voice possible, Amelia let out a loud gasp. She never anticipated her to say anything similar to that "Oh my God! I cannot believe I'm hearing this from you."

"Don't laugh! It makes me feel so unladylike and embarrassed." "It's very normal for everyone to have these cravings." Amelia insisted while her laughter continued to make the young lady's cheeks redden. "There is no one preventing you; you can always do it whenever you are ready."

"Well, not necessarily now. We aren't even wed yet." The girl exclaimed, putting her index finger to her lip and starting to wonder. "What is getting married related to this?" Questioned Amelia. "Isn't having intercourse before being married a sin? I would feel terrible."

"Are you kidding? When did you start practicing religion? Additionally, I was fine doing it before I got married."

"To be fair, you did become pregnant at a young age." As she squinted at her pal, Marina retorted. She was taken speechless, and Amelia stared at her. "That...

Listen, he loves you and you love him. Absolutely nothing can be lost. Don't push yourself to do it, but also don't think about it too much." She sighed. "It's a very wonderful experience... two people who deeply love each other and desire to be more intimate and linked." Marina's eyes widened as she cast a worried glance at her partner, who was deep asleep. The unexpected prospect of having a sexual relationship with him was both appealing and horrifying. To control her exuberance, she started to twist the ring on her finger, but she soon stopped and turned to look at it. She decided to give Amelia the ring after turning to gaze at her and her sons once more. Instantaneously taking it off, Marina clasped her friend's hand.

"I am aware that I made numerous mistakes, and I can understand if you would never pardon me for them. But I would like to at least perform this act of kindness for you by giving you Rocco's ring. When your sons are older, give it to them; they deserve to own a memento of their father. They are his legacy." Amelia started to cry when Marina stated it. She had entirely forgotten about Rocco's ring, which brought back memories of how she could always feel it when she held his hand. "Thank you so much. Do you know that I preserved every painting he gave me?" Questioned Amelia. She advised the young lady to simply look around since they are all hung on the walls when she inquired about their location because she was curious. "I can't believe your husband let you have them inside the house!"

"Well, Carlo doesn't mind because he is well aware of my past. Whatever makes me happy, he says. Additionally, the paintings are stunning."

"They are. My brother had artistic talent. If he were still living, I sometimes wonder what his life would be like." When Marina looked at the time and realized how late it was, she sighed and decided to send Amelia to bed with her husband. The young lady approached Gabriel and gave him a light shake, saying, "Wake up, we need to go. It is quite late." "Are we leaving already?" he murmured as his eyes slowly opened. "You've been asleep for thirty minutes now." Marina said as she glared at him with her large eyes wide open. He then turned to look around and saw two boys sleeping on him, so he cautiously rose to avoid waking them.

Marina thanked her friend for the coffee and for letting her come inside uninvited as they approached the doors to leave. "I welcome you and Gabriel at any time. I'd like to see you more frequently. I want us to be in a good relationship at least so my sons have an aunt in their life. However, I must warn you that a lot of Naples residents still hate you and refer to you as a witch." Amelia warned her as she encircled her nightgown with her husband's robe.

"God, society keeps going backward rather than moving forward," Marina groaned as she clenched her fist in rage at people labeling her a witch in the year 1911. "Didn't know you were so well known here." The captain remarked. "I lived in the wealthiest neighborhood of Naples," Marina snorted aloud. "The most well-known restaurant in my city is owned by my father, who also authored a cookbook. Of course, I'd be well-known." She had never told him that about her father, so he cast a perplexed glance in her direction. "Well, Amelia, farewell. Thank you for everything." Saying "Goodbye, Marina." Amelia grinned at her. Marina gave her a kind wave before starting to leave with the captain. Marina clung to her dark green shawl as they moved. "Tonight I came to the understanding that I never take the time to appreciate the moment I'm in. I have a tendency to keep looking at the past or take things for granted. I never tried to approach Mia, so I didn't even know about my nephews."

"I suppose that's the appeal of life's lessons. Throughout your life, you continually pick up new skills. When you become aware that you are doing morally well, you immediately become aware that you are then acting unethically once more, and so forth."

"I suppose that's a philosophical way of putting it."

LV Polcic

"It is true, but not many people take this into consideration. But I am proud of you for coming to terms with your friend. You're not anymore the little girl I met that day." the captain said with a delightful nod. She wrinkled her eyebrows and offered him an affectionate grin as she turned to face him. She lightly touched his jawline with her hand. "Thank you, Captain, my most beloved and dearest."

April 20th, 1911

Moving toward Antoni's cabin was Marina. Her current nightgown is too huge and quite outdated, so she asked him to make her a new one a while ago. And she planned something special with it "Have you finished stitching my nightgown, Antoni?" She questioned eagerly. She was impatient for it to finish.

"Why are you so impatient? It's merely a nightgown." He questioned her. She couldn't wait even a minute longer for it to be finished, which puzzled him greatly. "I'd rather not say it." It was starting to get hot outdoors, so Marina responded while biting her bottom lip and flapping her fan. "What is it that you find so awful that you don't want to tell me? Me!" He laughed at Marina as she pressed her fan against his chest. "Believe me, you don't want to know why I'm so impatient." she said. He was beginning to be intrigued about it, but he chose to brush it aside. "If you'd like, you can try it on right now, and I'll alter it to fit based on your dimensions." Marina quickly clapped her hands together as she said, "Wonderful!" and grinned broadly. Antoni was starting to interrogate Marina while having needles in his lips as Marina put on her new nightgown and he was straightening it. "You know, ever since you and Gabriel had gotten together. He and I are starting to talk less. It seems as if he wants to spend every second with you."

"Oh, I'm sorry. I didn't want you two to—"

"No, it's not a problem. I'm glad he found someone who makes him happy. He won't accomplish anything if he remains dependent on me forever. Not to add that I'll be leaving quite soon." He said and Marina cried out, "Ah! You're moving, what?" "Well, yes. I came to the realization that remaining here won't do me any good if I want to pursue a profession. Although a little frightening, I think that's what makes it exciting."

"I'm at a loss for words. You will be missed by me. You are the first person here who didn't despise me." The young girl sighed and said, "And I'll miss getting from you always free gowns!" as she gave him a sad look. "I can't believe you're only using me to stitch your gowns."

Antoni chuckled. "That makes me sad to hear." He sarcastically added.

She rolled her eyes at that, but as the needle unintentionally stabbed her leg, she loudly exclaimed, "Ouch! You're going to make me bleed out before I even get to wear this nightgown for bed!" "Stop being so dramatic!" he said as he raised an eyebrow in her direction. "I'll drop you off in St. Helena, where you may be buddies with Napoleon." She groaned while swallowing her spit. "But please promise me that you'll persuade Gabriel to finally find a place to call home since this isn't life. Despite my best efforts, he never pays attention to me. He might listen to you more because you two are closer."

She felt special hearing that from D'Angelo. The fact that Antoni and him have been friends since they were sixteen years old and Gabriel considers her as a person more closer to him, truly makes her feel adored by him and special. "I'll try." Antoni nibbled the little thread still attached to the needle as he finished sewing the nightgown. "There! Ms. Marina Rivalli, it's finished. I wish you well with your gift." Marina lifted her very long, curly hair and gave it a twirl. She checked to see if the nightgown enhanced her features and figure, and it did. At that moment, she knelt and gave the man a tight hug. "I'm grateful. I sincerely hope you succeed in being Italy's top tailor. No! You deserve it more than anyone in all of Europe." Antoni laughed at her beautiful thankfulness, but he also thanked her for it.

Marina visited the captain's cabin later that evening. He was meant to be in awe of her, therefore she was wearing her new nightgown. She positioned herself so she would look attractive when she sat down on his bed. In anticipation of his arrival, the young lady waited there for hours. "What am I doing? I appear helpless because of this." Marina partly opened her mouth and appeared frightened as she questioned herself as she gazed down at her nightgown. "Perhaps it's a good thing he's working right now. He shouldn't see me like this."She started to doubt herself and frantically grabbed the collar of the nightgown. Even though it was getting quite late, Marina continued to wait for him because she was desperate for his companionship.

The captain eventually arrived. His black hair was a complete mess, and he appeared worn out. While Marina was already fast asleep and appeared to be waiting for him, he looked down at his bed and noticed her. Mr. Santarelli pouted and expressed his annoyance with himself for working nonstop. He hardly saw her yesterday and the day before, and he didn't even see her today. He took a few long breaths to calm himself down after becoming so angry with his job and his life. The captain sat down on the bed near the girl, to take off his shoes. The young lady awoke from her nap and opened one eye to look at him when he sat down. She didn't move and remained silent. When Gabriel moved his head to look at her again, he wanted to savor her beauty even while she was asleep, but he saw she wasn't. "Why aren't you sleeping?" He worriedly questioned, "It's three in the morning."

"I heard some noise and it woke me up." He began to feel awful for disturbing her awake when she said that. She kept telling him that he shouldn't apologize for anything as he started to apologize to her. She knelt and put her hands on his shoulders. He was strained, thus Marina offered to give him a massage to help him unwind. The captain groaned, "My beloved." and tilted his head to the left as she caressed his back. That caused Marina to chuckle and move her face closer to his ear before asking, "What is it?"

"My heart is so full of love for you that it seems like it will burst." As he shut his eyes, Gabriel uttered. Marina kept quiet. His remarks overjoyed her and startled her at the same time, and she wasn't sure how to react. "Ah, how impolite of me. Your new nightgown didn't even get my attention." At that moment, Marina nervously smiled and pulled one of her hair strands. Her cheeks turned scarlet. "As a surprise for you, I had Antoni make it."

"For me?" He turned around and asked, completely perplexed. She released her hold on his back and inhaled deeply through her nose. He leaned in closer to Marina, but she froze, crossed her arms, and swallowed her spit as she frightened and stood up. After she rose, the captain reached for a fold in her brand-new nightgown. "It truly is wonderful. It complements your lovely olive skin." He spoke while lowering his gaze to the nightgown. Gabriel approached Marina and grasped her hands while she clenched her lower lip in apprehension.

"I've never seen a woman more lovely than you are. I am unable to look away from you. To be able to gaze up at you every night and admire you, I would replace you as the star Polaris." He muttered. As she continued to glance up at him, Marina's lips took on the shape of an O. When she looked at him, her eyes glistened. She leaned in close to him, put her hand on his chest, and put her lips on his. To get a better grip on him, Marina stood on her tiptoes and hung her arm around his neck. He clung to her firmly and didn't want to let go.

Marina made a noise as he started kissing her from her face to her collarbone. "Ahh..." he paused at that very moment as he drew a breath. "Are you—" Before he could even finish his remark, she abruptly cut him off. She blinked her eyes shut and said, "Yes, yes, I want this." He stared her in the eyes and they kept eye contact for good 20 seconds, during which time Marina pursed her lips and bit them uncomfortably. They were both pretty anxious and unsure of what to do next. He placed his hands gently on her waist as she rubbed them while grinning at him and saying, "I'm very nervous." She confessed. Gabriel grinned warmly and sighed, adding, "I am as well."

"I thought you'd engaged in sexual activity before?" He was questioned by the young lady. "Not with someone I love." He responded. Marina cautiously smiled and started to chuckle at him. By grabbing her hand and placing it on his deep-blue sweater, he started to lead her by signaling for her to pull it off of him. She continued to ogle his chest as she did so. She cracked her knuckles while clenching her jaw as the sight of his chest excited her. The girl was frightened as the captain started to delicately untie her nightgown from the back and remove it from her. Her nightgown fell from her body as she turned around to assist him. He held her firmly and put his hands on her breasts, and she let out a faint gasp. She continued to inhale deeply as he lowered himself to kiss her behind. He did it in such way that he kissed each beauty mark that was on her back. She felt as though she had no control over her sentiments because they were so erratic. He was down on his knees admiring her beauty as she turned around to face him.

Mr. Santarelli suddenly got to his feet and started kissing her once more. In that instant, not even an earthquake could stop him from kissing her; he adored kissing her. "Gabriel..." she whispered. As he undid his trousers, the captain put her on his bed. He then removed his pantaloons while Marina continued to gaze down at his crotch region. The sight caused her eyes to widen as she took a breath and swallowed her spit.

Mr. Santarelli climbed up onto his bed and got on top of her. "I find it hard to comprehend we're doing this." Marina said as she kept her gaze fixed on him. "I cannot either." He was the first man she had sexual relations with and the one who will deflower her because it was her first time. He felt anxious and shivers down his spine at the mere notion of it. He wanted it to be a positive first experience for her and didn't want to ruin it. The girl pondered, "I keep feeling as if we're committing a sin because we aren't married."

"So it's a good thing I don't believe in God, you might say." Marina nodded as he cautioned her, "This could hurt for a moment." He briefly considered whether her hymen broke on the day of her wedding. He made the decision to brush it off, but even if he had, it wouldn't have mattered because this was the exact moment she felt as though her purity was being taken away. He inserted it into her and took a thrust. In short pain, Marina moaned while pursing her lips. "How does it feel?" He inquired. "Weird, pleasant, and hurts a little." She replied with a trembling chuckle. Gabriel put his palm on her cheek, grinned sweetly, and continued to reassure her that everything is alright.

She gritted her teeth. "Please continue." After
swallowing his spit, the captain started to slowly thrust.
The multitude of emotions Marina was experiencing at
once astonished her. She gripped him firmly by pressing
her nails into the skin on the back of his neck. He was
continually being drawn within by her. She even
wrapped him with her legs. Gabriel cracked up at her
responses before taking several rapid breaths. As soon as
he could, he would keep on complimenting her: "Your
skin is so beautifully soft and smooth... I simply want to
kiss you all over." He mumbled. "O-Oh, God." In a sharp,
high-pitched voice, Marina spoke. She was having such
a good time that tears started to well up in her eyes. The
young lady covered her mouth with her palm so that no
one could hear her speak aloud. As the captain continued
to penetrate and kiss her body, she continued to let out
sweet little cries. One of her legs was taken by him, and
it was slung over his shoulder. Since she was doing this
with a man she adored, she was enjoying every second
of it.

The captain then swiftly jumped off of her and
ejaculated on an old piece of clothing that he had taken.
In the interim, Marina covered herself with bedsheets
and fixed her already ruined hair. Mr. Santarelli
crouched down on the bed and kept trying to take a
breath. He approached her and started kissing her body
again. "How was it? Was everything alright? Did I

accidentally injure you?" Not wanting her to be upset over her first time, he cautiously questioned. "I enjoyed it. Even though I still feel a little awkward about it, every minute was wonderful."

She grinned as she relaxed on the bed with her eyes closed. "It's fortunate that we still have work to do." He got under the sheets and began nibbling her thighs as she pondered what he was talking about. Before Marina could respond, she grabbed her hand onto the covers as he ran his tongue lightly along her labia before placing it on her clitoris. She let out a loud "Aah!" as he grabbed for her breast. After that, "Haah!"

Marina bit her bottom lip and pressed her knees on his head. She thought she was going to pass out from the experience as Gabriel pulled away from her. After he sat down next to her again. The man put both of his hands on her face and gave her one last kiss on the lips. She continued to look at him, laughing, and breathing deeply as he muttered, "My love. I'm all yours." He told her. "And I am yours." She replied, laying her head on his sweaty chest. At that very moment, he sniffed her hair and noticed that her hair smelled of lavender. "I just realized that your hair smells like lavender, is that right? When was the last time you used rosemary to wash your hair?" The captain inquired. "Since I discovered lavender soothes you and you've been sniffing my hair constantly." His eyes started to brim with tears, and he started crying. "Don't cry..." the young lady said as she started to wipe the tears from his face while looking up at him and pouting her lip. "Please!"

"How am I supposed not to cry? You care so deeply about me that you're putting lavender in your hair to ease me down, how sweet of you!" She firmly grasped his hand and placed it over her chest. The captain's eyebrows were furrowed as he gazed at her with his dark brown eyes *"Est osculo gratum speculari semper amatum."* He murmured. Marina chuckled at him "What?" She questioned as she didn't understand what he had told her "Beholding the beloved one is a big pleasure for the eyes." He caressed the girl's nude body as she grinned sweetly at him. She never wanted to be without him or him without her. It was a moment in which they loved each other deeply. Blood stains were visible on the bedding as Mr. Santarelli looked down at them. He simply grinned at the girl while maintaining silence. "What are you smiling so much about?" Marina questioned him as she snorted at him and he smiled at her out of the blue. Instead of explaining to her why he was smiling, he chose to lie on her chest and nod off.

Chapter XXI

May 1st 1911

In his cabin, Mr. Santarelli was the only person. He was noting the precise location for where he would drop the goods off next. He carried a pen in one hand and a full glass of whisky in the other. He started drinking regularly, and he felt that he couldn't operate without alcohol in his system. He attempted to dip the pen into an ink container, but he unintentionally kicked it, causing the ink to flow all over the page. The captain yelled as he got to his feet and looked at the disaster he had created. He kept banging himself in the head because of how foolish he was. "Good Lord! Every action I do results in a mess." He sighed. His already jam-packed schedule was getting even more hectic as a result of this. Back in his chair, Gabriel took a closer look at the whiskey bottle. The man decided to immediately drink the full bottle since he was so furious at the moment and wanted to forget what he had done.

Hours later, Marina entered the cabin in worry. The captain missed lunch, and she was concerned that he wouldn't eat, so she went to bring him a plate of food she had prepared for him. She gazed at the captain as soon as she entered. He was scruffy in the hair and clung tenaciously to the empty whiskey bottle. The young lady

was stunned speechless, and the man appeared to be
extremely intoxicated. When Mr. Santarelli discovered
she was his lover, he glanced at her and immediately
covered his face with his arms in humiliation. "Stop! G-
go away!" Marina moved aggressively in his direction.
"Why are you doing that!? Have you consumed the
entire bottle on your own!?"

"P-please just go away." She wouldn't want to see him in
this state, he thought. He found himself disgusting.
Marina, on the other hand, was irate and irritated. She
was also gravely concerned for his health. As he turned
away from her, she fiercely squeezed his arm. "This is
not how you can live. You can't drink! If you don't care
about yourself, at least consider how your actions are
harming me!" He was forced to look at her as she held
him by the cheeks and said, "I want to help you, but if
you're going to continue like this, then I'm leaving." As
soon as she said those words, he started to feel anxious.
Even though he didn't want her to leave him, he couldn't
resist the impulse to drown his troubles in alcohol.

"Don't leave me, please! " He yelled as he firmly grasped
her arms that were encircling him. The young lady
withdrew her arms and turned away from him. When she
went looking for more bottles to toss away from him, the
man stared at her with a broken heart, believing she was
about to abandon him. He was fighting the impulse to
approach her and steal those bottles, but he knew that if

he did, he might have to bid Marina farewell. She dumped each bottle into a can and warned him that she would never forgive him if she caught him drinking again. More than the fact that she would possibly leave him, that comment devastated him more. He gave her a startled, silent gaze.

"You should get some fresh air. You've been in bed with me or on the ship for days. You need to go for a walk." She took hold of his hands and supported him as he stood. Because he was embarrassed by himself and had no idea what to say to her when she offered to help him, Gabriel refused to speak to her. Giordana was outside on the deck and observed them two as they left his cabin. "And where are you two going? I assumed that both he and you still had tasks to complete in the kitchen." She inquired. "We're taking a quick stroll and will be back soon." The young lady replied. "Fine, but don't whine when you're overworked," the woman exclaimed. With her back to Giordana, Marina rolled her eyes at that and scornfully imitated the latter's speech. The girl gripped his hand tightly (even too tightly at times.) and they walked along the street by the sea. She worried about his health and didn't want him to become fatally intoxicated one day.

She had her eyes wide open, and tears started to form in them. She looked up in order to stop her tears from rolling down her cheeks since she needed to be strong in this circumstance. At that very moment, Marina inhaled deeply and said, "I'm sorry if I was overly critical of you earlier. I was very concerned because I didn't want to lose you to alcohol." To get herself to stop being so upset and to calm down, she fluttered her hand close to her face. "I know." He spoke as he looked down in humiliation. She helped him straighten out his untidy hair and suit as she placed him down on a bench. "All I want to do is ask you. What makes you drink? Did I possibly do something wrong?" She inquired. "It's not you, it never was and it never would be." he sighed. "I've always consumed alcohol, just not recently. I sometimes think that drinking will help me forget some of my challenging life experiences." He responded. "Then why did you begin drinking so much recently?" She put her hands on his hand and demanded to know. "It's completely ridiculous, but watching my father drink made me want to start drinking again. He additionally degraded me, which was another factor. Then, if I felt furious with myself, I would drink. Day by day, it all just started to pile up all at once. Particularly this work is turning me become an alcoholic as well from how... upsetting it makes me feel."

"Then leave."

"What?" He gave her a perplexed expression at that point. "Let's leave. There is no future for us on this ship. You hate your job and it's preventing you from achieving your goals and mine. And if I had to work, the last job I'd wish to do is be a maid." He laughed in response to what she said. Since he lacks any relevant work experience and hasn't completed any higher schooling, leaving the ship would have been impossible. "I'm not kidding. I have some money saved up, and you might have too! My folks could even be able to assist us if I go see them."

"Marina, in all honesty, your parents would think you're insane for showing up at their door unannounced and asking for money right away." He gave her a relaxed look "Hmm, you might be right about that. However, my point remains. I mean, wouldn't it be great if I started my own bakery? Additionally, you might land a better job. Even if it's not your ideal career, it's still more beneficial than you losing your mind on this ship right now." She spoke passionately to him about her intentions for the future while holding his hands "We might as well get married... I take your name... Even have a bedroom of our own. You can't possibly say it wouldn't be amazing, can you?"Gabriel sighed and said, "It would... Yes. Alright. I'll start looking for homes in Rome. I recall you telling me you wanted to move there and start your wonderful bakery." The captain grinned as he glanced at her. She gave him a kiss on the cheek because she was glad he remembered that. "You won't regret it." She said, putting her head on his shoulder. "You were right; I needed to go for a stroll to feel better. I'm suddenly much happier. I am more optimistic when I feel the sun's warmth on my skin." Gabriel said as he let out a sigh.

He caught Marina's chuckle. "Yes, I am aware that I am always correct."

"When did you last get something right? You insisted that the sun revolves around Earth only the other day." "Alright sir, I apologize for not being as smart as you are," she moaned. Looking up at the sky, Gabriel grimaced and put a finger to his lower lip. "But you are smarter than I am... I am constantly tempted to drink bottles and bottles of alcohol, therefore my knowledge in mathematics, history, and science is useless."

The young lady put her hand on his jawline and gave him a mournful expression as she wished he would look at her at that precise moment and state, "It's alright... I'm right here to assist you now. But we need to move on right away." she said, grabbing the fold of her garment. "Work needs to be done." At that, Mr. Santarelli nodded before rising. As they started to walk towards their ship, he took her hand and along the way, he noticed a wooden pole with a flier attached to it. His eyes brightened as he took a closer look and noticed "Maria Santarelli! That's the name of my mother."

The young lady picked up the poster and read the entire message, "It seems she's in an opera? I had no idea your mother performed in opera." she questioned as she continued to study the flier. "I didn't know either. I was aware of how strong her voice was. But I didn't anticipate this from her at all... If that's the case, I wonder if that's why she left my father." The idea of his mother appearing in an opera, let alone serving as the primadonna lead singer, baffled the captain. While he was pleased with her achievements, he couldn't help but question whether he was to blame for her failure to pursue her aspirations.

"We're going to see her." He said. "I want to see my mother and congratulate her on achieving her dreams." the captain said, raising his fist and pointing at the flier.

"Are you certain? Gabriel, are you sure you want to see her? I'd love to go to an opera but I'm just concerned."

"Yes, I'm positive. I'll try to sell some fish these days to neighborhood markets in order to raise money for two tickets." Marina remained dubious about everything. She was unable to avoid feeling uneasy about every aspect of it. She felt that since his health was already deteriorating if he went through a stressful situation once more, he would drink even more. The young girl made the supporting decision to go to the opera with him in the hopes that at least that would make him happy.

Along with her close friend Antoni, Marina went to drink coffee with, one particular morning. She was still upset by seeing Mr. Santarelli so intoxicated. Days went by, yet she couldn't help but worry excessively about him. "Antoni, I'm not sure what to do. I worry that as he continues to drink, he'll get worse." As Antoni continued to deliberate over how to respond to her, he looked up and then down. "I don't necessarily agree." he said. "He used to drink much more recklessly than he does now. He put me through hell, and he never made good on his commitment to stop drinking."

"He did not? When I threatened to leave if he chose booze over me, he vowed to stop drinking right away. I realize it was a little harsh. however, he gave me no other options." Marina said as she clung firmly to her coffee. "I believe you made the proper choice. Although that might have been harsh, there wasn't much else you could have done. It was either that or keep letting him drink." Antoni said. When Antoni described the circumstance to Marina, she sighed. Then, she recalled how he had informed her that his drinking was worse, and she was curious to find out more. D'Angelo strained to recall everything that had transpired in the past.

"Well. He was exceedingly angry and disappointed when he first took the title of captain. On his deathbed, Dante, the previous captain, pleaded with Gabriel to succeed in replacing him. To him, Gabriel was like the son he never had. Despite the fact that I did nothing wrong, for some reason, he didn't like me." He groaned "However, I didn't give an inch of thought. There will never be another father like the one I had. Gabriel, on the other hand, felt a connection to him because Dante was the only person who truly resembled a parent to him. He was extremely devastated by his passing, and to make matters worse, he had promised Dante that he would take his place as a captain." Marina scowled in response. She was unaware that Mr. Santarelli's promotion to captain was due to that. She had always believed that he had simply shown up one day with Antoni and demanded to be a captain. But when she realized what had happened, she was heartbroken.

"That's terrible. It must have been tremendously stressful to suddenly be in charge of the ship, everyone on it, and the finances." Marina answered. When the man heard that, he nodded and stated, "It was. For him to truly fall asleep at night, I had to buy him lavender oil." Antoni went on to elaborate. He regretted all the times his friend had been hurt and wished he would never experience that again. To better assist him, Marina anxiously turned away and bit into a biscuit. What recommendations do you have for someone who is an alcoholic? It was her. "Truthfully? Continue your previous course of action when around him. It seems to function."

At that, Marina pursed her lips. She was unsure of how to respond. She continued blaming herself for his inebriation because she was the one who insisted on taking him to see his loathed father, which she couldn't shake from her mind. "Ah, look at the time." Antoni said as he turned to face the time. "My train to Rome is going soon. I should have moved more slowly. He commented.

Marina got up to give him a hug. She found it unbelievable that he had already left. She had just met him, and it seemed like yesterday when he had fashioned her a gown to make her feel more at home. She pulled him with such force that Antoni thought he would not be able to breathe. "I still find it hard to believe you're going."

"I've got to. But don't worry, we'll still write to one another. Gabriel is familiar with my grandparents' home's address." At that, Marina grinned. Later, everyone gathered on the deck to wish D'Angelo farewell. He was carrying a suitcase containing all of his possessions. Mr. Santarelli struggled to accept the departure of his friend. He was sorrowful and resisted saying goodbye. "I find it hard to comprehend you're leaving me."

"I won't abandon you. Be less dramatic; our friendship still exists.

"You're my brother, not my friend. We experienced so much growth together. Why won't you remain?" Dark brown Gabriel's eyes started to well up with tears. He wouldn't let his friend leave as he stared at him in despair. "Please stop saying it that way; your words are going to make me cry." Tears streamed from his eyes. The captain approached Antoni and grabbed hold of him. "I don't know how I'll live without you." he said in a frustrated tone as he squeezed his hands onto his friend's clothing. "You were a huge part of my life. If you hadn't found me that night and assisted me in standing up, I would have died."

"Gabriel, you don't need me." Antoni said as he brushed away a tear from his cheek. "I must begin my own life, just as you must begin yours. She is the one you need if anyone." He cocked his head toward Marina's direction. The captain continued to cry and nodded at that. As Antoni put his hands on the man's cheeks, he hardly cracked a smile and said, "Please write to me, brother. I'm hoping to see you as soon as I can." Gabriel's voice started to break at this point since he was unable to even form words. He was merely shaking his head because he was too emotional to speak. They eventually parted ways because D'Angelo had to go. Marina raised her white napkin in the air and waved him off. She comforted the captain by holding his hand with her other hand. He had been sobbing hysterically that his eyes were bloodshot. The captain and Antoni's brotherly affection brought tears to the girl's eyes. They truly were soulmates, but each in their unique manner.

"Goodbye, Antoni! Farewell!" Margherita, an elderly woman, exclaimed as she waved him off. His leaving didn't appear to bother Francesca much. The day Antoni finally stood up for Marina, she despised him. She was no longer able to stand anyone aboard the ship. D'Angelo stopped even trying to be on good terms with her; anytime he tried to speak to her, all she did was roll her eyes up at the sky. Mr. Santarelli sighed deeply as he saw his friend go away. All of a sudden, the ship felt empty without him. He will miss Antoni's daily jokes and hearing about his strange encounters with new women. He will also miss having brotherly affection from him and a shoulder to constantly lean on when he needs support or counsel the most.

"We ought to prepare for the opera. I desperately need something to distract me from this." In that instant, Marina gave him a lethal glance. "Not booze." He said, " I meant that I want to watch the opera."As she stroked his shoulders, Marina grinned at him and said, "I can make you a chocolate cake tomorrow with sour cherries to make you feel better." "Well, if you did, it would be extremely nice. Though I haven't eaten anything sweet in a—" he stopped himself as he looked at her with a grin on his face "I did, not too long ago." Her mouth fell open and her ocean-blue eyes widened in horror as he told her that. "Stop it! Do not say such things in front of everyone!" She lightly kept hitting him on his shoulders and back. The man continued to chuckle at himself as her cheeks reddened and was hoping no one had heard that. "I haven't anticipated something like this from you!" She let out a groan as she gripped his arm firmly.

They both dressed that evening and made their way to the opera. Both of them were pressed for time and had no idea where to start when it came to getting dressed. "Marina, would you kindly adjust my necktie? I can't seem to do it properly." The captain asked the girl as he crouched down a bit for her, and she assisted him in tying his necktie. He gave her a brief kiss on the forehead. "Where is my money!?" he said as he hurried to find the rest of his supplies. He yelled in fear because he was running out of time to find everything. "Calm down, I put it in your coat's pocket." He responded with "Oh." as she explained. After that, he hurriedly grabbed a bouquet he had bought for his mother and urged Marina to get out of the cabin.

As they approached the Opera house, they hurried to purchase their tickets. When they arrived, there was already a long queue of people standing in line to purchase tickets. That made Marina sigh; she has a terrible case of impatience and hates having to wait for anything. Gabriel, on the other hand, waited patiently, though he did become frustrated quite a few times when the young lady kept asking him how much longer they had to wait to pay for their tickets about every second. Gabriel spoke with the person in charge of booking when it was time for them to make a payment. "Which seats are you interested in?" asked the booking clerk. "What are your least expensive seating options?" questioned the captain. "The least expensive rows in the orchestra are P 3 and P 5, which are directly on the side rows." As Gabriel asked to reserve two of those seats for him and the young lady, Marina heard that, and she exclaimed, "What!" and rushed over to the captain. "They are the worst seats!" She yelled, "You buy the tickets the next time when you have the money for the good seats." He said, casting a short glance her way because he didn't want her to complain about the seats.

She rolled her eyes. After a lengthy absence of not going to any special events, Marina was eager to put on an elegant gown and attend an opera, but the one time she goes, she is given the worst seats. As soon as they were seated, Marina pouted her lips and appeared utterly uninterested in trying to watch the play or listen to the symphony. She was impatient for everything to be finished. Gabriel couldn't wait to watch his mother perform. He was interested in how she would act as a primadonna. Her name is printed in large letters on flyers, therefore she must be excellent.

Maria Santarelli appeared on stage as the crimson curtains were raised. She had gorgeously arranged high hair and was dressed in a long, grey dress. Mr. Santarelli inhaled deeply and turned to face his mother. As he continued to stare in astonishment at his mother, he experienced a heavy feeling in his chest. "For heaven's sake! Nothing is visible to me. This man in front of me is wearing an excessively long hat on his head!" exclaimed Marina. "I'm already not tall, so in this position, I have no chance of seeing anything." She turned her head to the captain and whispered aggressively. "Shh! Keep quiet. I know you find it very challenging to remain calm, but try it once." He mockingly whispered to her as he urged her. She put her lips together and sat back down. Her inability to see anything annoyed her, and she additionally had the worst seats in the entire opera house.

"I don't even have theater glasses to help me see the primadonna better." In response, she heard Gabriel chuckle, "No, but I've brought my binoculars." He gave her his pair of marine binoculars so she could see more clearly. "I have a feeling we're the poorest people that have ever gone to an opera." Marina chuckled at him repeatedly as she put her hand on his shoulder. "Sit on my seat." he got up and added, "I'm taller so I shouldn't have a problem seeing on your seat." She sat down in his seat as soon as she got up. The lovely girl pursed her full lips and even utilized his binoculars. "She has a lovely voice." As she heard the captain's mother performing, she informed him. Sighing, he happily acknowledged that she does. The fact that Maria was his mother made him feel proud at that moment.

After it was all over, the captain hurried backstage to visit his mother and congratulate her on her new, lucrative career. He clung tenaciously to the rose bouquet, thinking she would adore them. He yelled, "Mother!" as soon as he saw her. When Mrs. Santarelli turned to face him, she saw a tall man approaching her. She briefly worried and was perplexed when she mistakenly believed the gentleman in front of her to be Mr. Alessandro Santarelli, only to find that it was her son, who she had assumed had long since died. "Gabriel?" She wondered.

When he saw her, he grinned broadly, and she was able to identify him. "Well, I didn't expect you to bother showing up. What do you want?" Years had passed since his last encounter with her, so the man awkwardly stated that he wished to see her. He then turned to look at the bouquet. "This is for you," he said as he handed it over to her. "Hope you appreciate it." Maria frowned as she regarded the rose bouquet, asking, "Roses? You couldn't have purchased a more remarkable and unique flower for your own mother than a standard rose, could you? Hm."

Mr. Santarelli stroked the back of his neck and replied, "I'm sorry, mother." He apologized. "However, I thought your performance was exceptional. I am proud of you for accomplishing what you want in life." Before turning back to face her son, Mrs. Maria Santarelli gave the other vocalist the bouquet of roses and instructed them to place it anywhere they wanted. "Oh, I'm delighted. I would have done it a long time ago though, but I was forced to look after you." His mother caught Marina's narrowed eyes as she started to become irritated by her degrading remarks.

"And who is this young woman you have with you?" Maria said with a questioning query and a menacing smirk. "This is Marina Rivalli." Maria made a disgusted look as Marina extended her hand for a handshake and stated "I don't touch women with dirty skin." Wide-eyed and in complete shock, Marina exclaimed, "Dirty!? I always wash myself—" The captain interrupted her and stated, "Mother, you cannot talk to her in such a way." He didn't want anyone to start an argument right now. He calmly expressed as he extended his arm to stop the young lady from advancing ahead. She was irritated with him for not letting her defend herself.

"Whatever. He'll eventually have an affair. He is just as pitiful as his father." Maria added. "I won't. I cherish her. Why on earth would I have an affair?" He questioned her.

Maria kept laughing uncontrollably at him. "Ask your father why he had an affair at that time. With our maids and the wives of other men." When the captain heard her say that, he exclaimed "I'm not my father! I was never like him!" With her hands behind her back, his mother started to encircle him. He was starting to feel uncomfortable because of her statements, so she kept beaming menacingly at her son. Maria always knew when it was appropriate to cause someone significant harm. "You are equally as unattractive as him, look at yourself. You possess his face, hair, and vacant brown eyes." She grabbed his arm and pulled up the sleeve of his suit to see the scars on his arms as she exclaimed.

"You still have burn scars on your arms, I notice." She took note. To prevent anyone from seeing the scars on his arm, Gabriel pulled the sleeve down right away. When he was a little child, his mother used to know to press her cigarettes on his arms whenever she became angry with him. He was speechless at that point since he was too afraid she might do anything worse to him.

The fact that his mother was making fun of him for having scars on his arms which Marina was unaware of because of his arm hair covering them, infuriated her. "Maybe you can talk to him in such a way because he still loves you, but I'm tired of you talking to your son in such a way," she said. "You old hag!" When she heard that, Maria's green eyes widened and her rounded brows raised. She approached the young lady and asked, "You dare speak to me in such a way?" She looked Mrs. Santarelli in the eye. Marina was told to stop by Gabriel because he didn't want her to dispute with his mother. One of Maria's coworkers walked by and said, "Your husband and son want to see you."

"I'm right here." Mr. Santarelli said, turning to face the person. At that moment, Maria's eyes widened in panic. "Are you Matteo? You grew quickly." The coworker laughed. Gabriel glanced at his mother with an angry expression in his eyes as he was perplexed as to who Matteo was. "Do you have another son, mother?" He inquired. "I do, and he's five years old." She stated while exhaling and glaring at her son. "Why?... You treated me so badly that I believed you didn't like children. Instead, you simply didn't care for me." When he started blinking, his face broke out in tears. "You've always preferred father to me... Despite the several times I have protected you, you have never stood up for me. I suffered for you. Even after all the times you hurt me, I still loved you." He was having trouble breathing.

"Will you stop crying, you aren't a woman. It's uncomfortable to watch you cry." His mother said while gagging in disgust. Mr. Santarelli's heart had been broken by that. "Leave him alone. No wonder your husband wishes you were dead." Maria looked across at Marina and laughed. "He claimed that? Ha, he talked a little too quickly." and grinned ominously. They were starting to irritate her, so she made the decision to get rid of them. The woman in her early fifties went to her room to retrieve a letter she had received, then returned and presented it to her son, saying, "Your grandparents sent this to you. I don't know what it says."

As Gabriel puzzledly regarded it, she said. "Get out of my face right away, now. I never want to run into you again in my life." The statement made by his mother shocked Mr. Santarelli. She treated him in this manner despite everything he had done for her. Gabriel was persuaded to depart by Marina since staying in the opera house any longer was not worthwhile. Since he remained immobile, she tightly grabbed his hand and continued to look at his mother with a devastated expression. That night, she completely broke him, and he was feeling crushed. As he walked away, Maria gave him a threatening stare while grinning. It frightened him.

"Please don't even consider her. Your mother is awful." Marina spoke on, but he didn't hear a word since he was fixated on the letter he was holding in his hands. He tightened his grip on it while looking at him with wide eyes and a pursed lip. "Do you want to read the letter? I'm interested in hearing what your grandparents said to you." "N-no." He gave her a quick look. "I don't think I'll open it... I'm not interested in hearing anything from my family." He explained as he sighed and tucked the note into his suit pocket. Although she tried to ignore it,

Marina couldn't help but be curious about what was in the letter.

In his cabin several nights later, the captain and the young lady had fallen asleep. It was around two in the morning and everyone else on the ship was asleep while Marina was continually coming back to the letter in her mind. She was interested to hear what his grandparents had to say. Though she felt bad for doing it, her curiosity was killing her. The captain was sound asleep as Marina sat on the bed and observed him. His hair was lifted out of the way of his drained eyes by her hand moving it from his face. She then stood up and draped his dark blue sweater over her exposed torso. She searched through his closet for the suit he had on for the opera and discovered a letter stashed inside its pocket. She moved softly, even walking on her toes to completely not make any sound. Marina took a deep breath and then opened the letter. But after reading the letter, she dropped it on the ground unknowingly.

"Dearest, Gabriel. In the hopes that you are still alive and well when your mother, 'Maria Santarelli,' hands you the letter, we have sent this letter to her since we do not know your current address. On April 10th, 1911, 'Alessandro Santarelli' your father, passed away. Because you are his one and only son and the firstborn in the family, you are legally entitled to everything considering he was an heir to the family's fortune. This

includes; the family's wealth, vineyards, a mansion in Rome, the wine industry, wine stocks, and a country home in Capri... Best regards, L.S. & A.S. Your grandparents." Marina covered her mouth with her palm. Her eyes widened, and she started to feel apprehensive. She was worried that if he read the letter, he might run away from her for wealth. She unintentionally dropped a vase that was on the captain's work table at that instant while she was still in denial. Fortunately, even though it fell, it did not break.

In any case, Mr. Santarelli heard something fall and realized all he could feel when he extended his arm to touch his sweetheart was her chilly pillow. "Marina?" the man asked the girl as he sat on his bed, his eyes barely open. "What are you doing?" he demanded. She pursed her lips, attempting to come up with an excuse as quickly as possible. "I simply couldn't fall asleep. I went to the window to observe the waves." She clarified. He mumbled "Oh... alright." as he fell asleep without delay. Then Marina clutched the letter and knelt to take it. She concealed the letter between the pages of a book she was reading in the hopes that he won't ever see the letter after her tears fell on the letter and crumpled it. She returned to bed. The man put his head on her back and grabbed her tightly around her torso.

Marina was making breakfast for everyone on board the ship the following morning in the kitchen. She was preparing an asparagus omelet. At least she was able to relax while cooking and temporarily shut her mind off. The captain entered the room, sat down at the table, and began reading the newspaper. Each home in Rome that he thought would be a worthwhile investment was circled. He received his omelet and black coffee from Marina when she moved closer to him. "Have you found a house yet?" She inquired. "Not really, no. Although I did find a handful, they are still significantly more expensive and outside of our price range." That caused Marina to sigh. As he took a better look at her, he pulled down his newspaper and observed, "You've been acting strangely all morning. Has anything happened?" He put his hand on hers and asked her. Every morning, Marina often had a beaming smile on her face. But she was acting strangely today and even last night. even stranger than she already is.

"Nothing happened, therefore why do you think that?" She was being self-aggressive because she didn't want him to find out the truth. "In the morning, you usually smile and flash both of your sweet dimples."

"Good lord, I don't have to smile every morning." She responded impolitely while crossing her arms. He gave her a perplexed look and replied, "Alright, you're right. I apologize for the question." After responding, he resumed reading his newspaper. He was completely perplexed by Marina's conduct as she pouted her lip and furrowed her brows before returning to cooking. The captain assumed he had done something wrong for her to be angry with him. After finishing his breakfast and coffee, he walked back to his cabin to continue estimating the time of arrival. He spent the entire day inside the cabin, not even for a little break he spent outside.

On the other hand, Marina spent the entire day cleaning since she preferred to be engaged with that activity than to think about the letter all the time. She went out that evening with an old broom to sweep the deck. As she was doing so, she felt a few raindrops land on her face and clothing. She sighed and wrapped her shawl securely around herself. The captain exited his cabin at that very moment and emerged with a grave expression on his face. "We should talk." He demanded. The girl clung to her broom & demanded to know his reasoning. "What happened?" "I searched trough my suit and can't find the letter anywhere." he retorted.

"I'm sure you put it somewhere else." she said as her lower lip was bit and she tried to convince him he put the letter somewhere else. "I haven't, no. You've been acting strangely today, and now the letter is gone. Confess that you stole it."

"Stole is a powerful word." "No, it's not when you deliberately invaded my privacy," he responded. "To open that godforsaken letter is the one thing I swore I would never do! What did you do then? You read it after stealing it! If you had stabbed me 23 times, it would've hurt less. It is your betrayal towards me that hurts the absolute most!" As he approached her closer, he exclaimed. With her mouth trembling and her eyes wide open, Marina stared at him in terror. "I just— I just wanted to know—" she said. She was terrified because he never raised his tone at her and she didn't know how to react at him yelling at her for something she had done to him.

"Marina, if my wish was not to read that letter, there is no way for you to know what was written inside! With my family, I don't want to do anything! Why is it so hard for you to comprehend that?" Marina collapsed upon boxes after tripping on one as she continued walking backward. "Ahh!" She screamed as she fell. Additionally, she hurt herself. The captain instantly turned his expression to one of worry as she let out a painful moan, wanting to assist her in standing up. He tried to assist Marina, but she swatted his hand away "Don't touch me!" She yelled while squeezing her eyes shut and crying uncontrollably.

Mr. Santarelli was bewildered by her acts and unsure of how to respond as he stared at her. At that moment, it started to heavily rain, and the wind was getting harder by the second. The girl started to take big, sharp breaths while glaring at him as her hair fell on her face. He was unclear about what to do as he stood there. Marina sprung into a sprint and started to flee from him and the ship. She exited and hurried past the marine, but the wind continued making her move more slowly.

"*Marina!*"

Gabriel didn't let her get away from him and he instantly went for her. The storm was too much of a barrier for Marina to run through, so she screamed. She remained motionless while hyperventilating. As soon as he reached out to her, he grabbed her by the arms and kept asking her what was wrong in a frightened voice. "I am sorry! Although I shouldn't have, I did read it!"

"So why did you keep it a secret from me?" He yelled. "Because I'm afraid that if you read what the letter said, you'd leave me!" Her mouth trembled further as she sobbed and glanced down. The man was surprised and exclaimed, "Why would I ever leave you!? What was it in the letter that made you think I would have left you, exactly?"

Marina inhaled deeply and quickly. "It stated that your father passed away, you inherited everything." Gabriel exclaimed, "Oh." He wasn't expecting the letter to say that, and he was unsure about how he should feel about it. "Alright... But why exactly do you believe that I would have left you for my father's wealth?" He inquired since he was still perplexed by her thinking. As she nervously bit her lip and rubbed her fingernails against her palm, Marina created the shape of a crescent moon. "My fiancé only married me for my wealth. Because I don't have any money and you struggle with money as well, I panicked thinking that as soon as you inherited something, you would leave me in an instant." She wailed as she continued to struggle for air after crying hysterically for so long.

"I am not Matias. Never will I be him. If I had married you, it would have been out of pure love." He said, resting his hand on his chest. "You're lying!" yelled Marina. She found it difficult to believe him since Matias managed to scar her so severely that she now believes any man who performs an act of compassion for her is deceiving her. Putting both of his hands on her heart-shaped face, the captain stated, "I love you! Whether you think it is true or not." He gazed up at Marina, who sniffed and put her hands on his "Now, will you kindly come? I don't want you to go away from me." Marina pursed her lips and nodded as he questioned. While she also wanted to stay with him, in a moment of terror and humiliation she only wanted to leave her problems behind and thus ran away from him.

The captain helped her change into a dry nightgown once they were inside the cabin and wrapped her in blankets. To help her relax, he even went to the kitchen to brew her some rosemary tea. He slumped into his table and groaned during the entire time the young lady remained silent. "Are you upset with me?" She asked quietly, holding her tea in her hands. With a bewildered and concerned gaze, he turned to face her. "What? No. I'm disappointed that you ignored my advice, though."Marina cried once more. "*I'm sorry.*" She apologized in a high-pitched voice, her throat throbbing from so many tears. "It's alright." Mr. Santarelli firmly gripped her hand as he sat down next to her. "Please try not to cry." He brushed her wet bangs away from her upset face and stated, "I love you and your silly 1800s bangs." He smiled at her and chuckled. She looked up at him with wide-open huge blue eyes, surprised by his remark, "You know they're 1800s?"

"I do, of course. I pay close attention to all of your details." In response, Marina grinned while squeezing her lips together. He didn't even care that her long hair was sticking to him as she put her head on his shoulder. "What are you going to do with the money you inherited?" She enquired curiously, "We could use that chance to buy a house." "You're right." Gabriel thought as he clasped his index fingers together and regarded her. "However, I find it distasteful to use my father's money. Knowing that I didn't make so much money and that my father would have purchased the house, I feel horrified."

Marina averted her eyes and sighed, "I understand you." She answered. Before saying anything, she gave it some thinking. "This might sound insane, but I think I want to go see my parents." He turned his head "Are you sure?" the captain asked, staring at her with confusion. "Really, do you want to see them? Naples is a simple course to set."

"I'm certain. They should at least be aware that I am still alive. Although they might disagree with my choices in life, it's been much too long since I last saw them." The young lady wrapped her blankets tighter around her.

Chapter XXII

June 12th, 1911

Regarding her entire choice, Marina started to experience conflicting feelings. She questioned whether her parents would embrace her or possibly even hate her and deny that she was their daughter. Her fears filled her thoughts. She got dressed pretty that day so her parents don't think that she's homeless perhaps or has been kidnapped. She was dressed in her soft blue dress, gloves, and hat with a large feather on top. Because her parents, especially her father, are very critical, the young lady wished to make a good impression on them and even requested the captain to dress fancier.

"Will your parents approve of this?" questioned the captain while fixing his light blue necktie. "It's lovely. How do I appear?" She questioned him "Exceptional." The man replied. Marina kissed his cheek and gave him a grin. While walking to Vomero, Marina repeatedly used her fingernails to graze the skin on her arm. She was frustrated and her skin turned red. "You need to calm down, so stop doing that. They will be overjoyed to meet you." Mr. Santarelli reassured her and made pleasant comments about the circumstance. "I sincerely hope so. I'm worried they'll view me negatively when they see me again."

"Therefore, their loss. You are a wonderful daughter who has changed up a lot in a short period of time—not even a full year." He kept attempting to assure her that nothing negative would occur. They boarded the funicular to make their way to the area where Marina lived. Vomero was positioned directly on a hill in Naples. It offered a wonderful view on the city. Mr. Santarelli was at Vomero for the first time, and he was captivated by the view of the city and the sea, saying, "This is beautiful... you can even see the volcano Vesuvius!" He examined it closely and stated, "We should go to Pompeii sometime even! There, they discovered recent excavations." Marina grinned at his question. "I've been there numerous times. However, we'll travel there together of course."

Gabriel was taken aback by how beautiful the neighborhood looked when they eventually arrived, saying, "Southern Italy never ceases to amaze me. It's absolutely beautiful." he said. "I got tired of it." Said the young lady as the man surveyed his surroundings and was transfixed by the view of the city and the volcano. "We don't have time to go sightseeing here." Marina softly reminded him as she took hold of his hand. "We must move forward. I do not wish to speak with my folks for only five minutes before departing." The captain nodded his head in agreement. They eventually arrived at Marina's parents' home. She had left it exactly as it appeared last July. Just as she approached the doors, she heard someone walking inside the house. The young lady hesitated a little before knocking, but the captain comforted her by holding her hand, which gave her more confidence. She gave the doors two knocks and waited for her parents to answer.

"Who is it right now?" As he was getting ready for work and looking at his wife, Mr. Rivalli inquired. He opened the doors, and she followed him there. Upon seeing the doors open and her parents standing there in complete disbelief, Marina pursed her lips. "Marina!?" As he stared at her, her father exclaimed. He and his wife both gave their daughter an eerie look as if they were seeing a ghost. Miss Annabella passed out and fell on the ground, which caused Marina to call out, "Mamma!" She yelled in fear at the fact that her mother would suddenly pass out. As soon as possible, Mr. Rivalli lifted his wife and seated her on a couch in the living room. He yelled at his daughter to enter the house immediately as he entered the living room.

Gabriel hurried inside the house with the young lady after being surprised by her parent's reaction. They took a seat on the couch across from Marina's parents. As his wife grew hotter and lost consciousness, her husband continued to flail a fan above her face. "Marina, please bring me some water with sugar in it." He asked his daughter. The girl went straight to the kitchen, fetched a glass of water, and gave it to her father. The moment her father's hand touched hers, he was overcome with emotion at the knowledge that his daughter was still alive. He also felt her touch once again which made him emotional. His wife awoke after he gave her water to drink. "I thought I saw Marina!" Miss Annabella gasped as she cast a wide blue-eyed glance at her husband. "I believe I may have suffered a concussion." She cried out for air. "It's because you did see her!" her husband said.

Mrs. Rivalli looked confused as she moved her head to see her daughter once more. The moment Marina got up, her mother ran up to her. She sobbed uncontrollably, "Mari!" as she closely hugged her. "My lovely and precious daughter!" She gave the girl a full-face kiss that injured the girl's cheeks. Marina was rendered frozen by Mrs. Rivalli's strong embrace. Then Mr. Rivalli ran over and gave her a tight hug as well, continuing to kiss the top of her head while saying, "We thought we lost you." He sobbed. "No, I'm fine, I was fine the entire time."Marina said as she started to cry.

Her parents were overjoyed to see their daughter there, alive and thriving. Mr. Santarelli kept staring at the three of them, and the image of adoring parents made him feel warm within. He was pleased for Marina to have parents that love her and have been deeply concerned for her throughout her entire life. Then Mrs. Rivalli grasped the girl's face angrily and said, "You look different! You look so worn out and like you lost so much more weight!" Marina furrowed her brows and rolled her eyes. She answered, "Well, I have been working a lot." Mr. Rivalli asked her in a perplexed manner, "Worked? Where did you work?" He inquired. The young lady pointed at the captain and started to say, "I've worked as a maid on his ship."

"Who is that, Marina?" She just now noticed a strange man in her home and questioned her daughter. Marina gazed at her parents while tightly gripping the captain's hand. "Gabriel Santarelli. He's my lover." Her parents yelled at her, "Lover!?" as soon as she said that. "Have you lost your mind? You have this... man as your lover after the Matias controversy, how is it possible?" They weren't pleased to hear that, and Gabriel wasn't pleased to hear her parents yell at her because of him. "I realize it's stupid! But it's true. This year, he saved me and gave me a lot of support, and I will always be grateful to him." Marina told her parents how she felt about Mr. Santarelli while putting her legs up on the couch and resting her head on his shoulder.

"No, absolutely not at all." Mr. Rivalli said. "This is ridiculous and unheard of. I've been worried sick about you, only for you to go around and be with other men!?"

"Papà! That is not how it is! I love him." She yelled in an obnoxious tone. Mrs. Rivalli, who supported her husband, expressed her displeasure with what she had heard, saying, "You need to end this immediately. What will people say? Here, they already hate you." Marina's eyes widened, and her brows furrowed. "No. You're not going to be controlling me."

"We are your parents! Get this man out of my house!" her father yelled at her as he pointed his index finger at her. At this moment, Marina was furious and refused to let them speak to her loved one in this manner. "You make him leave, and I'm leaving with him instantly." She said while giving them a frightening glance. Her parents were surprised by this and questioned whether the captain might have influenced her thoughts. "You! Have you poisoned the mind of my daughter?

Gabriel gave him a puzzled look. "No!? I never would have! I genuinely care about your daughter, sir." Mr. Adriano moaned and put his palm over his face. His daughter's continued immaturity infuriated him. He only wished she would return and that they could all live in harmony as a family. "Marina, why are you treating us like this? Do you realize how much money we gave to Mr. and Mrs. Marotta to ensure that they wouldn't ever report you to anyone?"

"What did you do? Why!?" In disbelief, Marina struck her thighs with her hands. "They arrived and threatened to report us if we didn't pay them." Miss Annabella explained as she worriedly eyed her daughter. Marina was furious and frustrated. "That man, *that!*—I detest him! I resent him to the core of my being!" She yelled. The captain took a look at her and told her not to worry about that crude and abhorrent man. "Why are you mad at Matias so much? You're the one that ran away from the wedding that I paid for and that was tremendously expensive!" shouted out Mr. Rivalli. The girl ground her teeth and clenched her hands as her face grew crimson with rage. She screamed, "I despise him because he raped me!" as tears ran from her eyes. "He raped me in my bedroom the moment papà left downstairs!" She rested on Mr. Santarelli's shoulder and started crying. He comforted her by wrapping his arm around her and lightly touching her face.

The girl's parents' mouths gaped in surprise. They were in disbelief. A man sexually assaulted their own daughter. They never considered the idea that their cherished daughter would experience something like it. To avoid passing out once more, Mrs. Rivalli grabbed her fan and started to flap it at her face. On the other side, Marina's father was furious. If he had the ability, he would have revived Matias Marotta and killed him once more. He turned around and started to cry in silence. Her father sobbed uncontrollably while covering his lips with his palm. He wished he could have stayed with her all day that day so she wouldn't have suffered any harm. He was so overcome with shame that he was unable to breathe. The mother of Marina couldn't help but break down in tears as well. The thought of her young daughter suffering harm pained her. "Is that the reason he died? Did you murder him?" asked Mrs. Rivalli "Yes. He wouldn't let go of me, so I killed him to defend myself." She heaved a groan in agony.

Her mother pursed her lips, thinking that asking additional questions about the circumstance would be detrimental to her daughter's memory of the terrible circumstances she had gone through. "You. Why is my daughter working as a maid for you? What kind of disgusting justification do you possibly have?" Mrs. Rivalli questioned the captain. "She approached me and begged me to assist her. She stayed on my ship for free, so as a way of my gratitude, I hired her as a maid. She willingly agreed to it. I will swear on my life that I never made her do anything." Replied the captain.

"How cheap are you to make my daughter work for you!" The girl's father yelled. "Do you not feel ashamed?" "I'm delighted he gave me the job position!" Marina snapped at him. "I gained the ability to be self-reliant, diligent, kind, and ready to experience life. I even picked up cooking and baking skills! Mamma and papà, you never suggested that I learn anything besides how to be a decent wife." Angry, she yelled at her parents. "You could have always asked me if you wanted to learn how to cook!" The famous chef and father of Marina, who is well-known across Naples, yelled in confusion.

"I repeatedly asked you for assistance, but you ignored me and instructed me to go sit down since I would only cause trouble." She made a pouty face while furrowing her brows. Her father never tried to let her assist him. "Instead of learning it from my own father, a chef, I had to learn from a sweet elderly woman who was ready to teach me." Marina grabbed a fold of her dress and felt like ripping it apart.

Her attitude was starting to irritate Mr. Adriano. "Young lady, I'm sick of your attitude. You have treated your parents horribly ever since you left." He shouted. When Marina heard that, she gasped in shock at her father's remark. "My attitude!? You've just been utterly awful to me today, and even to Gabriel."

"I don't care about some odd homeless man who came into my house! Out of every single person you could've chosen, you found some godawful sailor!"

Marina yelled. "He's a great man!" "You live near the sea!" he said, pointing at her. "You should be aware that

sailors are troublemakers." The captain rested
awkwardly on the couch and started to realize where
Marina had learned that all sailors are lousy men. "Out
of all men, you just had to find a captain. Why weren't
you able to wed the prince of Naples?" Mr. Rivalli
sighed. Having a headache from her parents, Marina
moaned deeply and put her palm on her head. "He's
married and much older than me, papà! And I would've
never married a man whom I do not love!" She scowled
because she couldn't believe her father wanted her to
wed a man solely for financial gain.

In that instant, Mr. Adriano Rivalli looked at his wife,
who was keeping quiet out of concern that the fight
might get worse than it already was. "What is your
opinion on this, wife?" He questioned, extending his
arms to Marina and the captain as he sent a frustrated
gaze her way. "We ought to all calm down, in my
opinion. The fact that our daughter returned safely
should make you and I delighted. We'll see what we
decide to do about the captain position later." She
muttered as she smacked her fan against her hand. In
response, Marina stood up and said, "Well, I'm leaving. I
had no intention of remaining here for so long. especially
now that you two completely lack support for me." She
was yelled at by her father "Sit back down! You've been
running away for a year, you're not going anywhere!"
The captain was unsure whether he should stay or leave
as the girl sat down angrily since she was upset with him.
"Should I leave you and your parents alone to discuss,
perhaps?" He crossed his leg across his knee and

LV Polcic

inquired. "Stay, please. I am unable to manage them on my own." Marina conveyed her want to go immediately as she sighed.

"Where is my cat?" She asked. As the young lady stood up and realized she couldn't see her cat anywhere, she asked. "He's here someplace. Most likely snoozing on your bed." Marina's eyes widened as she uttered, "*My bed*." Thinking of her bed and everything that had occurred on it made her uneasy. Gabriel hurried up to her and he put his hands on hers as she started to make her way upstairs to get her beloved pet. "Would you like to have me come with you?" He questioned. "I'll handle it on my own. I am capable of entering my bedroom on my own." She pushed back. Worriedly looking at her, the man aggressively murmured to her. "Please, I cannot be alone with your parents; I'm terrified!" She left him all alone with her parents and he uncomfortably grinned at them, thinking he'd have a better impression on them. As he sat back down on the couch, Marina's parents kept looking at him with a judgmental facial expressions.

"It is very lovely to meet you."

"Be silent." Demanded Mr. Rivalli.

The young girl put her hands on the wall as she made her way upstairs to her room, remembering what it was like to live here as she glanced at the pictures hanging on them. She discovered her bedroom door was wide open and her cat was soundly dozing on her bed. When she walked into her bedroom, everything was exactly as she had left it, but for the fact that it was now cleaner than it had been the day of her wedding. "My kitty!" She exclaimed as she grabbed her fat cat, Cesare. He attempted to push away from her since he was upset that she had awoken him from his slumber. He was carried around by Marina like a baby, and she kept kissing his tiny nose. She held her kitty aloft while she lay on her bed and looked up at him.

She dropped her cat, who then fell on her stomach and caused her to grunt in pain, as all the memories suddenly came flooding back to her as she was doing that. She ultimately started breathing deeply, stood up, and leaned against the mirror. However, as she did that, she became even more frightened and put her palm on her chest, clutching it firmly while she continued to breathe rapidly. While trying not to cry, Marina tripped and fell close to her bed. She was unable to handle the thoughts of Matias raping her in this same room. She felt angry with herself for still being unable to let go of him. Her heart started to beat quickly, and she could feel it in her throat.

The captain was upstairs at the moment to avoid the girl's parents and to observe what she was doing in her bedroom. He hurried up to her and grasped her hand firmly as soon as he noticed her shaking on the ground. "What happened? Talk to me!" He begged her to explain what had occurred. She struggled to take big breaths and yelled, "I can't— I can't breathe!" as she continued to take shallow breaths. He lifted her tightly and carried her to another bedroom that was empty after realizing that her current bedroom was making her uncomfortable.

She was placed on another bed, and he firmly gripped her hand. "Are you all right?" She was starting to calm down and breathe properly when he questioned. "I'm fine, I just had a moment of distress after entering my bedroom."

"Ah... Please tell me whatever else you need from there, and I'll go get it." He said as he tucked a curl that had fallen on her cheek behind her ear. "I'm grateful. I'm irritated at myself for not being able to enter my bedroom without thinking of him!" She cried out as her fists slammed against the bed's edge. "You cannot rush healing with your wounds. Plus you say that, meanwhile, you became more comfortable even uttering out what happened to you and you even became more comfortable with intercourse." Her lips curved into a smile in response to the captain's smile. Then her fat cat entered the room and leaped onto the bed, "Cesare! You sensed I was sad and you came to me!" Marina cried joyfully.

Judged For Mercy

She was overjoyed to see her cat seek to comfort her
(Which wasn't the truth. He just wanted to sleep
somewhere.)

"Your cat is named Cesare?" He queried. "After Giulio
Cesare, yes." She answered. She caught Gabriel's
attention as he momentarily considered, "I was born on
the same day as him, what a coincidence." The girl
chuckled as she asked him a question. "When is your
birthday, then? Actually, you've never even told me."

"July 12th, 1889." He responded as Marina's eyes
narrowed, enlarged, and wrinkled her nose in response.
"It is July 12th today." He didn't tell her that he was born
on this day or that he turned 24 years, she exclaimed in
annoyance. "I didn't consider it important. I also didn't
want to bring up the subject at all because of the whole
issue with your folks." Marina sighed at him as he
continued to explain. He proceeded to tell her that he
doesn't like celebrating it either way, and she threw
herself to the bed. "Im upset at you still for not telling
me that, but now I'm not sure what to do with my parents.
They want me to remain." She replied while putting her
hands over her face.

"Then, to resolve everything and in comfort for them, I
believe you should stay for a few days." He explained,

but he was aware that she detested doing this far more
than she should have. "Will you stay with me?" the
young lady said as she nodded and looked up at him. He
inquired "I can't, maybe for a day, and then I need to
leave and drop off cargo." He sighed and then gave his
response. At that, Marina scowled and crossed her arms.
"But I'll be back as soon as I can, I swear. Then we'll
leave." The man's hand caressed her soft, freckled cheek.
She clutched his hand with both of her hands while she
closed her eyes. "Alright, if you say so. Then let's
continue our conversation downstairs."

They clasped hands securely as they made their way
downstairs, and the girl was grinning from ear to ear.
Seeing her so close to a sailor made her father sick to his
stomach. "After speaking with Gabriel, I decided that I
would stay here for a few days. But only if you two
listen to what I have to say and refrain from disparaging
the man I care about as I speak." Her fists were on her
hips as she pleaded with them to acknowledge her as
their daughter once more. "I—" Mr. Rivalli started to
dispute, but his wife interrupted him. "Certainly,
sweetheart. as long as you're with us here." Miss
Annabella answered calmly while firmly placing her
hand over her husband's mouth to prevent him from
saying anything further he might later regret. "Can we
talk in the garden? I detest spending all day indoors."
Marina asked her parents while furrowing her brow.
They all moved toward the garden behind their house
after her mother agreed.

In the garden, an enormous lemon tree had been planted, and there were chairs and a table there as well. As Marina was about to sit down, Mr. Santarelli hurried up to the chairs and pulled one back. While her mother watched them, her daughter kept laughing at the cavalry. She had grown accustomed to the captain and loved how protective he was of her daughter in contrast to Matias, who was only interested in dominating her. Miss Annabella went to the kitchen to prepare a cool beverage after grabbing a few lemons. The captain and the girls' father were seated outdoors alone. Mr. Santarelli tried to be friendly with her father while he continued to glare at them, saying, "You have a very beautiful garden, sir."

"Thank you." Mr. Rivalli responded in a lifeless tone. Then, as Marina tried to bestow praise on Gabriel for his abilities in math and history to her father, the captain pursed his lips awkwardly. "He speaks a variety of languages as well!" She shouted. "If you're so talented, why are you working on a ship?" her father chuckled. "Because I ran away from home, I was unable to complete my schooling or pay for further study to secure a better job." Mr. Adriano Rivalli cracked his knuckles and gave his daughter the side-eye, not believing what a man his daughter had found. It would have been preferable if she had wed a goat instead.

"You're forgetting, papà, that I was expelled from school for punching a girl in the nose with a book." She reminded him as she leaned against the table with her arms folded. "This is different since you are a woman. Your sole straightforward task was to find a wealthy man and be married to him; you don't need to work to have money." He yelled. "You're such a hypocrite, honestly," Marina banged her palms on the table. "When mamma first met you, what should she have done? You were a poor butcher! Does that mean she could've treated you like garbage because she was an affluent Austrian girl!?" She managed to trap her father in such a way that he was struck speechless. Mrs. Rivalli entered the garden at the given moment while carrying a tray of drinks.

"I see all of you are screaming like barbaric cavemen again." As she set the drinks down, she said. The captain welcomed her arrival since he was sick of Mr. Rivalli's screaming. After tasting it, Gabriel thought it was wonderfully hydrating. "This is incredibly good and soothes you off in the heat of the summer." He praised Mrs. Rivalli's drink. "Thank you, this is just plain lemonade juice with black pepper and mint. This lemon tree produces excellent lemons." She spoke as she looked up at the lemon tree. "The tree was a gift from Marina's Sicilian grandparents when she and her brother were born. Every time a member of my husband's family has a child, it is customary for them to plant a tree." The captain grinned at that; he thought their family tradition was lovely and wished his own family had it in place of constant conflict.

The smell of her garden during the summertime calmed Marina immensely, and she continued glancing at the butterflies and bees flying around and close to her. Even her cat came out to the garden to sit on her lap as Marina straightened the large pink bow that was around the cat's neck. "Why did you give Cesare that pretty pink bow?" Questioned the captain "Because I want other female cats to purr the moment they see my handsome little fat kitty." After hearing what she said, Mr. Santarelli started laughing and would not stop. Cesare sprang out of Marina's lap as soon as she started laughing because the trembling from her laughter terrified him.

He continued to sit on Mr. Rivalli's lap instead. At first, her father didn't like the idea of having a cat in the house, especially a black cat because he thought black cats were extremely unlucky, but over time, he warmed to the notion and eventually came to adore him.

"Alright, Gabriel. I wanted to know whether you had any plans with my daughter." questioned Marina's mother. She was curious as to whether the captain had anything planned with Marina or if he was merely taking advantage of her youth for his amusement. "Well, we had intended to move to Rome soon and settle down. Hopefully, also get married." He spoke while firmly gripping Marina's hand on the table.

"Over my dead body." Marina's father exclaimed. His
wife gave him a warning finger and stated "Silence! No
one asked you to talk!" She screamed at him because she
was sick of his attitude. Infuriated, Mr. Rivalli crossed
his arms and turned his head away. "In Rome, I had
originally intended to start my own bakery. I feel quite
passionate about cooking and baking since I've gotten
good at it." Marina explained "She really is a terrific
cook, it's true. She must be like her father, I suppose."
The captain tried to be kind to Marina's father, but he
was angry the entire time and didn't even acknowledge
his compliment.

When Mr. Santarelli realized he still had a lot of work to
do at the ship, he glanced at his watch and said, "Dearest,
I must leave right away. I recalled that I needed to
determine the coordinates, monitor the shipment, and go
get new ropes. I'll visit tomorrow." He said as he kissed
the girl's hand. "You're already leaving?" She questioned
while giving him a sad expression. Unfortunately, he had
to leave, so he nodded and said, "It was a pleasure
meeting you, Mr. and Mrs. Rivalli, but I have to leave
for work."

The young lady watched him depart, and her mother
waved him off as he walked away. The minute Mr.
Rivalli wanted to speak to his daughter properly because
the captain had left, Marina got up and excused herself,
saying, "I'm going to wash myself and get ready for

bed." She expressed her displeasure that the captain had to depart in a monotonous voice. Without Mr. Santarelli by her side, she didn't want to make any effort to talk with them more, which her father could not believe.

Later that evening, Marina was braiding her long, curly hair while dressed in a nightgown. It felt strange to her to braid it without Gabriel's assistance for the first time in a while, especially since she was about to go to bed without him. "Rina, may I come in?" her mother asked her before coming in as Marina was seated at the edge of the bed. In her response, the young lady said that she could. While holding a plate of strawberries with sugar sprinkled on top, Miss Annabella sat next to her daughter "I sincerely hope you still like them." Her mother enquired. "Oh, mamma. I'm not somebody altogether different. I am still me." She spoke while maintaining eye contact with her mother. "I know." Sighed Mrs. Rivalli "I simply don't want to annoy you."

"It's fine mamma. I'm just frustrated that papà won't take my advice."

"You should give him a bit of time. He finds it difficult because of the chaos that followed your wedding. Due to your poor reputation in the city, he nearly lost his restaurant and later had to give away a lot of money." She gave her daughter a cheek pat. "Whether or not you realize it, your father loves you in his unique manner.

You need to give him some more time to adjust to this whole situation." As she attempted to explain to her daughter the circumstances surrounding her husband, Mrs. Rivalli smiled awkwardly.

"I only hope you don't make the same mistake you did with Matias again. And disregard your father's advice, never get married for money. I didn't, and I'm quite content." The remarks made by Marina's mother gave her comfort. She gave her a firm hug. She placed her face on her mother's chest and whispered, "Oh mamma..."

Miss Annabella broke down in tears when her daughter hugged her. She hadn't felt her hug in a year, and when she did, her heart cried with happiness.

Days went by... Marina was starting to open out more to her parents. Even her father started to feel more things for her besides just being resentful of everything she did. He was so proud of her that one night they even made dinner together. He questioned how she was able to perfect his recipes without ever seeing them.

Her mother gasped at the dinner as Marina set the pasta with clams and garlic on the table. "I knew you said you learned how to cook, but I didn't know you were this talented!" She exclaimed. The young lady put her hands on her hips and grinned confidently. I even made quickly a dessert for later."

"Papà is incredibly proud of you!" her father said as he gave her a strong kiss on the cheek. As he continued to kiss her face, Marina pursed her lips and wrinkled her nose. In order to arrange her hair because the curls kept tripping over her face, the young lady removed her mittens. The captain rushed in at that moment and muttered, "I'm sorry if I'm late! It takes so long to get here." He sat down at the table, trying to regain his breath, and started to apologize for being late for dinner. He handed a bouquet of tulips to Mrs. Rivalli "I hope Miss you love tulips. They compliment your features beautifully." Mrs. Rivalli gasped and was so in love with the tulips. She thanked him and immediately went to put them in a vase to admire them.

Marina raised a brow at him "Where is a bouquet for me?" She questioned. He handed her then a beautiful bouquet of daisies "Don't be so impatient, of course, I thought about you as well." The young lady smiled widely and kissed him on the lips for his generosity towards her and even her mother.

As soon as the father of the girl side-eyed Mr. Santarelli, his demeanor abruptly changed. "What wonderful dish did you cook?" He inquired. "Oh, I just made some clam and garlic spaghetti." She answered as she put away her daisies. He eagerly rubbed his hands together and smiled. Before starting to eat, the man waited for her to take a seat. For them all to enjoy while eating, Marina brought a bottle of white wine. She strained to open the bottle and was so frustrated that she nearly broke it.

Gabriel assisted her in standing up and stated, "You have to center it in the middle before screwing it up." As he started to open the bottle and place a towel underneath it in case anything spilled, he explained. Everyone's glasses were filled with wine by the man. He struck Miss Annabella as such a gentleman and she smiled at the thought of him being her son-in-law.

After dinner, Marina went to bring a homemade dessert: a glass of pudding with raspberry topping. The tray she was holding became too heavy for her, causing her hands to start shaking, and the captain stepped in to assist her. He set everything down and told her to go sit back. "You see how he aids her, right?" enquired Miss Annabella at her spouse. "I do and I don't give a damn. She was capable of bringing the tray by herself." He muttered as he lost all desire to even think about or even look at the captain. After taking a drink of her wine, Mrs. Rivalli inquired, "Oh! How long have you served as a captain, Gabriel?" "For a few years now." he responded. "I've never desired this job. I just needed to be hired right away so I wouldn't be homeless." The same way her daughter did, Miss Annabella puckered her thin lips and said, "That's such a shame. If you ever get married, what kind of job would you desire to have?"

"Since becoming a lawyer would need years of education and the best university for it is in England, where I have no intention of ever moving, if I could then, I'd love to be a professor." "I didn't know you gave up on becoming a lawyer." Marina asked him with concern as she turned to face him. "It's fine. It's a prudent choice because if I didn't, I wouldn't be able to provide for you financially, see you very little, and it would take me much longer to become one." As he continued, Marina put her head on his shoulder and said, "I'm sorry you want to give up your dreams for me." She was a little upset that he was giving up his dreams for her.

"I desire to be with you. All that matters is that." He gave her a reassuring grin as he gazed into her lovely ocean-blue eyes. "You just cannot be with my daughter if you do not have a reliable source of income to support her." The girls' father yelled angrily as he rose and scowled at them. "Adriano!" yelled his wife. Saying "Stop it!" She pushed back. "Sir, I don't mean to offend you, but I'm not homeless. I still have a substantial amount of savings, and I know I can get another work to keep our finances stable." Gabriel made an effort to defend himself, but the father of his beloved wasn't sympathetic. "I could care less! It makes me uncomfortable to see you close to my daughter.

Godawful sailors like you could easily manipulate her since she's young." He yelled as he violently banged his hands upon the table, causing the plates to jump up a little bit in the air. "Stop! Do not address him in this manner! You should be grateful because he repeatedly saved my life! Gabriel saved me from drowning and being nearly killed by a robber." Marina raised an eyebrow and exclaimed.

"What!?" Do you not hear yourself!?" her father shouted. "Because of him, you've come close to passing away several times!" Her father continued as he placed his arms on the table and was slowly beginning to push things off of it "Papà stop!" Shouted his daughter. "You would have been fine and well if you had never been on his ship! I will lock you inside this house if it meant of you to *never* leave with that man again!" Mr. Rivalli said as he pushed everything off of the table aggressively, smashing the plates and ruining the meals his daughter had made. Marina gasped, placed her hands on her lips and was bewildered. She shook her head in denial as the captain placed his hand on her shoulder for comfort. He couldn't believe what her father had done, simply for them loving each other. Miss Annabella as well was frustrated and resented her husband in that moment. With a stern expression on her face, Marina exclaimed, "No, I wouldn't. You would have rather kept me inside the house shut and prevented me from leaving. To me, that is torment, not life. With Gabriel, I once again experienced life. I was happy." the young lady said, pausing to gather her thoughts and calm herself as she bit her bottom lip. "You kept comparing me with Rocco. I experienced a sense of living under his shadow. Father, for the first time in a very long time, I felt like my own person while I was aboard his ship. Someone for once cared about me." Tears rolled down her cheek as she shut her eyes. As Mr. Rivalli started to feel regret, he moved closer to his daughter. She pleaded with him to let go of her and moved her arm away from him. Going upstairs, she said with an upset tone in her voice "Thank you for destroying the dinner I worked so hard to prepare."

Being angered by her father, Marina immediately walked upstairs and sobbed. She could no longer stand to hear him. The captain got to his feet as well, stared at the girl's father as he left, then turned around to go after her since he could tell she was furious. Mrs. Rivalli gazed at her husband while inhaling sharply and deeply. She had never been so furious with anyone in her life. "You are such a moron." She declared. "Me!? You're referring to me as a moron?

"I am, yes. If you even get to sleep in the same bed as me tonight, consider yourself lucky." His wife raised an eyebrow and expanded her eyes to warn him. Like her daughter, she was fairly intimidating when angry and didn't hold back on her insults. Mr. Rivalli was left alone in the catastrophe of a dining room, which was

something he didn't want to happen, as Miss Annabella
went to her bedroom as well. He was furious with
himself for shouting during dinner, but his rage
overcame him.

Marina was pacing around the bedroom she shared with
the captain while speaking quickly. She raged against
her father and spoke nonstop while gesturing with her
hands to convey her feelings, saying, "I cannot believe
him! Such a frustrating man, he is! Gabriel, I'm going to
leave them without saying anything and pack up
immediately."As the hair on her face fell, she yelled.
"Do not do that." Mr. Santarelli, who was sitting at the
edge of the bed, tried to convince her. "That will just
seem incredibly immature. You need to calm down even
though I can tell you're quite angry." She was advised to
take a seat next to him and to cease being so negative.

"You aren't understanding me at all! He has no right to
tell me what I should do with my life! I can do whatever
I want to because I'm an adult lady. I want to shout and
cry at the same moment when I see him." She yelled,
making a fist out of her hands and letting out a long,
loud groan. "Do you realize that when I first saw you,
you reminded me exactly of him? You annoyed me, too,
but it wasn't the cause of my sudden want for the worse
for you." Marina turned to face him, scowled at him with
her menacing blue eyes, and pointed a finger at him as

he tried to explain. "Do not displease me tonight either, dearest." She pushed back.

"You can be angry all you want, and I will understand you since I'm as furious with him. Do you think I enjoy hearing your father make fun of me every time I see him? No, I don't, but if you're not going to be reasonable with your father, at least be reasonable with your mother, who loves you a lot and seems to be trying to be kind to you." He softly took her hand and motioned for her to take a seat next to him. Marina was so furious at the exact moment that she was on the edge of striking her fist into a wall as she pulled at her hair and looked down. The captain took her trembling hand and gave it a gentle kiss while she continued to shake with stress and rage. "No matter what, I'll be here for you."

As she laid her head on his shoulder, Marina sighed quietly "I envy you for being so calm." She mentioned her desire to sometimes be as composed as him. "What will we truly do when we are settled? How will we be able to live in Rome on our budget?" She asked because she was concerned that starting a bakery would be extremely difficult and expensive. "Well, after giving it some thought, I'll take my father's fortune. As a result, we receive both money and a mansion." The girl widened her eyes and leaped out of the bed, and he glanced at her.

"You're making fun of me, aren't you? Do you intend to take the money? That would be amazing, Gabriel!" She grinned broadly, shrieked with delight, and leaped up and down in response to how happy she was to hear it from him. "I don't want to be so bitter about my father; he should be dead in my head too. Additionally, if Hell exists, I hope my father is crying in Hell since his feminine son got all of his money." As the girl leaped on him and they both fell on the bed, he laughed.

He put his hands on her waist and she gave him a passionate kiss on the lips. His eyes were entirely hidden by her hair, which tickled him. "However, I must break some awful news." She pulled her lips away from his as he mumbled to her. "I have to leave Naples tomorrow, and I'll be gone for at least a week but no longer than two weeks. I have cargo to deliver in the Ottoman Empire." Mr. Santarelli rolled his eyes since he didn't want to travel for such a long time.

When she heard him say that, she asked "Should I come with you?" Marina became upset. "No, remain here a little longer with your parents. Although I'm sure you'll despise me for it, I believe it's for the best. If I took you away from them for two weeks, they would kill me." He stated that he didn't want her to be too sad over his leaving her as he took both of her hands. "It has been awful to sleep without you." The captain said. The young girl nodded in agreement and commented on how strange it was for her to sleep alone after getting used to having him by her side.

"The fact that you don't pull me by the hair in the middle of the night is equally strange." He was the target of her hysterical laughter. "Every time I do it, I apologize to you. I truly apologize." As he attempted to apologize to her once more, his eyebrows scrunched. "Soon, it will just be the two of us..." he said as they lay down on the bed, holding hands and looking at each other. "No Francesca, no Margherita and Giordana, no your parents—just the two of us spending time together." As he started to tell her about their near future, Gabriel stated. "I wish to decorate the garden at the mansion, so we have somewhere to sit and talk while outside." As she flashed him a condescending smile and glared at his drooping hooded dark brown eyes that she admired, Marina asked. "It's all yours, my dearest Marina."

August 10th, 1911

Second, minutes, hours, days, and weeks have passed, but the captain is still nowhere to be found in Naples. Every day, Marina would walk to the marine and spend hours waiting for her beloved there. Due to how frequently she was seen, many started to recognize her face. Some even felt sorry for her because she was constantly waiting for someone who never appeared. Everyone would think she'd lose all hope for the man to return, but she never did, even when people told her to give up. In particular, her father told her that she should be glad that he never returned. One day when she arrived at her house after leaving the marine, she took off her hat and was welcomed inside by her parents who were holding a gift for her. They wanted to give it to her right away. "Mari, I know you're disappointed that he hasn't returned and probably won't, but that's not the reason for you to be upset today on your birthday." her father said.

"I'm not unhappy; I'm just concerned if something were to happen to him." Marina sighed as she cast a glance at him. "Well, let's hope he's fine." Mrs. Rivalli said while kissing her daughter's sweet cheeks. "Happy twentieth birthday, however, to my lovely and beautiful daughter." They couldn't believe their daughter was already twenty as they both gave her a full-face kiss and continued to hug her. It seemed like yesterday when she was still an adorable baby who sobbed nonstop.

She grinned at their parental love for her as they seated her on the couch. She exclaimed in shock at the size of the present they presented her. "Open it!" Her mother urged her. When Marina opened the box, she saw a gorgeous pair of brand-new white shoes inside.

The young lady took them out and gazed at them. "You shouldn't have; buying them must have cost a fortune." She continued to stare at them as she spoke. "Buying you something is not a problem, especially for your birthday." Her father added, "Plus you've been so sad lately due to Gabriel leaving you."

"He didn't abandon me!" Marina growled at her father. "He's traveling aboard a ship! Why do you have so little hope? When I departed, did you have the same thoughts?" She inquired in anguish because she couldn't believe that her father wanted her to have the same lack of hope as he did. "He's been gone for a month, Marina. In all honesty, you can forget about him because he won't ever return and is likely already seeing someone else." Mr. Rivalli crossed his arms and knees and gave his opinion. While Marina pursed her lips and appeared to be crying, his wife narrowed her eyes at him and struck him on the arm. "Say you're sorry to her now!" Miss Annabella yelled at her husband and demanded an apology. "I'm tired of you, you old man who's so sour! I did not marry you for you to act like this toward our daughter!" She exclaimed. Instantaneously, Marina threw her gift-received shoes to the ground.

She turned around and headed away, looking at her father, "I hate you." she grumbled. Her father chased after her as she ran out the doors, out of fear that she was fleeing once more. "Marina, stop!" As Miss Annabella moved closer to him, he yelled at his daughter, "Leave me alone! You ignored me repeatedly, and now you suddenly want me back?" As the wind whipped in her face and her hair stuck to her cheeks, she yelled in confusion. "I'm sorry for treating you so poorly. Although I should be, I'm not the best father."

"Sorry is not enough." She said as she left the house and headed back into the city. "She is right. We've done a lot of damage to both of our children and look what it led us to! You want to keep Marina inside the house, knowing that she's upset without Gabriel!" Miss Annabella exclaimed while glaring at her husband who didn't know how to fix his relationship with his daughter.

Even though Marina would have preferred to see the captain, at least the feel of the sea gave her a sense of peace. She passed the marine again, but his ship was still nowhere to be seen.

The young lady headed for a nearby beach and spent several hours there. She simply didn't think about anything while lying on the sand all afternoon, letting her hair drift in the water. The girl found it to be peaceful, and she treasured the sensation of the warm sea in the summer. In that instant, she even felt a connection to the sea. She eventually got to her feet and dried her long, curly locks in the sun while looking for pretty seashells to collect and store at home. It seemed strange to her at times that she was back home in Naples. Not at all in a nice manner. She was aware that she didn't belong here and that she was once more feeling confined.

After her hair had dry, she turned back toward her house and strolled past the marine once more. She became distraught as she stared at the ships and briefly lost faith that her beloved would not come back to her. She worried that he might have perished in the sea, become lost on an island, or be drifting somewhere in the middle of the sea. That notion made her heart start to beat more quickly. She took another glance at the shimmering sea to calm herself before spotting a recognizable figure there.

It was Gabriel's ship. He finally arrived after all this time. She instantly started running as fast as she could in his direction. Everyone regarded her strangely and wondered why she was rushing. Although Marina's feet hurt from sprinting in her shoes, she didn't care at the time because all she could think about was him. She held her dress up so she wouldn't trip over it. The captain quickly exited his ship once it had anchored while carrying a big bag with him. "Oh, my heart!" He said as he grabbed his chest and turned to face Marina. She leaped into his arms when she saw him since she was so excited to see him. He then dropped his bag and spun the girl around.

They couldn't believe they were seeing each other at that very second and started to cry together. "You're alive! You're alive!" Exclaimed Marina as she cried hysterically and smiled widely at him. "I am! Even if I had passed away, I would have returned from the grave simply to see you." He continued to smile at her while saying with a brittle voice. He sincerely missed her. He missed everything about her—her eyes, her lips, her dimples, the feel of her hands. "How come you brought a bag with you?" She touched his face as she felt his stubble short beard poking her fingers, and inquired.

"My clothes are in it..." he said. "I sold the ship. The crew just dropped me off here. I couldn't bear another minute without you, I want to start a new life with you!" She sobbed even harder as he shouted at her and she closely clutched him. The young lady's tears started falling like a waterfall since she was unable to control them any longer. "I didn't bring you anything for your birthday, I'm so sorry." Said the man in an upset tone as he was frustrated at himself for not being able to gift her anything "Having you be here with me is the best gift I could've ever received." Marina grasped onto his back tighter, she adored being able to touch him. Being without him was the most miserable she's ever felt.

Marina hastily gathered her old belongings and headed up aboard the ship. After gathering everything, she went to the elderly women to express her gratitude for everything they had done for her, particularly to Margherita. "I appreciate your patience with me. To me, you acted as a godmother." The girl wept. The kind old woman gave her a forehead kiss and told her to have a good life. Finally, she turned to face Francesca, the girl who had nothing but animosity for her from the beginning to the end. "Francesca, I hope one day you find your peace." The young lady said this as she reached out to shake her hand. The young woman with red hair slapped her arm. "Leave already, please." Francesca said. Marina gave her a fleeting glance before averting her gaze. Francesca was very resentful that Marina had left the ship and started an affectionate relationship with the captain. The captain and the young lady gave everyone one more wave before departing.

Since the ship was ultimately the reason they had met, they were both feeling emotional at that very moment. They both felt as though this was the end of an era, but instead saw it as the start of a new era. It was there that they declared their affection to one another and even shared their first kiss. To inform the girls' parents that they would soon be traveling to Rome, they traveled to Vomero. Mr. and Mrs. Rivalli heard two of them laughing as they unlocked the entrance to the residence. "He's back?" asked Mr. Rivalli. "He loves her, so of course, he returned." As she got to her feet and walked toward her daughter, she yelled angrily. Marina and the captain received warm embraces from Miss Annabella, who said, "It's good to see that you're well!" The woman addressed Mr. Santarelli. "Thank you; I know it must have seemed strange for me to be gone for so long." Although he apologized, the young lady's mother kept begging him not to.

At the hallway's entrance, Mr. Adriano Rivalli approached them. He kept quiet because he was speechless. He merely extended his arm to Gabriel and said, "Welcome back." He spoke softly. He was thanked and Mr. Santarelli extended a handshake. In that instant, Marina beaming with happiness said, "Me and Gabriel have news to tell you two." Her father sighed and hoped she isn't pregnant with the man.

"We're departing to Rome. Forever." The girl smiled while tightly gripping Mr. Santarelli's hand, who was also beaming. "Leave? But how? Aren't you engaged in nautical work? And how are you going to pay to leave there so quickly?" asked Mr. Santarelli, Marina's mother. "I'm not anymore. I sold the ship. Additionally, I was born into a wealthy family and inherited everything." He spoke while looking at Marina's father, who was unable to speak. "I inherited all the money, and we'll have our own mansion." When she heard it, Miss Annabella gasped because she hadn't anticipated that he would genuinely be wealthy and come from a wealthy family.

After that, Mr. Rivalli started to feel guilty about assuming Gabriel was quite impoverished when in fact he wasn't and he realized that he truly cared only about money.

"When do you plan to depart?" curiously asked her mother. "We're boarding the first train tomorrow." Answered Marina. Mrs. Rivalli found it incomprehensible that her daughter was already leaving for Rome and had begun a new life. Mr. Rivalli wanted her to simply stay with them forever but was in denial about it. He felt such great pain in his chest from thinking about letting her get away with Mr. Santarelli, which was painful to see.

Marina and Gabriel prepared that night for their departure to Rome. They were eager to leave and couldn't stand to be in Naples any longer, particularly Marina, who wanted to have her own space and not live with her parents forever. When her parents were about to fall asleep, Mr. Rivalli sobbed to his wife, "I can't let her go! When I consider my daughter leaving once more, my heart begins to tear up! I'm worried she'll sustain another injury." "You need to let go of her; she is no longer five years old." his wife told him as she turned away from the book she was reading. "Gabriel and she are in love, and that is the end of the narrative." She gave an explanation because she was becoming tired of seeing him weep over their daughter. "Why can't you be more consoling toward me, you're acting so coldly toward me?" He looked at her and questioned. Miss Annabella tapped him on the face three times with her hand while keeping her eyes firmly fixed on her book, saying in a monotone voice, "There, there." and kept reading her book.

"My impossible daughter..." he sighed as he kept thinking about his dear daughter who he loved with all of his heart.

The girls' parents were at the railway station the following day with Marina and Mr. Santarelli. They awaited the departure of their train. They were saying their goodbyes in the interim. Miss Annabella continued to adjust her daughter's hat as she adorned her neck with a pretty bow. "Please send me letters as frequently as you can. And if you could, come back more often." she cried. While her mother was sobbing, Marina frowned and said, "Mamma don't cry... I'm not moving to America." "You're not, but it feels like you are!" Her mother couldn't stop sobbing. Even though he came to grips with it, Mr. Rivalli still didn't like the notion of his daughter leaving the house with Mr. Santarelli. If the man made her happy, there was nothing more he could do, and he realized that keeping her inside the house would cause more harm than good. He approached Mr. Santarelli and warned him, "I'll slaughter you if you fail to take care of my daughter." Gabriel pursed his lips and said, "You don't have to worry about it sir, I would've died if it meant protecting her."

"Good." said her father. "We should head inside." Marina said while wiping her eyes of tears and turning to face her parents. The young lady and her beloved picked up their bags and started walking toward the train. Before entering, Marina gave her parents one more affectionate hug. Although she regretted leaving them, she understood that if she wanted a life, she had to make this decision. "Goodbye, look after Cesare while I'm away. I'm hoping I can bring him along when I come back for a visit." As they pledged to take care of him, she grinned at them. Finally boarding the train, Marina sat down and peered out the window at her parents.

Her parents waved to her as the train pulled away and continued to do so until they lost sight of it. As she was leaving the city, she kept turning to look at it. She felt as though she was at last liberated and had the opportunity to start living the life she wanted. In an effort to calm herself down, Marina started to take deep breaths. She was feeling guilty for leaving and feeling like a horrible daughter. At that same moment, Mr. Santarelli seized her hand and said, "I cannot believe we're starting our life together." He murmured as he gave her a kind gaze. "Like you, I can't believe it. It doesn't seem real." She sighed and said, "Thank you for letting me on your ship." The girl's large ocean-blue eyes met his as she turned to face him. He added, "And thank you for being in my life."

Epilogue

December 15th, 1913

Marina was in the bedroom she shared with her husband. She yelled in pain, tears, and sweat streaming down her face, and a doctor and midwife were standing close by. "Push Mrs. Santarelli! Push!" She was yelled at by the doctor, who urged her to keep pushing. "I can't! I can't do it anymore!" At them, she screamed and sobbed. She vowed to herself that she would never become pregnant again in her life since everything ached. Mr. Santarelli was outside waiting for his wife to give birth. He was anxious in case she passed away during labor or their child did as well. His friend Antoni, who was standing next to him, persuaded him to be calm and wait, saying that nothing bad would happen. "Soon you'll be a father! That's exciting, isn't it? And I'll be an uncle." He declared. Gabriel chose to go against the custom of fathers staying outside of the room where their wives were giving birth since he could not wait any longer. "Gabriel, wait!" Antoni yelled. Gabriel was frightened as he banged the doors open and saw his wife in pain and the midwife trying to calm her down.

"Is she alright!?" In distress, asked Mr. Santarelli. "*Gabriel!*" Marina wept. Whimpering, she lowered her head to her pillow. Her hair was so wet that it was sticking to her face, and her face was completely crimson. Her husband quickly approached her and tightly gripped her hand. "She needs to give it one more push, but she won't." The midwife said as she gave Mr. Santarelli a worried look. The man turned to face his sobbing wife. "Please push once more to end this." The young lady scrunched up her eyebrows and nose. She whimpered, "It hurts so much..." At that instant, her spouse kissed her hand. "I know it does, but please, you need to do this one more time. The pain will then stop and we'll he happy together."He advised her. "This is all your fault for putting this baby inside me!" growled Marina.

"I know, I'm sorry for that." As he rolled his eyes at her, he sighed. She gave his hand such a strong grip then that she almost snapped every bone in his hand. "*Ahh!*" Marina yelled as she pushed. She inhaled deeply, and soon a baby's sobbing could be heard. While still holding her hand, Marina's husband stood up, and she gasped.

"Congratulations, it's a healthy boy." As she was holding their son, the midwife said. When Mr. Santarelli realized he had a son, tears began to fall from his face. The midwife took the baby after the doctor assisted in cutting the umbilical cord and took him away to go wash the blood off of him. Marina sobbed and extended her hands. Asking, "Where are they taking my baby?" Her voice was rough as she questioned. Because of all the yelling and screaming, her throat stung. "My love, she took him to wash him." As he started to kiss his wife on the forehead, lips, and cheeks, he remarked. He was overjoyed that she was still alive and well and was immensely proud of her. He even assisted in cleaning her face from the sweat by placing a cold towel on her forehead and cheeks.

Mrs. Santarelli received her son from the midwife, who said, "There you go, all nice and clean." as she left the two new parents alone. When Marina first held her son, she was already deeply devoted to him. She and Gabriel both broke down in tears of happiness. Marina remarked, "Hello little baby..." as she saw his tiny face, tiny eyes, tiny nose, and tiny lips. Mr. Santarelli extended his hand, and his newborn son completely encircled his index finger with his small grasp. When his son first touched him, he sobbed. "I swear I'd never, ever allow anything bad to happen to you or hurt you," He said as he kept staring at him.

"We need to give him a name." Marina spoke while barely offering her husband a smile. Taking a look at his wife "You're right, I forgot. Do you have any recommendations?" He queried. "He looks like Gianluca to me." She said as she softly rocked her newborn and caressed his cheek. "Gianluca Santarelli... my son."Gabriel spoke while keeping his eyes glued on his son. He was overjoyed to have his own family at last. "In our garden, we ought to plant a new tree." He told his wife "Why?" Marina asked while scowling at him. "I believe it is a custom in your family to plant a tree whenever a new family member is born?" He smiled at her and inquired.

For remembering that, Marina adored him, and she was happy that he wished to carry on her family's tradition. She was deeply in love with him at the moment and couldn't believe that after insulting and despising him in the past, she was now married to the captain of the ship and had a wonderful son with him.

The end.

Writers Note

Thank you for reading the story that I have created. I am very passionate about this book and it's the first one I successfully managed to write. English isn't my first language so this was all challenging to write fully in English, especially because I had to write like in the old days (Jane Austen style) because after all, this is a period drama. It's especially thrilling how I wrote all of this at only 18. I've been writing this book since I was 14y.o actually! So it makes me incredibly happy that this project is finally done and that I can finally and entirely share about my characters to everyone.

I know people are eager to know what happened in the future with the rest of the characters so here's all the information you'll need; Antoni did become a well-known tailor in Rome, and he helped his mother and sister a lot financially. Amelia stayed in Naples with her husband and sons, later had a daughter with him, and even decided to visit Mr. and Mrs. Rivalli from time to time. She and Marina still see each other and write each other letters, their kids are especially close with each other. Marina also opened eventually her bakery in the center of Rome, which was very successful. Gabriel became a history professor in a private school that Antoni helped him get the job position because he helps tailor the uniforms for the children there and that way managed to get his friend into the school. After they had a son, Marina, and Gabriel four years later had a beautiful daughter and their lives were incredibly joyful... They still loved each other dearly and their love for one another never changed but only grew more and more each day.

And a big thank you to my friend Lety for always being by my side and helping me out a lot with writing. Would've never finished this without you. There have been moments in my life where I felt awful and wanted to quit writing. Lety was the only one in my life to encourage me to continue writing. As I said before, if it weren't for her I would've never finished writing my very first novel, so thank you a lot my dearest friend.

Printed in Great Britain
by Amazon

31766938R00264